Design for Holidays and Tourism

Edward D Mills CBE, FRIBA, FSIAD

Butterworths
London Boston Durban Singapore
Sydney Toronto Wellington

First published 1983

© Butterworth & Co (Publishers) Ltd, 1983

British Library Cataloguing in Publication Data

Mills, Edward
    Design for holidays and tourism.
    1. Tourist trade – Great Britain – History
    I. Title
    338.4′79141   G155.G7

    ISBN 0-408-00534-3

The Butterworths Design Series for architects and planners

General Editor: Edward D. Mills CBE, FRIBA, FSIA

Each book in the Butterworths Design Series takes an in-depth look at the design approach to a particular building type or building problem. Basic design philosophies are analysed in the context of the needs of the building user. Truly international in scope and coverage, the series draws on abundant worldwide examples of the best of modern design and planning.

All the books in the series have been specially commissioned from leading architects and specialists of worldwide repute. The Butterworths Design Series complements the publisher's *Planning* Series, and will be an invaluable reference for practising architects, schools of architecture and design, and departments of urban and rural development.

Titles in the **Design** series

Design for Safety
Eric W. Marchant

Design for Health Care
Anthony Cox and Philip Groves

Design for Holidays and Tourism
Edward D. Mills

Design for Leisure Entertainment
Anthony Wylson

Design for Shopping Centres
Nadine Beddington

Design for Sport
Gerald A. Perrin

Photoset by Butterworths Litho Preparation Department
Printed in Great Britain at the University Press, Cambridge

Foreword

by Richard England

The phenomenon of mass tourism, in less than a century of existence, has become one of man's most highly developed and professionally run 'industries'. The major factors which have contributed to the rapid growth of this activity have been the increased free hours in the fast changing work-leisure equation, the advent of relatively cheap travel and the failure, on environmental levels, of contemporary urban-planning schemes modelled on rationalist architecture's sterile thought-patterns.

Many of today's holiday-makers, seductively lured by sophisticated advertising systems to their 'away from it all' holiday, end up facing traumatic mirror-images of the nightmare cities which prompted their exodus in the first place. The search for change inevitably ends in boring predictability. The process leading to these catastrophic end-products is repeated with alarming consistency: unspoilt places with unique characteristics attract tourists; the need for accommodation produces change, to such an extent that the original tracts are transformed, more often than not, into tragic paradigms of dense high-rise urban fabrics.

Modern man, in a world already environmentally threatened by industrial chemical spin-offs, can ill-afford to discard kilometres of precious coastal areas, together with the rarer man-made cultural centres. Tourism, with its goals focused on the enjoyment of natural and man-made beauty spots, when not carefully controlled, becomes one of man's worst forms of 20th century pollution. Ironically, tourists become involved in a process of destruction of the very qualities which attract them in the first place: a form of genocide of all the geese which have laid the golden eggs.

Much of the onus and responsibility in avoiding these tragic situations and of consequently producing solutions for housing these travelling masses, without committing environmental suicide, rests squarely on members of the architectural profession. As planners, designers and policy-makers there is much we can contribute to ensure that while the necessary economic aspect of foreign-exchange earnings and employment is not stunted, accommodation can be achieved *without* spoilation and pollution, and that the preservation of natural and man-made beauty spots together with the retention of the essential qualities of the 'genius loci' are carefully preserved.

My own particular experience, as designer and defender, in a country of such exigous proportion as Malta, has enabled one to bring into close focus (in the form of a microcosmic case-study) the complex problems of an island with the basic touristic requirements of sun and sea, together with an extensive number of high-quality architectural momuments. These problems may be examined in this context, with a clarity that is not possible or practicable in extended cases. This scale, further emphasizes the urgent necessity of sensitive planning together with the vigilant care required in a fragile and vulnerable ethnic ambience, if this is to survive against the greedy aspect of man's money-making speculative ideals.

The architect of today, involved in tourist projects must consider architecture as a journey involving and linking the past, present and future of his particular site. He (or she) must remember that the ultimate aim is the production of an architecture which relates to both time *and* place. An expression embodying a complex multi-faceted approach which involves the architect in not only being the designer of the future, but even more so, the defender of the past, in so far as the past constitutes the natural and man-made heritage, which forms the particular ethos and identity of *place*. Architects should constantly be reminded that the most important joint of all in their manifest concepts is that of the building of its site.

The situation today in the planning and architecture of tourism leaves much to be desired. What is required is not to doctor the effect but to remove the cause. This excellent book is a most valid and timely contribution in this direction. It provides valuable material and pointers not only for architects but for all who are involved in tourism and its immediate effects.

This century has unfortunately been responsible for the removal of much of the sense of the *wonderful* from our everyday lives. The architecture of tourism, if thoughtfully planned with solutions in keeping with, and relating to, the uniqueness of place, together with adhesion to necessary scale-requirements, is still one of the rare fields where the element of *wonder* is still possible. It may in this context (as an antidote to the oppressive everyday environments of modern man) be considered as an essential 'functional' requirement' fundamental to the practical solution to the problem.

If architects are, in their designs for holiday environments, capable of again causing an emotive response in man, not only will we be making a valid contribution in once again establishing our profession as an Art, but we shall be ensuring the survival of much greater and crucial values. We shall be providing reassuring glimpses that man and his environment, with proper design discipline and control still have a basic potentiality for future survival.

Preface

Design for Holidays and Tourism is third of a trilogy of books in the *Butterworth's Design* series dealing with leisure activities, the other two are *Design for Leisure Entertainment* by Anthony Wylson and *Design for Sport* by Gerald Perrin.

The post-war years have seen a world-wide increase in leisure time for millions of people in both the developed and the developing areas of the world. Shorter working hours, greater individual prosperity, faster and cheaper travel and the impact of radio and television have all helped to make the leisure and travel industry the fastest growing industry in the world.

The employment potential of this growth has, as yet, only been partly appreciated by Governments; it has been estimated that every thousand tourists generate sixty new jobs and help to circulate foreign currency. In the UK, incoming tourism brings in nearly £4 billion in foreign currency annually and the British tourist industry employs three times as many people as the car industry and earns four times as much foreign revenue. This pattern can be repeated in most developed countries of the world and as tourism spreads further afield developing countries are looking to the holiday and tourist industries to boost their economies.

The dilemma to be faced is the fact that while tourism can bring wealth and development, it can, at the same time, destroy the things that attracted the tourists in the first place. This book looks at this problem and tries to suggest ways in which provision can be made for tourism and holidays without bringing destruction to irreplaceable historic and natural treasures.

Holiday hotels need not be intruders, built of imported materials, with foreign staff. Tourist facilities can be integrated with the landscape, and bring benefits to the host country as well as the visitors, and tourist income can help to preserve historic buildings, endangered wildlife and areas of great natural beauty. The essential requirements are genuine commitment, long term planning and sympathetic design skills applied to buildings, landscape and infrastructure.

When opening an exhibition concerned with churches and tourism prepared by the English Tourist Board in conjunction with the Church of England Council for Places of Worship in 1980, the Archbishop of Canterbury, Dr. Runcie, said he was an 'unashamed supporter of tourism – one of the enrichments of life'. Tourism can offer relaxation and mental and physical recreation, it has an important educational role to play in the modern world and can help to break down barriers of colour, creed and class. Young and old, fit and disabled people should be able to enjoy the benefits of holidays and tourism on both near and remote parts of the world in ancient cities or unspoiled natural beauty spots, but these places must not only be available for today's visitors, their preservation must be guaranteed so that future generations may also enjoy them.

This book outlines the history of tourism and holidays and briefly considers the reasons why greater leisure time is available to many more people than ever before; the economic and physical problems that arise from the growth of tourism are examined and means of avoiding the destruction and dereliction that can follow unplanned and ill-considered tourist expansion. The relationship between tourism and conservation is one of importance for they can be mutually supportive, and the role of tourism in bringing new economic opportunities to the Third World cannot be overlooked.

Throughout the book the importance of sympathetic development is stressed and illustrated by thirty-two Case Studies, drawn from twenty different countries covering a wide range of building including Game Lodges in remote African reserves and sophisticated holiday hotels in Mexico and Cyprus.

Restaurants, museums, farming centres, shopping precincts, holiday apartments, villas and cabins are all part of the building needs of holidaymakers and these are illustrated by photographs or Case Studies in order to underline the importance of architectural design that respects the physical environment of which it is a part and provides the facilities needed by large numbers of visitors without destroying the attraction they seek to enjoy, whether it is a sandy beach, a wildlife sanctuary, or an ancient city or historic building.

Any book on a subject as wide as this can only be regarded as an introduction. For readers wishing to pursue the subject in greater depth a short bibliography has been compiled which will provide details of further reading material.

It is hoped that this publication, like the other volumes in the *Butterworth Design Series* will be of interest to architects and designers concerned with the leisure industries and in particular to developers, governments, national and international bodies concerned with holiday and tourist development throughout the world; particularly in those areas as yet unaffected by the tourism boom. Many of the ideas set out could assist in the preparation of long term plans, and legislation which would help to reduce the harmful effects of large scale tourism and at the same time ensure that the host country could reap the undoubted benefits that can be gained from a carefully planned and controlled tourist industry.

In the preface of his book *Design for Sport*, Gerald Perrin underlines the necessity for good design, and

sensible planning backed up by intelligent management in relation to all free time activities including sport, entertainment and tourism. The author believes that architecture has an increasingly important role in improving the quality of life in both developing and developed societies. This book endeavours to promote this point of view, it cannot offer ready-made answers to the problems that holiday and tourist development presents but it endeavours to offer guidelines that can lead to more acceptable solutions to some of these problems.

Special thanks are due to my wife who has accompanied me on the many journeys all over the world; to the staff of the Publishers for their continued support and practical help; to my secretary Irene Trezies, who has deciphered my almost illegible manuscript and assisted in many other ways, and to those responsible for the design and production of the book.

Constructive comments and suggestions from readers would be most warmly welcomed so that they can be considered for inclusion in later editions.

Edward D Mills

London

This book is dedicated to my wife in appreciation and gratitude for many happy journeys in the past and in expectation of many more such travels in the future to 'far away places'.

Contents

Foreword *iii*
Preface *v*
Acknowledgements *viii*
List of Case Studies *ix*

1 A brief history of holidays and tourism 1
Holidays 1
Tourism and travel 1
The railways 3
Air travel 4
Holiday patterns 5
Tourism 6

2 The human problem 8
Changing work patterns 8
Mobility 11
Instant communication 12
Far away places 13

3 The economic problem 15
The international dimensions 16
Tourism as an industry 17
Tourism and the developed countries 18
Tourism and the developing countries 19
Benefits of tourism 21

4 The physical problem 22
The urban scene 22
The tourist resort 25
Far-away places 27

5 Planning for tourism 29
Road travel 29
Roads and access 30
Roads and tourism 31
Car parking 31
Tourist pressures on the infrastructure 33

Evaluation and forward planning 34
Design for special needs 35

6 Building for tourism 37
Camping accommodation and caravans 37
Camping sites 38
Static caravan sites 40
Permanent non-serviced accommodation 44
Serviced accommodation 64
Planning for disabled people 78
Remote places 81
Other buildings for tourists 83

7 Tourism and building conservation 101
Castles, chateaux and country houses 103
Churches and religious buildings 106
Other buildings 108

8 The developing pattern of holidays and tourism 113
Multi-ownership or time-sharing 115
Agriculture and tourism 116
Country parks 120
Country and folk museums 120
'Honey potting' or diversionary attractions 125
Crafts and tourism 128

9 Tourist planning for the future 132
Planning for the future 132
The role of the design team 134
Building materials and techniques 135
Alternative ways of travel 141
Conclusions 146

Bibliography 147
Index 148

Acknowledgements

The preparation of any book for publication requires support and assistance from many sources. The collection of material for this book has spanned many years and involved travel to many parts of the world, discussion with many people and organisations connected with the holiday and tourist industry world-wide, and the co-operation of developers, architects, designers and tourist authorities whose assistance and collaboration is greatly appreciated and acknowledged.

The following list of individuals and organisations cannot be complete and the author's apologies are offered in advance to any who have been inadvertently omitted.

Scottish Tourist Board
British Tourist Authority
The Society for the Protection of Ancient Buildings
Snowdonia National Park Information Service
Wales Tourist Board
The National Federation of Site Operators
The Librarian, British Architectural Library
The Camping and Caravanning Club
Thomas Cook Group Ltd
Isle of Arran Tourist Organisation
The Wildfowl Trust
British Railways London Midland Region
British Airways
The Anglo-Japanese Economic Institute
Club Mediterranée
Camino Real Cancun
Proalgarve Holdings S.A.
Spel Products
The Automobile Association
The Reo Stakis Organisation Ltd
Travel Alberta, Canada
Multi-Ownership & Hotels Ltd
The National Trust
American Automobile Association
Republic of Turkey Ministry of Tourism and
   Information
Ambassade de France

Parkhotel Wasserburg Anholt
Chalk Pits Museum
The Weald and Downland Open Air Museum
The Broome Park Estate
Zambia National Tourist Board
The Castle Museum, York
Thomas Bates & Sons Ltd, Thorndon Hall
The British Airport Authority
The Greater London Council, Dept. of Architecture
Kenya Tourist Development Corporation
Treetops Outspan
Welsh Folk Museum
Telford Development Corporation
Historical Aviation Service
German National Tourist Office
Colonial Williamsburg Foundation
Saga Holidays for the over 60's
Museum of Finnish Architecture
Scarborough Borough Council
Buckland Manor Estate
Gulf Leisure Developments Ltd
Twickenham Travel Limited
The National Motor Museum, Beaulieu
Crafts Council of Great Britain
Skansen Foundation, Sweden
Pontins Ltd
Gast in Schloss
Swedish National Tourist Office
Fiat Auto (UK) Ltd
Elizabeth de Stroumillo

Thanks are also gratefully expressed to architects who have loaned photographs, drawings and information for the Case Studies and illustrations; individual credits have been included from other publications. The help given by architect Richard England and permission to quote his writings on Architecture and Tourism; by John Weller for information on the relationship between Tourism and Agriculture, and the Shankland Cox Partnership for material on Strategic Planning for the Tourist Industry has been of great value.

List of case studies

1 Holiday Cabins 42–43
Kernton Forest, Herodsfoot, Cornwall, England
Architects: Hird & Brooks

2 Holiday Town Marina 46–47
Vilamura, Algarve, Portugal
Architects: Eric Lyons, Cunningham Partnership in
association with GEFEL

3 Apartment Complex 48–49
Mellieha, Malta
Architects: England & England

4 Villa Group 50–51
Provence, France
Architect: Santa Raymond

5 Danish Holiday Centre 52–53
Mellieha Bay, Malta
Architect: Hans Munk Hansen

6 Holiday Cabins 54–55
Lochanhully, Carrbridge, Inverness-shire, Scotland
Architects: Shankland Cox Partnership

7 Holiday Housing Complex 56–57
Stazzo Pulcheddu, Gallura, Sardinia
Architects: Alberto Ponis & Aldo E Ponis

8 Family Holiday Villa Group 58–59
Canakkale, Dardanelles, Turkey
Architect: Sedat Gurel

9 Holiday Housing Complex 60–61
Portmadoc Harbour, Caernarvonshire, Wales
Architects: Phillips, Cutler, Phillips, Troy

10 Holiday Village 62–63
Belle-ile-en-Mer, Morbihan, France
Architect: Danielle Cler

11 Hotel and Conference Centre 66–67
Kampala, Uganda, E. Africa
Architects: Robert Browning in association with
Edward D. Mills & Partners

12 Beach Hotel 68–69
Djerba, Tunisia, N. Africa
Architect: Hans Munk Hansen

13 Beach Hotel 70–71
Camino Real, Cancun, Mexico
Architect: Legorreta

14 Bargaf Jall Ski Hotel 72–73
South Lappland, Sweden
Architect: Ralph Erskine

15 Amathus Beach Hotel 74–75
Limassol, Cyprus
Architects: The Architects Collaborative and Fotis J.
Colakides & Assoc.

16 Hotel Oberoi 76–77
Bogmalo Beach, Goa, India
Architect: Uttam C Jain

17 Nature Reserve Visitors Centre 84–85
Arundel Refuge, Mill Road, South Stoke, Arundel,
W Sussex, England
Architect: Neil Holland

18 Wildfowl Refuge 86–87
Martin Mere, Redcat Lane, Burscough, Lancashire,
England
Architects: Building Design Partnership

19 Safari Lodge 88–89
Semliki Game Reserve, Uganda, E. Africa
Architect: Hans Munk Hansen

20 Safari Lodge 90–91
Nile Falls National Park, Uganda
Architect: Hans Munk Hansen

21 Visitors Centre 92–93
Risley Moss Nature Reserve, Warrington New Town,
Lancashire, England
Architects: Building Design Partnership

22 Café and Tourist Centre 94–95
Tollymore, Newcastle, County Down, N. Ireland
Architects: Ian Campbell & Partners

23 Day Study and Information Centre 96–97
Witley Common, Surrey
Architect: Michael Cain of Casson, Condor & Partners

24 Tourist Information Centre 98–99
Brodick, Island of Arran, Scotland
Architects: Baxter, Clark & Paul

25 The Market 110–111
Covent Garden, London, England
Architect: F. B. Pooley, Superintendent Architect to GLC

26 Recreational Farm Centre 118–119
Flevohof, Flevoland, Holland

27 Wellington Country Park 122–123
Stratfield Saye, Heckfield, Hampshire, England
Architects: Leonard Manasseh Partnership

28 Museum and Visitors Centre 126–127
Beaulieu, Hampshire, England
Architects: Leonard Manasseh Partnership

29 Tourists' Guest House 136–137
Sevagram, Wardha, India
Architect: Uttam C. Jain

30 Game Lodge 138–139
Chobe National Park, Botswana
Architect: Bill Birren of Mallows Louw Hoffe & Partners

31 Serena Beach Hotel 142–143
Shanzu Beach, Mombasa, Kenya
Architects: Archer Associates

32 Holiday House 144–145
Moduli 225, Prefabricated house kit, Finland
Architects: Kristian Gullichsen & Juhani Pallasmaa

Chapter 1
A brief history of holidays and tourism

This chapter traces the development of holidays in the UK over the past centuries and shows how the various methods of travel over the last few decades have changed and made it easier for people to travel long distances.

Holidays

The idea of periodic breaks in the normal flow of human life and work is not of recent origin, man has always felt a need for organised interruption in the regular pattern of his routine activity. Not only is sleep necessary to all living things for the purpose of regeneration in a regular cycle, but longer breaks at greater intervals are also essential.

It is not without interest that the biblical story of the Creation records that the Creator completed the work in six days and rested on the seventh – in modern terms took a holiday or 'day off'. The word 'holiday' is a corruption of the original 'holy day' and all the religions of the world including Christian, Jewish, Moslem and Buddhist have a regular calendar of festivals, saints' days and holy days. In pagan times such festivals celebrated the natural changes of the seasons Winter, Spring, Summer and Autumn that made up the cycle of the year.

In the western world many Christian celebrations such as Christmas and Easter were grafted on to the earlier pagan festivals. Shrove-tide in England, Mardi-Gras in France and Fastendienstag in Germany are all successors to the pagan Spring-tide festival celebrating the coming of new life to the earth. The word 'Easter' denoting the Christian celebration is derived from Eostre, the pagan Goddess of Spring. The hare was sacred to Eostre, this became the traditional 'Easter Bunny'.

Just as pagan celebrations were adopted by other religions, so were some of the original descriptive words. A 'barbecue' was originally the pagan altar framework on which a sacrificial ox was roasted on feast days. Other festivals have equally early origins, May Day (the first day of the month of May) was originally the festival of the Roman Goddess, Maia the mother of the god Mercury: it was revived in Medieval and Tudor times and the Maypole, still a centre of festivities in many European villages, has a link with pagan tree worship. May Day became International Labour day only as recently as 1889 and still more recently in England became an official secular Bank Holiday. In Britain, the Bank Holidays' Act of 1871 was related to Christian Festivals with the exception of the August Bank Holiday.

In Europe many of the Christian Saints' days were celebrated in the Middle Ages by Fairs, which often lasted for several days, St. Bartholomew's Fair in London and St. Giles' Fair at Oxford are two examples. These fairs were not only holiday occasions for the people, but also important commercial events, where goods and produce were sold, and employees hired; they were the forerunners of the modern Trade Fair or Exhibition. The original fairs declined with the industrialisation of the nineteenth century, but many of the dates remain in the European Christian Calendar.

Tourism and travel

Before the Industrial Revolution travel was largely a matter of religious pilgrimage or for official or business purposes. Mass travel of a private nature was unknown, as long journeys were difficult, expensive and sometimes dangerous. In Medieval times overseas travel was generally limited to individual pioneers, explorers, traders, official government representatives and envoys, and those engaged in warfare.

In the 16th and 17th centuries the fashion of the Grand Tour developed in Europe, this was to become an essential part of the education of a young man of quality. Such tours were long and expensive and limited to the very rich or those with wealthy patrons. For example, in 1775, Lord Herbert (later the 11th Earl of Pembroke) at the age of sixteen started a tour with his two tutors which lasted five years and included Germany, the Netherlands, Austria, Poland, Russia, Switzerland and Italy. His diaries reveal that this was not merely a sightseeing tour but a carefully planned educational programme, during which the principal European centres of art and culture were visited.

"When Samuel Johnson contemplated a tour of Italy in 1776, Boswell records him as saying . . . 'A man who has not been in Italy, is always conscious of an inferiority, from his not having seen what it is expected a man should see. The grand object of travelling is to see the shores of the Mediterranean . . . All our religion, almost all that sets us above savages, has come to us from the shores of the Mediterranean.' In this sentence lies the concept of the Grand Tour, the peregrination through Europe, by which the wealthy young might become civilised by exposure to European art, architecture and manners by which they might also enrich their country houses at home."
(*Extract from Tourism by A.J. Burkart and S. Medlik, Heinemann*)

The foundations of the international tourist industry as we know it today were established in the 19th century. With the change-over from agriculture and craft industry to the mechanised industry of factories and mills the annual holiday was originated in the mills of the northern industrial towns of England, where the Wakes weeks were instituted. These were basically holiday weeks when the mills closed down for maintenance and repairs to machinery and plant, and the workers enjoyed a well-earned break from the tedious labour of the preceding year.

Seaside resorts (dealt with in some detail by Anthony Wylson in his book *Design for Leisure Entertainment*, in this series), began to develop to cater for

An artist's impression of a modern popular holiday resort in Britain, once a quiet fishing village (*from a drawing by Alan Price*)

ALAN PRICE

Scarborough, Yorkshire, Britain's oldest holiday resort. South Bay where the discovery of the Chalybeate Springs in 1626 led to the development of this small seaside town. In the foreground are restored Victorian Spa buildings (*Scarborough Corporation*)

the annual mass invasion. Blackpool, Yarmouth, Scarborough, Southend and Brighton, for example, started their expansion from quiet fishing villages to meet the growing holiday demand.

The Victorians also travelled for health reasons, although before the 18th century sea bathing was unheard of in Europe. In the 18th century the motivation for bathing was almost entirely for health reasons and Scarborough was the first and only seaside resort in Britain to flourish between 1730–1750, largely due to the discovery in 1626 by a certain Mrs. Farrow of the Chalybeate Springs along the Scarborough Cliffs. Scarborough rapidly became a bathing resort and holiday town. At the same time travellers visited the spas of Europe in France, Germany and Italy.

The use of natural springs first started with the Romans and those at Buxton and Bath in the UK and many others in Europe are still in use. In Central and Eastern Europe the spa as a health resort has never lost its appeal and today many of the traditional 'watering places' such as Vichy in France and Cheltenham in England are making fresh plans to attract visitors.

The railways

The advent of the railways made travel easier and the effects of this will be discussed later, but the major advance in mass travel was due to the foresight of Thomas Cook, who was born in 1808 the same year as the first steam locomotive was displayed in what is now Euston Square, London. The locomotive worked, and was a source of considerable local interest, but no-one took it seriously until some twenty years later. In 1841 Thomas Cook, who was a publisher and temperance reformer in Leicester, organised the first cheap railway excursion from Leicester to Loughborough and back. Five hundred and seventy-five passengers bought tickets for one shilling each (5 pence) which included tea and buns in Mr. Paget's Park. Thus the great Thomas Cook travel business was started and the foundation of cheap tourist travel was established.

The ticket issued by Thomas Cook for his first cheap railway excursion on Monday 5th July 1841 (*Thos. Cook & Sons Ltd*)

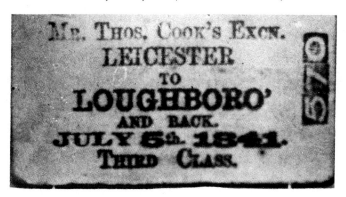

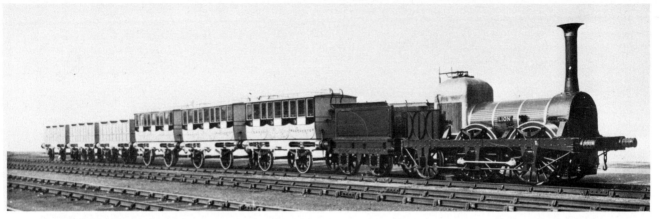

Lion was built for the London & Midland Railway in 1838. A train of this kind was used for Thomas Cook's first railway excursion. The Lion is probably the oldest original working steam locomotive. Restored by the LMS in the 1920's to its original colours dark green, with banded boiler and copper fire box, it is now in the Merseyside County Museum and has appeared in many films and exhibitions. (*British Railways, London Midland Region*)

As the railways expanded in Great Britain, Europe and America, long distance travel for large numbers of people became a practical possibility. The first UK seaside excursion was organised by Sir Rowland Hill (originator of the Penny Post) in 1843, and by 1851, the year of the Great Exhibition, regular rail excursions were common in England. The invention of the Wagon-Lits in France 1869 and the Pullman coach in the USA 1867 made long distance rail travel more comfortable and convenient, and Queen Victoria's holidays on Lake Como in N. Italy gave continental holidays Royal Patronage and respectability.

The 1914–18 war disrupted the everyday life of the early 20th century, but resulted in vast numbers of members of the armed forces of many nations being moved around the continent of Europe. When peace was declared the world was inevitably a smaller place, travel was no longer solely for the wealthy and influential; it had become the right of everyone.

Air travel

At the end of the 1914–18 war it was apparent that the aeroplane had an enormous potential in peace time as a means of fast travel over long distances. The world's first regular, scheduled civil air service began on August 25, 1919 when a converted wartime day bomber left Hounslow (the London Airport of that time) at 09.10 for Le Bourget, Paris where it arrived 2½ hours later. According to *The Story of British Airways* the flight carried 'one passenger, small consignments of leather, Devonshire cream, newspapers, mail and several brace of grouse'.

In the first ten weeks of operation one-hundred and forty-seven flights were made on the London-Paris route. This was the beginning of the age of air travel.

The pay load in those days over sixty years ago was absurdly small by modern standards – 400 lbs, or two large passengers. A modern jumbo jet (such as Boeing 747) can carry five hundred and seventy five passengers across the Atlantic Ocean non-stop.

In January 1923 the UK Parliament appointed a committee to examine Civil Air Transport and as a result of its recommendations a single British company – Imperial Airways Ltd – was formed to take over the operations of the four original air operating companies. On 26 April, 1924 the first Imperial Airways service to Paris commenced. The story of the development of British Airways can be read in the British Airways' booklet *Highways in the Air*. This describes the growth from those early days from eighteen miscellaneous aircraft with a very small passenger carrying potential to the present-day organisation that in 1978 carried 13 370 000 passengers over a distance of nearly 30 million miles.

Other world airlines can tell a similar story, but it is of interest to note that Britain can rightly claim a

A de Havilland 4a converted day bomber similar to the one that opened the world's first international scheduled civil air service from Hounslow to le Bourget on 25th August 1919 (*British Airways*)

A British Airways Boeing 747. The first of the wide bodied jets with a range of over 6000 miles (9655 km), cruising at 600 mph (965 km/hr) at between 25000 and 45000 ft (7620 and 13716 m) (*British Airways*)

number of firsts in addition to the world's first scheduled civil air service, all of which have had an important influence on mass air travel:

April 20, 1935 The first 'through' passenger flight from Britain to Australia. (Journey time 12½ days).

May 1, 1951 World's first *tourist* fare introduced on the Atlantic route.

May 2, 1952 World's first jet scheduled passenger service London-Johannesburg with Comets.

Aug 12, 1959 BOAC first regular round-the-world service.

June 10, 1965 World's first automatic landing on a scheduled airline service.

Dec 30, 1972 World's first aircraft of an international scheduled service (BEA Trident at Heathrow) to land in Category IIIA weather conditions.

Jan 21, 1976 World's first supersonic passenger flight inaugurated by BA Concorde London-Bahrain and Air France, Paris to Rio de Janeiro.

Aug 10, 1978 100 000th Concorde passenger carried.

Holiday patterns

While the enormous changes in the patterns of travel through the railway, the airplane and the motor car were taking place in the first half of the 20th century, the pattern of holidays and the growth of mass tourism was also developing. In 1936 Billy Butlin set up his first luxury holiday camp in England at Skegness to be followed by other operators in what had been the original seaside resorts of the Victorian days such as Clacton, Southend and Blackpool.

In 1951 the Club Mediterranée in France was formed and its camps inspired by primitive Polynesian villages have been established on deserted stretches of beach in France, North Africa, Yugoslavia and elsewhere. The atmosphere of the camps was deliberately primitive, grass-roofed huts, no radios or newspapers, informal dress and open-air living and recreation. The original formula was extremely successful and the Club has continued to grow over the last thirty years.

Camping, caravanning and similar forms of tourism also developed with the increase of the private motor car ownership. Ferry services to Europe enlarged the scope of the continental holidaymaker and tourist, as motorways were constructed on the Continent.

The enforced mass travel for vast numbers of people during the 1939–1945 war meant that a new understanding of world events was becoming more apparent and new forms of mass communication, radio, television, cheap books and newspapers all helped to emphasise the fact the world had become a smaller place.

The Jules Verne novel *Round the world in 80 days* when first published in 1873 described an almost impossible feat of rapid travel, but by 1959 it was possible to circumnavigate the globe in 61½ hours. Today the same journey could be made on scheduled

Pontin's, another holiday camp pioneer established their first camp at Brean Sands Holiday Village, Burnham on Sea, Somerset in 1946. Today their twenty-four UK centres and eight overseas centres provide over 800 000 holidays annually. (*Pontin's Ltd*)

air routes in 32 hours and 10 minutes. In 1981 the American manned space shuttle circled the globe once every 90 minutes.

Tourism

Mass tourism is a relatively recent phenomenon which has arisen partly through the technological development in the field of transport in the last twenty years. The frequent movement of millions of people outside their home environment is an inevitable result of modern urban life and as such, needs to be recognised and planned as an important element in the quality of life and as a major activity that influences the employment and economic well-being of very large numbers of people throughout the world.

Tourism is one aspect of increased mobility of people and goods for both work and leisure. Tourists are no longer a small privileged group of wealthy travellers, but a vast army of people travelling for pleasure in their ever increasing leisure time. The British Tourist Authority estimates that world-wide tourist recorded arrivals amounted to 25.3 millions in 1950: this figure had risen to 243 millions by 1979 and they forecast a further rise to 400 millions by 1985. Of these international movements, nearly 75% are for non-business purposes and they are themselves only part of a much larger log of travel movements that do not cross international boundaries.

It is clear from these figures that national and international travel and tourism is a growth industry that cannot be ignored. In the UK alone it is esti-

mated that tourist activity generates an annual turnover in excess of £15 000 million, and in the 1980s Britain alone can expect to receive up to twenty million tourists a year.

According to the Organization for Economic Co-operation and Development (OECD) tourism rose by 4% in 1979 and statistics show that some 270 million tourists went abroad during that year, about 70% visiting OECD countries.

The World Tourist Organization (WTO) the appointed United Nations tourist body, in a recent report covering 133 countries world-wide, estimated

The Club Méditerranée has catered for over 6 million holidaymakers in the last thirty years and now has over one hundred holiday villages in five continents, like this one at Playa Blanca (*Club Méditerranée*)

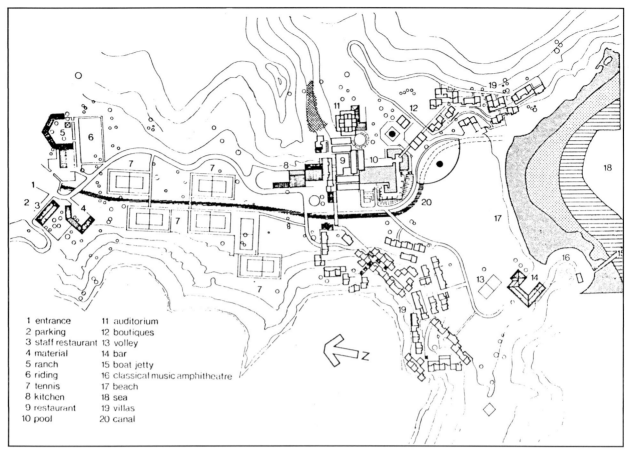

1 entrance   11 auditorium
2 parking   12 boutiques
3 staff restaurant   13 volley
4 material   14 bar
5 ranch   15 boat jetty
6 riding   16 classical music amphitheatre
7 tennis   17 beach
8 kitchen   18 sea
9 restaurant   19 villas
10 pool   20 canal

Playa Blanca – Layout of a typical Club Méditerranée holiday village

that in 1976 some sixteen million bed-places were registered, representing a potential accommodation capacity of 6000 million bed-nights per annum. The WTO forecast that this figure would increase to seventeen million bed-places by 1979: the survey covered hotels, motels, boarding houses, inns and other similar establishments.

The regional breakdown of the 1976 figures were as follows:

Europe	54.3%
The Americas	37.5%
East Asia and the Pacific	5.3%
The Middle East	0.7%
South Asia	0.7%

Of the total world accommodation capacity, some 85% is in the developed world leaving only 15% in developing countries.

In September/October 1980 the World Tourism Conference of the WTO was held in Manilla in the Philippines and in a report based on a document submitted in 1977 to the General Assembly of the World Tourism Organisation the following statement was made:

'The true significance of tourism has never been fully appreciated up to now, nor has the place that should rightly fall to it in the future social, economic and political life of a nation been properly assessed. This would seem to be the time for a change of attitude towards tourism, and thus for determining the role that should be played by it and the characteristics it is likely to have in tomorrow's society. This can only be done through a carefully considered, forward-looking analysis of the determinant economic and social factors and events in the lives of nations, their inter-relationship, and their impact on the development and expansion of world tourism.'

This underlines the importance of tourism in the modern world and emphasises the importance of the issues that will be considered in the latter chapters of this book.

Chapter 2
The human problem

The development of an urban life-style for the majority of people in developed countries following the Industrial Revolution of the 19th century has resulted in a large proportion of the world population seeking to spend part of their leisure time in an alternative environment. This has only become a practical reality on a large scale in the post-1945 situation which has created shorter working hours, paid holidays and greater personal mobility.

In Western Europe, North America and Japan people have between 30 and 35% of their time available for leisure pursuits. It is not surprising therefore that this has led to greater pressure on environments suitable for holidays and tourism such as sea coasts, lakes and mountains, the countryside and places of historic interest.

Tourism has developed largely in parallel with people's desire 'to get away from it all', and the fact that economic conditions and modern technological developments in travel have made available to millions the means of escape from the routine of every day life. Those who live in Northern Europe with a variable and unsettled climate seek 'a place in the sun', many Americans have as a tourist objective 'instant culture', while the Japanese tourist objective can be described as 'mass participation'.

Changing work patterns

The way in which millions of people work and the kind of work, if any, that they do has changed dramatically in the last fifty years, and will undoubtedly change beyond recognition before the end of the 20th century. To quote Professor Stonier (*The Impact of Microprocessors on Employment – The Micro Electronic Revolution*. Published by Basil Blackwell, 1980):

'At the beginning of the 18th century, 92% of the labour force worked on farms to feed the other 8%. Today it needs only 2 or 3% to feed the rest. That process, which occurred largely over the last hundred years or so, is now happening in the manufacturing industries. It has been going on for some time, but will probably be completed over the next two or so decades. It is highly probable that by early in the next century it will require no more than 10% of the labour force to provide us with all our material needs, that is, all the food we eat, all the clothing we wear, all the textiles and furnishings in our houses, the houses themselves, the appliances, the automobiles, and so on. In the near future, the vast majority of labour will be engaged as information operatives. The dominant form of labour in the 18th century and well into the 19th century involved farm operatives. From the nineteenth and well into the twentieth century it was machine operatives. Today it is information operatives.'

These changing patterns of work stem from the new technology of the microprocessor – commonly known as the 'chip' – and are already affecting those who work in industry, commerce and even the professions.

The micro-electronic revolution

Just as the change from handcraft to machine-based industry in the first Industrial Revolution ultimately reduced working hours and improved both economic and leisure conditions, so the new technology should, if properly managed result in shorter working hours, greater leisure time and a wider available range of leisure activities. These must inevitably include relaxation in the form of holidays and tourism.

The micro-electronic revolution should be capable of removing tedium and routine from daily activity, thus giving greater scope for creative activities, education, recreation and leisure activities of all kinds. This change is already taking place: the 35-hour working week is now accepted in the UK as the Trades Union Congress target; three weeks annual paid holiday in addition to statutory holidays is now normal and developments like 'flexi-time' in some work situations allows people to choose their working pattern in relation to other interests.

Other experiments like the 4-day week, where the accepted working time is divided into four instead of five days, result in a 3-day weekend giving further opportunity for leisure activities including 'local' holidays and tourist activity.

The subject of future employment opportunities has been the object of considerable crystal-gazing on the part of numerous experts in many fields: the resulting forecasts are many and extremely varied. Two UK study groups in 1978 estimated that unemployment in the UK would reach five million by the beginning of the 21st century if the British economy's future growth continued at the same rate as the previous twenty years, 'unless there were substantial reductions in working hours', and an increase in work sharing. These forecasts, relating to existing work patterns in industry, suggest that new patterns of employment are essential. The more advanced forms of industrialisation, automation and micro-electronic engineering will inevitably take over dirty, dangerous or boring repetitive jobs, which provide little job satisfaction because of their routine nature.

This should lead to a larger proportion of employees transferring to service occupations, which include those catering for tourism and holidaymakers.

It is not without interest that recent surveys have suggested that work which involves personal relationships, such as the service industries, produced the greatest job satisfaction. The Chairman of the English Tourist Board, presenting his Annual Report for 1981 said that the English tourist industry already employed over 1½ million people. He also said 'The service industries – and tourism is one of the most important – are a golden lifeline to future prosperity and employment for growing numbers of our citizens.'

Craft workshops and skills

The growth of craft workshops and similar activities, which have a genuine tourist interest in many countries, is not without interest in this context. Geoff Wright and John Garrett in an article in *Undercurrents*

A modern craft workshop. Janice Tchalenko at work in her pottery, her work is on display at the Craft Centre Gallery, London (*Philip Sayer*)

The Fiat Factory in Turin where the Robogate system operated by a central computer controls a series of robots around a gate so that they work as a team. In this illustration car bodies are being assembled by means of Robogate; increasing production but reducing manpower (*Fiat Auto (UK) Ltd*)

No. 27 (1978) suggest that the future lies not in a pre-industrial society but a new 'Golden Age' when automation frees people to participate in new, and socially beneficial, creative industries.

Handicrafts, like tourism, have become a boom industry for many developing countries, for through tourism, large numbers of western visitors are discovering the attractions of the developing countries of the world for the first time and returning home with souvenirs in the form of local handicrafts.

At their best, the Third World craft skills represent an authentic cultural heritage which, if properly organised could earn for the craftsman a better income from the world beyond his local workshop.

Personal involvement

The human race has a remarkable ability for adaptation and the field of work is one in which this adaptability can be clearly demonstrated. When it can be shown that machines can rationalise effort and thus reduce tedious, unsatisfying labour, the alternative of variety, change and personal involvement is of vital importance. Dr. Duncan Davies of The Department of Industry (UK) in a paper in the Chartered Mechanical Engineer (June 1978) quoted from *The Micro-electronics Revolution* (published by Basil Blackwell) makes the point very clearly:

'Those with the opportunity, craftsmen, for example, can and do change the operation and the product, according to a process apparently more complex than that of programmable learning. We could build random caprice into a robot, but human caprice seems to be different. Men did not like hoeing turnips in fields, where turnips are now grown using mechanical cultivation: with some of the time and effort so saved, men grow prize vegetables competitively in their allotment gardens. Men in affluent developed nations do not like assembling vehicles; presumably the job will now be done using machines plus micro-processors: with some of the time so saved, some men will build machines by hand, to their own design. The overall process seems to be the escape not from effort, but from routine, repetition and predictability (if vegetable growing were totally predictable, there could be no shows and competitions). Accordingly, man will continue to use himself both as a prime mover and as a servo-mechanism; if he does not, he will probably lose essential physiological function. But he wants choice and caprice.'

Even the Socialist Workers Party in the UK, which is not noted for its positive approach to the benefits of new technology, in a pamphlet published in 1979 says: 'We cannot give the impression we are against technology as such. We are for it, provided it is used to enable human beings to create more wealth and to lead happier, freer, fuller lives. After all, it is technology that enables us to envisage the coming reality of the age-old dream of a society without misery and drudgery.'

Clearly the means for creating greater leisure and thus more opportunities for travel, holidays and tourism exist; political, economical and social pressures will influence whether or not these opportunities are fully realised and developed to the advantage of the individual world-wide.

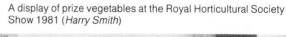

A display of prize vegetables at the Royal Horticultural Society Show 1981 (*Harry Smith*)

Mobility

If the first consideration in *Design for Holidays and Tourism* is the availability of time to enjoy such pursuits, then the second factor must be the extent of the infrastructure of transportation that allows for the movement of people and goods. Just as the social framework of older societies was based on caravans and trade routes by land and sea, today's world society is equally dependant on transportation by road, rail, canals, seaways and airways. Perhaps tomorrow's list should include space travel, but this consideration can reasonably be deferred until a later date.

In Chapter 1 a brief outline of the development of travel facilities was set in the context of the history of holidays and mass tourism.

Travel by car

The development of the mass ownership of the motor car has influenced personal mobility more than any other factor. When Henry Ford set out to build motor cars for the masses at a price every one could afford he not only established an international industry that would provide employment for vast numbers of people, but at the same time opened up untold opportunities for cheap travel. It is fashionable to describe the earth as a global village; perhaps a 'small town' would be more appropriate description for there are few places in the world that cannot be reached by air, sea or land in twenty-four hours.

In 1978 there were nearly 15 million private cars in Great Britain for a population of some 52 million and this pattern can be repeated throughout the developed countries of the world. Developing countries also regard the production and use of motor cars as an

The modern holiday rush in the UK on the Exeter bypass road. Cars and caravans in an endless traffic jam (*The Automobile Association*)

important factor in their economic progress. Even rising petrol prices in recent years has done little to reduce the importance of the private motor car, although less fuel thirsty vehicles are rapidly superseding the American style 'gas guzzlers'.

Rail and air travel

While the motor car made medium range journeys a practical possibility for vast numbers of people who a little more than a century ago depended on horse or foot travel, the dawn of the railway age 150 years ago introduced the era of mass long distance travel and laid the foundations for the world-wide tourist industry.

In recent years the world's railway systems have been fighting a losing battle against the ever-increasing competition from the world airways. Train speeds have increased rapidly in recent years in the USA, Japan and the UK. The British Rail Advanced Passenger Trains which travel at 200 km/hr (125 mph) and the Japanese Bullet Trains have replaced the glamorous Trans-Siberian Railway and the legendary Orient Express and provide transport for business and tourism on medium haul routes.

It is not without interest that the Orient Express was in 1981 brought back into service as a tourist attraction.

Henry Ford's 1914 model T car, the first mass produced car available at a price that millions of people could afford (*The National Motor Museum, Beaulieu*)

A British high speed 'Inter-city 125' train, part of the network inaugurated in 1976, capable of a speed of 125 mph (200 km/hr) (*British Rail*)

The major breakthrough has been the development of the long haul Jumbo jet aircraft with the ability to carry large numbers of people for great distance and at an economical cost. In the inter-war period the Atlantic crossing by large sea-going liner took up to two weeks, today the average airflight time needed is less than eight hours. Recently a London businessman and his wife set a new world record by leaving Central London by helicopter at 9.00 am, boarded Concorde at Heathrow and arrived in New York three and a half hours later, from Kennedy Airport the flight to Central New York gave them an arrival time of 8.30 am – a total flying time of 4½ hours.

Thus the age of total mobility has arrived and the impact on travel and tourism cannot be estimated.

The Japanese high speed bullet train (*Edward D. Mills*)

Instant communication

Not only has personal mobility in the form of rapid and comparatively cheap travel helped significantly to make the world a smaller place, but the instantaneous dissemination of information has helped to break down national and international barriers.

The new technology that is changing the work and leisure pattern of the world has also been responsible for what has become known as the 'information explosion'. By means of radio and television, in conjunction with communication satellites, world news and the coverage of world events, such as the Olympic Games, or the attempted assassination of a world figure can be immediately available to a large proportion of the world's population.

The transistor radio is regarded as an important status symbol in all developing countries. While colour television is commonplace in the developed countries of the world, in millions of private homes, in many villages in India, Africa and other places the communal television set has become the centre of community life where young and old meet to see the world in action beyond their village and even their country.

This visual breakdown of the barriers of distance between East and West, developed and developing countries, rich and poor means that ideas can no longer be confined by local or national boundaries. The age-old dream of a world family could become a reality if men can learn to live as a family and use the technology available for the betterment of mankind.

Travel and tourism could be a major contributor to better world understanding and does create greater interest in world affairs and a more sympathetic appreciation of 'far-away places'. In 1980 the devastating earthquakes in Italy received wide and immediate coverage by radio and television, resulting in practical help and assistance from all over the world.

Thousands of television viewers in Europe saw on their TV screens the ruined villages; places they had visited as tourists on holiday, and responded in a dramatic way by sending aid to the stricken areas in both money and kind. Modern technology when used properly can be an enormous power for good.

Television and radio have also created a universal interest not only in world affairs, but in national art and culture, conservation of the environment and the preservation of threatened wildlife, and has given millions of people the incentive to experience participation in such things. The facilities for mass travel and the international tourist industry can provide the means for such participation and for educational, cultural and leisure exchanges between one country and another.

Typical scene of earthquake damage, such pictures can be transmitted world-wide by TV within a few hours of the disaster, thus creating immediate interest and sympathetic support (*Edward D. Mills*)

Far-away places

Modern technology has improved global transport and made rapid, cheap and comfortable travel available to millions of people. The medium of the telephone, radio and television has made instant communication practical and economical.

Communication satellites have given the world population high quality twenty-four hours a day sound and visual communication. News is available on the air as it happens and the combined sciences of

aerospace, radio, TV and electronics have done more than any other 20th century technological development to make a reality of the visionaries dream of the world as a 'global village'. Far-away places have become very near to all of us.

The fact that vast numbers of people are able in remote African villages to hear of world events on cheap portable transistor radios or see on TV screens world events as they happen, has meant that the appeal of 'far-away places' has become universal. People of all nations now want to experience these things as well as hear or read about them.

This desire to see the world, encouraged by enforced migration resulting from two major wars and many lesser ones, means that world travel for business and pleasure, holidays and tourism has become the basis of an enormous and continually growing industry. By this means wealth and economic stability can now be brought to the poorer developing countries, together with employment to developed countries facing a technological industrial revolution. Hopefully, there will be a greater understanding between the nations as, through travel, the people of the world seek to understand each other's history, traditions, customs and culture.

Tourism is no longer a matter of the rich of the Western World seeking relaxation or refreshment in the cultural capitals of Europe. Today, tourists from Africa and Asia visit historic buildings in England, while Europeans seek the sun and natural beauty of the African continent. East and West meet in historic centres like Venice and Rome, and even political barriers which seem impregnable to politicians give way to the ever-increasing pressure of world tourism.

Russia, Yugoslavia, Poland, and more recently the Republic of China all, encourage tourists, for they have much to offer in terms of historic and cultural attractions and magnificent scenery. While some of these countries impose restrictions on visitors others, like Yugoslavia, allow complete freedom to travellers and by this means earns much needed foreign currency.

The appeal of 'far-away places with strange sounding names' to quote a popular song, is not likely to diminish. Those living in the colder northern climate, for example, will always be attracted to the sun, sea and sand of the warmer parts of the world. In 1980 the Managing Director of Britain's largest tour operator said that the increase in the demand for package holidays, 12% over the previous year's record of 5.08 million, indicated that a holiday was still top of the list for spending money in the UK.

Government figures published in March 1981 supported this view. These showed that living standards continued to rise in 1980 in spite of the world reces-

Canterbury Cathedral, Kent. One of the major tourist attractions in the UK that is visited by at least a million people a year from all parts of the world (*Edward D. Mills*)

sion, and real disposable incomes increased by 2.1% even allowing for inflation and taxation. The official figures also showed that people in Britain were spending less on their cars and homes and more on holidays and leisure. Spending abroad by British people increased by no less than 25% as they took advantage of cheap air fares, package holidays and tours overseas.

This indicates a clear trend in the pattern of spending. While this is good news for countries that are developing their tourist industry, it will undoubtedly pose serious problems as larger numbers of visitors demand more extensive facilities. The anticipated growth of tourism in the coming years must be properly planned and later chapters will examine the problems that are inevitable and ways in which they can be successfully solved.

Rome, the eternal city, where tourists from East and West meet (*Edward D. Mills*)

Chapter 3
The economic problem

We have already established that modern mass tourism is a comparatively recent phenomenon, even the words 'tourist' and 'tourism' have been in current use for less than two hundred years.

As we have already seen, in earlier times organised travel was limited to the movement of armies (and the consequent refugees), religious pilgrimages to places like Mecca, Jerusalem and Canterbury; student travel to universities such as Oxford, Paris and Bologna and merchants and envoys travelling for reasons of commerce or diplomacy. Travel for sport, recreation, holidays or personal leisure time fulfilment was rare.

While the medieval inn and hostelry was able to cope reasonably satisfactorily with the foreign visitor, such journeys were not always without hazards; bad roads, poor transport, doubtful hygiene and the highway robber all made such journeying suitable only for the young and rich or the dedicated and determined traveller.

Today 'tourists' of every nationality, creed and age have more exacting requirements and the ability to pay for them. Because of this the economic aspect of the international tourist industry is of considerable importance and for good or ill can have a major effect on the host country.

All tourists have different objectives; it has been said earlier, for example, that the Japanese seek 'instant participation', the Americans 'instant culture' and the Europeans 'sun, sea and sand'. This is, of course, an unsatisfactory generalisation, but tourists and holiday goals do, in general, break down into three broad categories:

1. Places of historic and cultural interest, cities with art galleries, museums, theatres and similar entertainment centres.
2. Places of relaxation and physical recreation: beach resorts, winter sports areas, mountains and lakes.
3. Natural and man-made sights such as wildlife reserves, bird sanctuaries, the Niagara Falls, etc.,

and ancient monuments like Ankor Watt, Stonehenge and the Temples at Luxor.

Each of these admittedly broad categories have a similarly broad geographical location: the first can be found in established urban centres and developed cities that have an existing infrastructure. The second, which relates basically to sea, sun and sand, is attracted to the coastal regions and accessible areas of countryside and mountains often based on an existing

Japanese tourists at a shrine in Kyoto, the old capital of Japan (*Edward D. Mills*)

European seekers of sun, sea and sand on the beach of the Adriatic at Rimini on the Italian Riviera (*Edward D. Mills*)

village. The third category is usually related to more remote regions, geographically dispersed and with no basic infrastructure.

The development of each type of tourism has different needs and different dangers, for the ever present problem – which cannot be too often emphasised – is that of the destruction or degradation of the particular attraction which originally appealed to the visitors, either because of its quiet separation, its ancient history or its beauty, or all three.

The international dimensions

Tourist development is supported at the highest international level by such authorities as the World Bank, the United Nations, UNESCO, the International Monetary Fund, the World Tourism Organisation and similar bodies, all of which attach great importance to the fact that international tourism results in considerable monetary transfer from country to country which have an important influence on world foreign trade balances.

In 1976 the share of such world trade estimated to be allocated to international tourism was in the region of 3.6% and this figure is reckoned to be growing at a greater rate than that related to world export trade. Thus the spread of international tourism is regarded as desirable for economic reasons. Until recent years the principal beneficiaries of such economic gains were the developed countries, the United States and the countries of Europe in particular, and this is still the case. Countries like Spain, Greece, Italy and even

Great Britain all regard tourism as an essential part of their economic activity.

A recent publication of the English Tourist Board 'Planning for Tourism in England' (1978) stated:

'Tourism is a major economic activity. Expenditure by overseas visitors to Britain makes a major contribution to the country's earning and provided a net benefit to our balance of payments of £1077 millions in 1977. Total spending by both British and overseas visitors in Britain in that year amounted to £4800 million. This expenditure generates employment both in tourist establishments like hotels and in other trades like shops and transport. The Henley Centre for Forecasting estimated that some 1½ million jobs were generated either dirctly or indirectly by tourism in 1975, equivalent to about 6% of total employment. Furthermore, in a period of increasing and/or high unemployment, the number of jobs in the hotel and other residential establishments sector has increased from 219 000 in 1971 to 264 000 in 1977. It is likely that tourism employment as a whole has increased at a somewhat greater rate given recent trends towards the use of self-catering accommodation.'

In 1963, a United Nations' conference in Rome declared that 'Tourism may contribute, and actually does contribute vitally to the economic growth of developing countries' (Recommendations on International Travel and Tourism). As a result, developing countries were encouraged to open up their frontiers to tourists and consider tourism as a major contribution to their economies, such efforts received considerable financial assistance from such bodies as the World Bank. Many developing countries such as Morocco, West African states like Sierra Leone, Senegal and the Gambia, and countries in the Far East, both large and small, began to encourage large numbers of tourists from the indutrialised countries of the world. In order to maintain the flow of tourists and meet their physical needs, buildings, services and supplies were all required.

Most developing countries were unable to provide these facilities without outside help and this meant the involvement of multi-national operators and international financial support. The danger in this approach lay in the fact that multi-national industries tend to draw benefits from their enterprises away from the countries in which they are based; in the case of tourist operations, this could defeat the original object of the venture, namely, to enhance the economy of the developing host country.

It is this dilemma that has led to considerable divergence of opinion among economists regarding the ultimate value to a developing country of the fostering and active promotion of a tourist industry.

The economic arguments for and against are beyond the subject of this book, but it must be realised that the international tourist industry exists, and is growing each year. Some of the reasons for this inevitable growth have been briefly mentioned in earlier chapters. The problem that must be resolved is the integration of tourism into an ancient or modern way of life in a way which produces positive benefits rather than destruction.

Tourism as an industry

It has been said that tourism is an industry without an end product. This is not strictly true for the end product is rest, relaxation, recreation and even education for those who enjoy the facilities provided by the host country.

The facilities required by the industry, the equivalent of the raw materials and plant needed by manufacturing industries have been mentioned earlier but as part of the economic structure they need consideration in greater detail. These are the aspects of tourism that need planning and design solutions which, together with detailed case studies, comprise a large part of this book.

To attract tourists and holiday visitors an area must have certain features which, singly or combined, appeal to a wide cross-section of people of differing cultural backgrounds, financial status and ethnic origin. These features can be broadly divided into three main categories:

1. Geographic and climatic.
2. Cultural and artistic.
3. Sporting and recreational.

These categories are not mutually exclusive and some

The Pyramids at Gizeh, Egypt built as Royal tombs over 5000 years ago now attract thousands of tourists every year (*Edward D. Mills*)

The ski slopes of the Austrian Alps where winter sport enthusiasts enjoy the sun and the snow (*Edward D. Mills*)

of the most popular tourist centres of the world can offer all three. However, all of these 'attraction features' require the back-up facilities of transportation, accommodation and service. While the need for these can be readily appreciated in an established tourist centre like Venice, Paris or the Spanish Costa Brava, they are still important in the game reserves of East Africa, the ski slopes of the Swiss Alps or the even more remote regions such as the Galapagos Islands. Here tourists can now, under strictly controlled conditions, follow in the footsteps of Charles Darwin to the islands where he first began his work on his theory of the *Origin of Species*.

This is the point at which the development of tourist facilities can destroy the features that originally attracted the tourists and holiday visitors: the next chapter will be devoted to this vital subject.

Tourism and the developed countries

Historically, international tourism began in the cultural centres of the Western world like London, Paris, Rome, Venice and Vienna. Later it spread to the USA, the USSR, and other regions where an existing infrastructure enabled gradual expansion to take place. Old coaching inns were enlarged to provide additional accommodation; roads and railway routes were extended and airports built. Other facilities such as shops, resort facilities and similar amenities were gradually added to the existing stock.

In this way the tourist industry was slowly integrated into the everyday life of the area. In some cases, like Venice, the industry ultimately took over the location so that Venice now exists principally for the holiday visitor.

The older holiday resorts in the UK are a good example of this process of gradualism and the integration of tourist and local resident is advanced. In such places both parties enjoy the benefits of improved local facilities and the host community gains from improved employment opportunities and other benefits. Environmental degradation can occur when the older established tourist centres are allowed to develop in a haphazard fashion, but proper planning can mitigate the situation.

Some of these old tourist regions, not only cities but also areas like Scotland, the Mediterranean region, the Alps and Egypt now depend heavily on tourism as part of their economic strategy and they are learning to plan ahead and control the industry that brings them much of their wealth. For example, according to

There are still many 'far-away places' such as Toby Bay, Jamaica where few tourists visit and where those who know the area can get away from the world outside (*Edward D. Mills*)

the Scottish Tourist Board's Annual Report 1979; in 1978, 13 million trips were made in Scotland, giving employment to 100 000 people and earning £523 million. One in ten of the visitors were from overseas, contributing almost one-third of the tourist spending. Since 1970 the Scottish Tourist Board has invested over £12 million, creating some 7000 new jobs and making tourism one of Scotland's biggest industries.

This example could be repeated for many of the established centres of the world and it is certain that developed countries will, in future, rely even more on the tourist industry to provide employment and economic stability.

Venice, once an independent State with a considerable influence in the Adriatic, now primarily a tourist centre (*Edward D. Mills*)

Tourism and the developing countries

The developed countries of the world still receive the major part of the world's tourist income which was established to be in the region of £18 000 million in 1976. The developing countries have a different problem to that of absorbing large numbers of short-term visitors into an existing infrastructure. Their problem is the sudden incursion of a tourist population into an undeveloped area of special interest and attraction.

Many developing countries have 'attraction features' of unequalled splendour: the vast areas of the National Parks and Game Reserves in East Africa; the

ancient cultures and historic monuments of the Far East; the sunshine and unspoiled beaches of parts of West Africa; the Pacific Islands and the Caribbean.

Many of these areas include spectacular scenery and natural phenomena, and each year new discoveries of ancient customs and crafts help to establish potential areas for new tourist expansion.

The sudden explosion of tourist population can permanently damage the unwilling host country if the development is not treated with great care. Where multi-national tourist industry operators have im-

Typical Scottish highland scenery of lochs and mountains that has helped to make tourism one of Scotland's largest industries (*Edward D. Mills*)

ported a standardised ready-made, almost prefabricated, tourist infrastructure, starting with the intercontinental airports, the development of foreign tourist enclaves naturally follows and the gulf between host and visitor becomes a yawning chasm. Once more the tourist industry destroys the very atmosphere the tourist wishes to experience and enjoy.

Integration of tourism

Just as the success of tourism and holidays in the developed countries has been in large measure due to absorption and integration, so this must be the basis of successful tourist development in developing countries. Firstly this involves the relating of any tourist facilities to the existing social context and by proper planning relating them to existing communities so that host and visitor can meet and live alongside one another, even for a short time.

Secondly, a cultural dialogue should be positively encouraged so that local folk festivals, pageants, and celebrations can be revived and developed for the cultural benefit of the tourist and the financial benefit of the local people. A good example of this is the formation of the National Dance Company of Sierra Leone which has achieved world-wide renown through its tours throughout the world as well as its performances in its homeland.

Thirdly, many local arts and crafts are in danger of dying out as the modern industrialised world replaces their products by the mass produced objects of the Western world. International organisations such as UNESCO are now advocating the revitalising of such dying cultures and industries which through planned careful commercialisation can not only bring much needed revenue to the local communities and craftsmen, but can also restore deteriorating cultural heritages.

A recent example supported by UNESCO has been the reconstruction of Borodur in Indonesia, near Yogyakata. This terraced Buddhist shrine nearly 140 ft high built in the late eighth and early ninth centuries, predates the great European cathedrals by four centuries and has now become one of the great centres of cultural tourism in the Far East.

By such means ethnic culture can be converted into artistic performance, enabling tourist receiving communities to safeguard or recover their own cultural identity and at the same time make their own special contribution to the common fund of universal culture.

Such developments have been greatly assisted by

An East African game reserve covering many thousands of square miles where great concentrations of wildlife attract tourists from all over the world. This tourist traffic has been a major contribution to world wildlife conservation (*Edward D. Mills*)

The Leonardo de Vinci international airport at Rome, one of the crossroads of the air carrying tourist traffic for all parts of the globe (*Edward D. Mills*)

the researches of Marie-Francoise Lanfant of the Centre of Sociological Studies of the National Centre of Scientific Research in Paris.

Benefits of tourism

To conclude, properly planned tourism can bring revenue to developed tourist areas; it can also provide much needed foreign currency and improved local living standards to developing areas of the world, and by such means help to build bridges between the developed and less developed communities.

The integration of tourism with the host country, mentioned earlier, is a matter of great importance in order to avoid the establishment of tourist enclaves that operate independently of the host country. In this respect the 'Tourist Friends Association' founded twelve years ago by Mohammed Fonly Sayed in Egypt is a unique venture.

There are now some 4000 members of the Association in Cairo and others all over Egypt, who on a purely voluntary basis welcome tourists and offer help and assistance to promote understanding and sympathy between the people of Egypt and foreign visitors, so that they can see how Egyptians and their families live in towns, villages and farms. The TFA is not in competition with the official tourist industry, but offers friendship and companionship on a personal and individual level, thus developing a bridge-building role between tourists and the host country – an example that could be usefully followed world-wide.

To quote from the editorial of the UNESCO International Social Science Journal No. 1 *The Anatomy of Tourism*:

> 'Tourism has become an industry, a vast, globe-encircling "system", the direct and indirect effects of which are still poorly understood and even less well controlled. It regenerates as it pollutes, pays off as it undermines its very base, represents a source both of constructive experience and cultural enrichment as of alienation and degradation. In short, tourism is a mirror of the contradictions inherent in the present state of world development. . . .'

...e National Dance Company of Sierra Leone which has ...hieved world-wide renown through its international dance tours ... well as its performances in its homeland (*Edward D. Mills*)

Chapter 4
The physical problem

In earlier chapters the inevitable problem of the physical impact of tourism on both urban and rural environments has been briefly mentioned. Before the planning and design solutions can be considered it is essential that the physical problems posed by large scale tourism should be analysed. Richard England, the architect, has summed up the situation very succinctly, as follows:

'1. Unspoilt place with unique character attracts tourists.
2. New buildings and amenities necessary to accommodate tourists bring change.
3. More tourists bring more change.
4. Loss of initial attractive character becomes the element responsible for departure of tourists.
5. Final result, environment, social and economic disaster.'

This tragic cycle from quiet isolation to environmental pollution and spoilation through the tourist invasion is not inevitable and can be avoided by means of proper planning and sympathetic design as later case studies will demonstrate.

The urban scene

Many urban tourist attractions have withstood the onslaughts of the elements and everyday normal use for centuries. In every major city of the world historic buildings and events now draw large numbers of tourists throughout the year, seasonal weather conditions have less effect on the urban tourist scene than the rural one.

In 1978 the cathedrals and greater churches of England received over 20 million visitors – as distinct from normal worshippers. In 1978 nearly twelve million tourists visited the 120 ancient monuments in Britain run by the Department of the Environment. They paid nearly £5 million in entrance fees, but the cost of maintaining the buildings they visited amounted to nearly three times that sum, £14.5 million.

The impact of tourism

The impact of vast numbers of visitors on any building fabric can be dramatic: the enormously increased tourist traffic in London's Westminster Abbey, for example, has resulted in the greatly accelerated erosion of the stone paving within the building as hundreds of thousands of tourists wearing modern footwear tread the centuries-old stone flooring slabs which were in bygone days walked on only by hundreds of religious pilgrims wearing a much softer type of footwear.

One of the world's greatest architectural tourist attractions, the Parthenon, built on the Acropolis in Athens BC 545–438, has received millions of visitors in its history extending for over 2000 years: it too has begun to deteriorate more rapidly in recent years due to the relentless onslaught of heavy-footed tourists. Twenty years ago a visitor could wander freely around the ruins of the Parthenon; ten years ago tourists were allowed only up to the perimeter of the Temple; today the whole area around the Parthenon is out-of-bounds because of the erosion of the marble paving through the endless wear of tourists' shoes. Tourists' wear and tear has, in a few years done more damage than normal everyday use over twenty centuries.

This situation applies not only to many of the world's great architectural monuments but also to smaller buildings now included in the tourist circuit. The National Trust of Great Britain owns and maintains over 200 buildings of architectural and historic importance, 88 gardens and over 450000 acres of land throughout Great Britain; these too are suffering from the problem of over use. A recent note in the *Architect's Journal* (September 3, 1980) reports on the concern of

Westminster Abbey, London. Originally the Benedictine Monastery founded by St. Dunstan in AD 960 and largely rebuilt in the 13th Century is one of the great London tourist attractions that is being adversely affected by the hundreds of thousands of annual visitors (*Jarrold and Sons Ltd*)

the National Trust about 'over visiting'. Certain of the Trust's houses and gardens are literally being worn out under the onslaught of a massive visiting public that goes on growing. For example, the restored 18th century curtains of Erddig – which opened in 1978 – fell prey to inquisitive fingers within three months. The dilemma lies in the fact that the National Trust needs the finance from additional tourists in order to continue its work of maintenance and preservation. It is clear that planning and propaganda is needed to avoid self-destruction.

Pollution and erosion

To be fair to the tourist industry, other dangers to the world's historic buildings should be mentioned, for these too can be eliminated by proper planning. One of the most famous monuments in the world, the Taj Mahal, the beautiful mausoleum built at Agra on the River Jumua by the Mogul Emperor of India, Shar Jahan, over 300 years ago, is slowly disintegrating as the marble of which it is built corrodes as a result of the pollution of the atmosphere by sulphur-dioxide.

The nearby oil refinery at Mathura adds to the

The Parthenon, Athens. A tourist attraction for over 2000 years (*Edward D. Mills*)

Sissinghurst Castle, Kent. The remains of a Tudor and Elizabethan mansion once the home of Harold Nicholson and V. Sackville West that became a National Trust property in 1967. The gardens are a special attraction, 126 000 tourists visited Sissinghurst in 1980. The National Trust magazine quotes Nigel Nicholson, who lives there 'Sissinghurst is too popular . . . or rather it is too much visited. This is not a unique problem among National Trust properties, but it is exceptional. If the garden is not to be slowly worn away by innocent feet, we must do something to control the numbers who go there' (*Lionel Browne*)

atmosphere of Agra a ton of sulphur-dioxide every hour. Together with existing industrial pollution the results could be catastrophic.

Clearly inadequate planning controls have been the major cause, but fortunately the recent (1980) Report by the Indian Heritage Society, accepted by the Indian Government, offers hope for the future of the Taj Mahal and its multitude of tourist visitors.

The Report recommends major re-zoning of industry in the area, and the establishment of a green belt around the Mausoleum to absorb the sulphur-dioxide (it is of interest to note that it has been discovered that Mango trees are particularly efficient in performing this function).

In other parts of the world pollution and erosion threaten historic buildings and monuments; the industrial development on the Italian mainland has endangered Venice, many of Egypt's age-old treasures are under threat, some will perish through neglect, others because of lack of town planning controls has allowed industrial development perilously near the ancient sites. It has been estimated that Cairo alone has lost one hundred and twenty Islamic monuments of importance in the last thirty years; seventy others are under immediate threat and two hundred may be lost in the next thirty years.

Yet buildings are an important part of a nation's heritage as well as being important tourist attractions. In these cases the tourist can reasonably claim that Governments are the destroyers because of their lack of planning or sensitive forethought.

The tourist 'pressure'

A further problem of tourism in urban areas is the impact that a seasonal influx of visitors has on the existing urban infrastructure.

In the holiday season the demand for hotel accommodation increases dramatically as the tourist saturation point is reached. Governments encourage the provision of more hotel bed-places often in a situation where local residents are in need of better housing. Buildings in city areas that are capable of conversion to housing accommodation are often converted to secondclass tourist accommodation. This fact, coupled with the fact that seasonal visitors put great

The Taj Mahal, Agra, India. This famous marble building has been suffering from air pollution by neighbouring industry; action has now been taken by the Indian Government, and the area has been declared a pollution-free zone (*Edward D. Mills*)

pressure on urban transport systems, buses, taxis and trains as well as causing traffic congestion on roads can lead to a growing antagonism between the local residents and the tourists.

Poor and unsympathetic hotel design is also often a cause of local irritation. It has been said that many new urban hotels 'will last two generations, took two years to build and look as though they took about two hours to design'.

Apart from living accommodation and transport, urban tourists put pressure on water supply, sewers,

Cairo, Egypt. A city of ancient monuments many of which may be threatened by lack of town planning control (*Edward D. Mills*)

police services, telephone and electricity supplies. They affect shops and shopping patterns and leisure activities. Tourist demands can also create serious social problems in large cities. In Mexico, 60% of the tourist revenue from the vast numbers of visitors who cross the border from the USA comes from the border town 'red-light' districts, described euphemistically by the Mexicans as 'zones of tolerance'. In other parts of the world gambling networks create problems, and drug smuggling is a permanent menace. There is always the danger that unplanned, misused tourist facilities can lead to the final spoilation of the very attractions that brought the tourists in the first place.

The tourist resort

Many of the problems arising from the influence of the influx of tourists into urban and city areas also apply to what can be described as 'resort areas'. These are usually, as described earlier, coastal regions and accessible areas of countryside and mountains.

Such places throughout the world have become popular centres for holidaymakers because of the beautiful scenery, the sunshine and clean beaches, or the availability of such facilities as winter sports, sailing, fishing or other recreational or sporting activities. The needs are transport, accommodation and facilities of a wide variety.

The problem arises because, in most cases, the development of such 'resort areas' has been haphazard and uncontrolled; too often any existing infrastructure has been completely swamped and the original character of the area completely changed. The coastline of Spain, the Costa Brava and Costa del Sol are horrifying examples of this despoiling of the countryside. The island of Majorca has also suffered in this way and considerable damage has been done to the island of Malta.

Siting of buildings

Firstly, the siting of new buildings has too often been unsympathetic with little consideration or understanding of the needs and demands of the local physical environment in relation to both manmade and natural features.

The familiar description of many cities of the West as 'concrete jungles' could be equally well applied to miles of Mediterranean coastline ruined by massive towering hotels and apartment blocks, insensitive in

An exceptionally ill-considered example of tourist development in Malta. A badly sited hotel has permanently ruined the skyline and the visual impact of the medieval Salina Palace built by the Crusaders (*Edward D. Mills*)

Once a quiet fishing village, Blanes, Spain, now a concrete jungle that has destroyed the original attractiveness permanently. Even the beaches have become unauthorised car parks (*Lionel Browne*)

design and often impractical in operation. These, together with the seemly endless regiments of monotonous holiday villas have converted the holidaymaker's 'dream' of a sunlit paradise into a cruel mirror image of the 'reality' from which the holiday period was intended to be the means of escape.

Sadly, in many parts of the world these so-called resorts are beyond salvation; the endeavour must be to ensure that a similar fate does not befall areas that are as yet unspoiled.

Caravanning and camping

Inappropriate tourist development of other kinds can also become a form of environmental pollution. Badly located and unplanned permanent and temporary caravan and camping sites with inadequate amenities and little control can have a serious impact on the countryside as can be seen from many examples in Europe.

In Sweden and the Canadian Rockies, for example, the problem has been handled with much greater sensitivity and many camp sites in forest and lake areas are models of their kind.

Traffic density

Traffic movement to and from countryside tourist areas can also cause major deterioration in local amenities. Increased volumes of traffic through hitherto quiet villages can be a major source of annoyance to local residents and can cause serious damage to ancient buildings and small residential communities.

The enormous growth of motor traffic means greater demands for car parking, toilets and refreshment facilities for the long distance traveller. Even walkers and picnickers can create lasting damage to places of natural beauty through the sheer pressure of numbers.

In Britain this problem has already been identified in the Lake District and the Snowdon area of Wales where serious erosion of footpaths has been caused simply by the vast increase in the number of visitors, over 400 000 a year; these very visitors seeking the peace and solitude of the mountains and lakes are contributing to the destruction of the very attraction that drew them to these areas in the first place. Mount Fugi in Japan is similarly suffering from the thousands of trampling feet that climb to the top each year.

An attractive forest camp site in the Rocky Mountains of Alberta, Canada (*Alberta Public Affairs Bureau*)

Litter

In all tourist situations litter is an increasing problem which affects both town and country and seaside. Litter can pollute water supplies, create insanitary conditions, endanger both farm animals and wildlife and inevitably reduce the aesthetic appeal of both urban and country areas.

It has been estimated that the Forestry Commission have to remove annually from the New Forest in England over 1000 tons of litter, and in Sweden on one day on a twelve-mile stretch of coastline near

Mount Fuji, Japan now threatened by the thousands of tourists that climb to its summit (*Edward D. Mills*)

Malmo, 500 youth volunteers collected over 700 tons of litter.

Far-away places

Tourists and holidaymakers in the inevitable search for even more remote places where they can escape from their normal environment are now able to travel much further afield to places as yet unspoiled by the onrush of the tourist industry. In such situations the danger of tourist pollution is even more acute for the visitor still requires man-made basic amenities.

There are still places on earth where man has not yet visited, but such spots may not remain undiscovered for very much longer. Wherever man penetrates the natural world he inevitably leaves his mark for good or ill. A few examples will highlight the problem.

In a remote Hawaiian swamp which is the last-known location of a certain native species it has been discovered that even a footpath used only by scientists once or twice a year has enabled a foreign species to invade the habitat and thus endanger the native species.

In a remote part of Yugoslavia severe losses of chamois and other shy mountain animals have been reported. They have fallen over precipices following disturbance by unaccustomed noises and disturbance caused by the unusual movements and highly coloured dress of tourists visiting the peaceful high peaks by means of a cableway.

Rare trees and plants can also become virtually extinct following the introduction of species from other countries infected with spores fatal to the local species. Hitherto inaccessible swamps, water glades and remote islands which have become the last refuge of rare animals and plants have sometimes been invaded by portable boats, hovercraft and helicopters and these creatures have become endangered because they have lost their last natural defences.

Visitors to remote island bird breeding colonies have kept parent birds away from their nests and eggs in unfavourable weather so that the young have failed to hatch, thus interrupting the essential breeding cycle to the detriment of the colony.

The damaging effect of some insecticides and pesticides on wildlife is well known, and the large scale clearance of rain forests in South America for both the

A deserted beach in the Gambia, West Africa as yet unspoiled, but for how long? (*Edward D. Mills*)

A safari bus in an East African game reserve watching a solitary lion (*Edward D. Mills*)

improvement of road systems and the exploitation of natural timber resources has led to a major reduction in the animal population of the areas. Cavers and inexperienced underwater explorers have caused considerable damage, often through lack of knowledge rather than deliberate vandalism and this can speed the destruction of the wonders of nature that they seek to enjoy and admire. Once more the danger of over-enthusiasm can prove fatal to the original feature of attraction.

Nowhere is this dilemma more obvious than in the vast Game Reserves and National Parks of East Africa and elsewhere. These last haunts of vast herds of elephants, wildebeeste, water buffalo, and other animals are one of the principal tourist attractions in these developing countries.

Kenya's growing tourist industry, which is a major contribution to the country's economy, is largely based on the wildlife of Ambroseli, Tsavo, the Masai Mara and the other Game Parks, but even here the conflict between the needs of tourists and those of game herds and local tribesmen and their cattle is obvious, and a reasonable balance must be struck.

A visit to the Nairobi Game Park at a holiday weekend when a solitary lion can be seen surrounded by a group of tourist safari minibuses underlines the problem, and it is sometimes difficult to differentiate between the watchers and the watched. One consolation is that big game hunting by tourists is now carried out with the camera and the telephoto lens with the aid of a camera and not with the high-powered gun with a telescopic sight.

Thus even in remote areas and far-away places the pressure of tourism must be regulated, planned and controlled. Otherwise these places may also suffer the fate of the Costa Brava and other desecrated areas of the world; destroyed by thoughtlessness rather than deliberate intent.

Professor Nelson H.H. Graburn, Professor of Anthropology at the University of California, Berkeley, USA, who has pioneered a course on *The anthropology of tourism*, described the course in the UNESCO International Social Service Journal, Vol. 1, 1980, mentioned earlier. The following extract from the course content summarises the problem and suggests solutions which can be reduced to a single phrase 'wise planning' which can be naturally extended to include 'good design'.

'The ecological and sheer physical impart of tourism is considered, by introducing the concepts of carrying capacity, land usage, infrastructure planning and parks and preserves to the students. The differential capabilities of various environments in withstanding the volume, behaviour and life-style of tourists are examined in case studies.

Damaging behaviour, such as hunting, collecting shells and plants, trampling vegetation and frightening wildlife, are considered, along with the effects of infrastructural developments, vehicular use, hotels, sewage, and bad examples for local populations of waste, litter and the sale of natural and historical items. It is also pointed out that it is the people of the industrialised world, who have seen their own environments disrupted, who carry the ethic of conservation and preservation to many Third World areas which, through of lack of education and the population explosion, may be rapidly destroying their own living spaces. Thus, *wise planning* for tourism may have a salutory effect on material and environmental destruction.'

Chapter 5
Planning for tourism

The first impact of the tourist is on the infrastructure of any society and, at the outset of any holiday, the journey from the place of residence to the holiday location marks the beginning of the vacation. This may seem obvious, but the effect of a massive exodus from the home base, if badly organised, can be just as catastrophic as the large scale visitor influx into a holiday area. The congestion at any major airport during the peak weeks of the holiday season is ample evidence of this problem and normal business travellers often avoid such periods of the year.

Tourist journeys commence by road, rail, air or sea and each mode of travel requires special consideration. For some tourists the journey is an integral part of the holiday, for others simply the means of getting to a particular place as quickly as possible. Ocean cruises, long-distance coach, minibus and rail tours usually make use of existing facilities for the regular stopovers, or in some cases such as minibus tours, carrying camping equipment for tented stopovers; the requirements of these short stay campers will be dealt with in the next chapter.

Rail enthusiasts can still cross the USSR on the legendary Trans-Siberian Express travelling from Helsinki in Finland in the West to Nakhodka in the East. Those who prefer travel by water can encircle the globe by luxury cruise liner, sail down the Nile from Cairo to Luxor and the Valley of the Kings, or explore the quiet canals of England, Sweden, Holland and other European countries.

Road travel

The availability of the motor car to millions of people and the development of the organised tour by motor coach or minibus has made road development throughout the world a matter of great importance. New motorways and road networks can speed travel but if they are unplanned they can cause great environmental damage.

On the positive side, by-passes around quiet villages can preserve the peace of a rural community, protect ancient buildings from harmful traffic vibrations and reduce air pollution. At the same time, new roads in hitherto undisturbed areas can upset the flora and fauna of an area and disturb established farming patterns.

The responsibility of the tourist industry in this field can be over-emphasised: in 1972 for example, some 280 thousand million passenger miles were covered by travellers of all kinds in Great Britain; 80% was by private motor car, but only about 15% of the total mileage was for holiday purposes. It is clear that on the basis of these figures the impact of tourism on travel facilities is minimal in total – the problem lies in the seasonal nature of the surges of the tourist traffic.

The Recommendations of the *Countryside in 1970 Conference* held in England in 1965 had a Study Group specially devoted to 'Traffic and its impact on the countryside'. The Conference recommended that action should be taken at once:

'To deal with the problems of motorised access to, and the passage of traffic through, the countryside on a national and regional level as an integral part of town and country planning. To press ahead with the channelling of through traffic on a national network of high-capacity highways; to provide intensive recreation areas near to large towns; to prepare local plans for access to the countryside in order to ensure that the motoring public can enjoy the countryside without spoiling it, and thus help to reduce the pressure of traffic over the countryside.'

Travellers in the UK will appeciate how relevant were these recommendations quoted from Robert Arvill's book *Man and Environment – crisis and the strategy of choice*. Over fifteen years later there are few signs that the advice given has been heeded. Those who think that the problem will solve itself as higher petrol prices makes private motoring ever more expensive will be disappointed by recent statistics that show that rising petrol prices have had little effect on the travelling habits of the general public in the developed countries of the world.

Roads and access

The development of any civilisation has always been related to road building. The Roman Empire followed the Roman road and invading armies sweeping across Europe two thousand years ago were maintained by the road system constructed to link the outposts of the Empire.

The Roman conquest of Britain included a formidable programme of road building: in four hundred years they constructed over 6000 miles of roadway cutting cross the country in long, straight lines, many of which have today becomes routes of our modern highways. Even today the remains of this road network can be found in Britain and elsewhere. (This manuscript is being written only a few hundred metres from the site of the road from London to the South Coast built for the Roman legions.)

Roads are essential for communication of all kinds, trade and commerce has spread throughout the world by roads within countries, by sea routes linking countries and in more recent years by air routes encircling the globe. The first overland routes were tracks through undeveloped country between human settlements. In Africa and other parts of the world these foot tracks are still used; later with the development of transport drawn by horses, oxen etc, the tracks became roads and the invention of the motor car finally established the modern highway pattern and the motorway.

This evolution was a gradual one until the early part of the 20th century. The mass ownership of the motor car and the consequent increased road traffic has resulted in the last fifty years in an enormous development of the road networks of all developed countries. Thus providing speedier communication but often at great cost to the countryside and landscape.

While roads did not develop for the benefit of the mass tourist industry, they are essential to it. Tourist traffic does cause considerable congestion, particularly in peak holiday periods as any journey to the West Country in England during August proves. Tourist development needs road access as a link with other transport systems such as arrival ports, airports or railway stations and as means of communication between tourist centres.

National and regional planning schemes for the development of road networks such as the motorway networks in the developing countries of the world are of great importance. The need to by-pass towns and villages to reduce urban and rural congestion has already been referred to, but the problem lies in the fact that such measures inevitably result in an intrusion into the countryside with the inevitable consequences that follow all forms of development.

This is particularly noticeable in the virgin areas of developing countries where the temptation to drive long straight highways across open plains or forest areas is great. New road networks in hitherto unde-

Part of the German autobahn network winding through the pine forests near Luedenscheid (*German National Tourist Office*)

A German autobahn roadhouse with terraced restaurant (*German National Tourist Office*)

veloped areas can be not only be dangerous to the wildlife of the area but are themselves often the least desirable form of road – long, straight and unbroken stretches that encourage excessive traffic speeds, and suffer severe weather conditions, such as great heat or heavy rainfall. This means that constant maintenance is necessary to avoid dangerous deterioration of the road surface. While engineering criteria are usually given adequate consideration, landscaping standards are often overlooked.

A road is a linear form of development, this suggests that the idea which has been developed along some motorways, namely linear Nature Reserves along the verges could be applied to any major road network; the incorporation of trees in a non-forest situation gives a background to the landscape on each side and enhances the road itself. Where forest areas are cleared the retention of tree groups adds to the landscape value of the area.

Roads and tourism

The single fact that roads are used by people for work or pleasure means that the development of essential amenities such as petrol stations and garages, toilets, overnight stopping places and parking areas are required. On long cross-country highways these facilities will need to be planned at regular intervals, and while they may often be associated with existing villages or hamlets, in many developing countries where such settlements may be very far apart, virgin sites may be the only solution. In all cases, careful planning, proper grouping of facilities and efficient signposting, together with imaginative landscaping, are all part of the contribution that planners and designers can make to ensure that the tourists 'escape route' does not spoil the countryside through which it passes.

There are many publications – books, Government reports, Codes of Practice and International Standards – relating to road design and road layout. Some of these are listed in the Bibliography at the end of this book and others can be found in *Planning*, published by Butterworths. These give the technical requirements for safety and efficiency in design. Standards of aesthetic quality can only be maintained by designers with an imaginative understanding of the long-term problems.

Car parking

One of the inevitable demands of all tourist activities, in this car-owning age, is that of parking space for the motor vehicle, private car, minibus or long distance coach. This applies to urban and rural situations in both developed tourist situations as well as undeveloped ones.

The design of car parking is even more important in developed tourist areas, now that one widely canvassed solution to the problem of over-visited beauty spots throughout the world, such as Mt. Fugi, the Snowdonia National Park, the English Lake District (and perhaps one day even Mt. Everest), is the control of access to these places and the creation of car-free zones. By this means motor cars can be parked at a distance from the vulnerable areas, where visitors can first have a distant view and then either walk or be transported to the site by minibus or similar conveyance.

This system has already been applied experimentally to the Snowdonia National Park in Wales. Here the visitor leaves his car on the periphery of the Park and travels within the Snowdon area by the 'Sherpa' bus service which also links with the public transport bus service. By this means greater control over the pattern of tourist use of the area can be achieved, and the visitor can enjoy the beauty of Snowdon more easily. This technique is applicable to many existing and developing tourist situations both urban and rural.

Many older cities have found the total prohibition of motor cars to be a particularly suitable solution to the problem of congestion and pollution. One of the attractions of Dubrodnik in Yugoslavia and Medina in Malta, and a number of other towns and cities throughout the world, is the fact that motor traffic is banned. Pedestrianised zones in major cities are now

The Sherpa bus service in the Snowdonia National Park in Wales. This carries tourists from periphery car parks to the Snowdonia area (*Snowdonia National Park Information Service*)

becoming popular and are regarded as an essential part of many new town plans.

This idea of control of the motor car, however, means that parking spaces are essential and if the cure is not to be worse than the disease such car parks must be designed and maintained with great care whether they are in urban or rural situations.

There are several essential factors that need consideration:

1 Means of access and egress should be adequate for the expected maximum load, and must be clearly marked, remembering that many tourists may have limited knowledge of the native language. International directional signs or easily understood pictograms should be used. If one car park is full, the location of an alternative car park should be indicated if the demand warrants this. The method of payment, if any, must be clearly shown; this may vary with local needs and customs.

2 The car park must not be too large: a number of smaller linked parks is preferable to one large characterless area. A simple means of identifying the location of the car when parked is essential. The fact that so many cars look alike can be frustrating to a foreign visitor who cannot find his own vehicle because of the lack of location identity.

3 In hot climates, shade is desirable to prevent unpleasant overheating of the cars; trees and well planned landscape will provide shade, will aid location, break up the visual monotony of large numbers of cars and give colour and interest to an otherwise uninteresting area.

Dubrovnik, Yugoslavia. An ancient walled town where motor traffic is excluded to the benefit of tourists and residents (*Edward D. Mills*)

The alternative to organised car parking. An inconvenient and untidy temporary car park at an English Country Show (*Edward D. Mills*)

4 Essential facilities such as toilets must be included in larger car parks. Where several parks are grouped together a small refreshment kiosk, first-aid post and police or traffic control point is desirable.

5 Heavy vehicles such as buses and coaches should have separate parking areas with special access points and areas should be set aside for motor cycles, bicycles and disabled visitors' vehicles.

Very large areas of uninterrupted car parking are both aesthetically unsatisfactory and inefficient. Landscaping, including planting and changes in ground level can humanise any car parking situation.

Beaulieu, Hampshire. Car and coach parks (shaded areas) are very carefully sited in relation to the buildings, screened by trees and divided into separate landscaped areas, convenient for the visitors and causing minimum disturbance to the natural environment (*Leonard Manasseh Partnership*)

A recent example of large-scale car parking designed with these criteria in mind is the National Exhibition Centre, Birmingham, where parking on the 300-acre site is provided for 15 000 visitors' cars, together with 500 motor coaches. The parking is dispersed in a number of areas around the periphery of the site and separated from the Exhibition Complex by a large manmade lake. Each car park is divided into smaller units by means of planting trees and grassed earth mounds to break up the visual impact of the cars. Local toilets and other facilities are provided together with a frequent visitor bus service from the car parks to the Exhibition buildings.

Automobile associations in many countries of the world can provide much useful advice on the design and operation of tourist car parking facilities and in many countries will also assist in traffic control, signposting of tourist attractions and the organisation of traffic diversions to minimise congestions at peak holiday periods. The service in these areas of the AA and RAC in the UK is well-known. Their breakdown and recovery services has been appreciated by many thousands of tourist visitors to Britain.

Tourist pressures on the infrastructure

While roads and other forms of access are clearly essential for the movement of large numbers of tourists and holidaymakers, it should be obvious that such tourist flows inevitably result in a massive increase in the population density of the place they visit.

Nowhere has the effect of this massive seasonal migration been more apparent and disastrous than the Spanish coastal areas and similar holiday areas. Many of these now overcrowded regions originally

A central London car park on the site of a demolished building, unsightly and inconvenient (*Edward D. Mills*)

consisted of a series of quiet fishing villages, self-contained and self-sufficient.

The arrival of the sun-seeking holidaymaker was rapidly followed by the uncontrolled development of huge, multi-storey hotels and other facilities placing a great strain of the infrastructure of the area which, in many cases was not developed to the same degree. Inadequate drainage and refuse collection facilities, insufficient electricity and water supplies, and under-developed telephone systems have all contributed to a saturation that is difficult to correct once it has arisen.

Advance planning could have prevented the inconvenience that now faces both local resident and visitor. While the visitors may have brought employment and wealth to the area they have also placed a considerable burden, both physical and financial, on the area they visit and much of this is related to the pressure on an inadequate infrastructure.

George Young's book *Tourism, blessing or blight* gives the following figures which were calculated in 1968, in relation to the cost per day for public services for each visitor to Hawaii:

	US dollars
Roads and highways	0.189
Airports	0.248
Sewerage	0.049
Police and fire protection	0.090
Local recreation facilities	0.111
Total per visitor per day	0.688

This may sound a small sum, but updating to take inflation into account would probably give a current (1983) figure of 2–2.5 US dollars per visitor per day. The fact that in 1977, Hawaii received half a million tourists from Japan alone, puts these costs into perspective.

Very few underdeveloped areas consider such costs in their overall plan (if they have one), when encouraging tourism in a new location. Such an exercise is a vital part of any tourism study, otherwise the benefits of a growing tourist industry can be outweighed by its cost to the local community. Another factor which cannot be ignored is that of the self-destructive effect on an inadequate infrastructure. Visitors will soon cease to visit a holiday area where water has to be rationed at peak consumption hours, where sewage and refuse disposal systems have reached saturation point and have become a health hazard and where telephone and electricity supply systems fail with alarming frequency because of overloading.

All these problems have been experienced in many parts of the world, where unplanned, and unco-ordinated tourist development has overwhelmed a hitherto low population density area. To specify particular places would be unfair, but most travel agencies receive constant complaints about such shortcomings and clearly a holidaymaker who has suffered from such deficiencies will be very reluctant to revisit the place in question; such rejection of a previously popular area can be the beginning of an irreversible decline.

The solution to the problem of tourist saturation and its effect on the infrastructure of a region, whether it is an existing tourist centre or a projected one, either in an urban or a rural setting, is neither simple or cheap.

Evaluation and forward planning

The future development of the tourist industry, whether in the context of an existing tourist area, or one that is at present undeveloped needs forward planning if the natural benefits are not to be outweighed by the disadvantages. This applies equally to urban, rural, and remote regions. Such planning must deal with the following issues:

1 Tourist demand in the region and the establishment of a saturation level in relation to the local community.
2 Accessibility by road, sea or air and the capacity of existing facilities or their possible expansion.
3 Accommodation for visitors in a variety of forms – hotels, motels, apartments, caravan and camping sites – and other forms of accommodation, including car parking.
4 The impact of large numbers of seasonal visitors on the infrastructure of the region with particular reference to sewage and refuse disposal, electricity, water, telephone and other supplies, as well as fire, police and coastguard protection (where appropriate). The adequacy of local health services and hospital facilities.
5 The increased demand for recreation, leisure and shopping facilities generated by a temporarily increased population.
6 The need to protect the existing landscape, historic or natural assets which attract the tourists and holidaymakers in the first place.
7 The impact on local employment and incomes, and the effect of foreign visitors on the local traditions, customs and culture.
8 The ways in which tourist development can contribute to the improvement of the environment, through the conservation of wildlife, forest areas, coastlines, scenic beauty and historic buildings.
9 The contribution that tourism can make to local,

regional and national, social and cultural structure of the host country by encouraging a policy of integration rather than separatism.

The need for structural planning of this kind is clear, so that strategic policies can be formulated in relation to existing and future tourist demands. Such forward planning is already in operation in varying degrees in many parts of the world. Strategic planning can be applied on an international, national or regional scale, and can be equally effective at all levels as the following random examples indicate.

The English Tourist Board is a strong supporter of planned development as their Advisory Document *Planning for tourism in England* shows. This publication gives a great deal of valuable advice on the question of strategic planning which can be applied universally.

In 1975 the Government of Morocco in conjunction with the Federal Government of Germany published a Tourist Master Plan for that country and in 1970 the International Union of Tourist Organisations approved a report entitled *Tourism planning*.

On a smaller scale, in 1977 *The Snowdonia National Park Plan* was published and The Snowdon Management Scheme is now in operation as a result of this Plan.

Tourism is now one of the major international industries and the indications are, that because of increased leisure time throughout the world together with cheaper and more rapid travel facilities, it will continue to grow and expand. It is essential, therefore, that existing resources must be used more wisely and managed with greater skill, and the development of tourism throughout the world must be properly planned and controlled to ensure that both hosts and guests receive equal benefit.

When a particular environment, urban or rural, is destroyed it can never be replaced, and the world becomes a poorer place – FOREVER.

Design for special needs

The year 1981 was designated by the United Nations as the 'International Year of Disabled People', and facilities designed by holidaymakers and tourists need to be considered in relation to their use by disabled visitors.

At the same time the elderly visitor also needs consideration; many popular holiday resorts in the UK and abroad now endeavour to attract older visitors during off-peak periods by offering lower rates for long stays. This not only helps pensioners and others by making accommodation available in places where the weather is still pleasant, but also gives year-round employment to hotel staff.

In many Mediterranean holiday areas these winter holidays at low rates are extremely popular with elderly people who can then escape the worst of the Northern European winter weather. Sir Winston Churchill in his latter years appreciated the benefit of such a break from the English winter and always spent this part of the year in the pleasant climate of Morocco.

At least one travel organisation in the UK specialises in holidays for pensioners and the range of opportunities offered include not only deck chairs in Bournemouth but long distance cruises on specially chartered liners, wide ranging overseas tours and many other options. As the age level of the world population increases, and people expect to live longer,

Saga holidaymakers on a cruise; age does not limit the capacity for holiday enjoyment (*SAGA*)

the needs of older people need to be considered in the holiday and tourist context.

Amenities for holidays and tourism must therefore be planned for the convenience of all from nursing mothers and young children to the elderly and the disabled.

It is impossible to estimate the proportion of the world population that suffers from some form of disability, but it is now generally accepted that people of all ages with physical impairment must not be segregated from the rest of the community.

The integation of disabled people into society should mean that special buildings are generally less important; special provisions for disabled people in all buildings are therefore essential, so that they can take a full and creative part in the life of the community.

The rather unhappy term 'disabled' can mean many things and does not necessarily imply that the person concerned is confined to a wheelchair. Some people need similar forms of aid to mobility such as a walking stick, crutches, walking frames or similar devices. Sensory disabilities are often overlooked; hearing and sight have an important bearing on a person's mobility and much can be done in interior design to assist in such circumstances.

Age is not necessarily a major factor, for physical and sensory impairment can affect children and the middle aged as well as the elderly. Disablement need not even be permanent, as many over enthusiastic skiers can testify; a broken limb or convalescence after a serious illness has made many people temporarily 'disabled'. It has been said that 'disabled' people become 'handicapped' only by the way their physical surroundings emphasise their disability.

The international logo that should be displayed wherever special facilities for disabled people are available

Chapter 6
Building for tourism

In common with all industries, tourism requires buildings. The range of buildings catering for the holiday business is very wide extending from accommodation – in all its forms – buildings for entertainment and leisure activities, transport buildings, shopping facilities and an endless variety of essential amenity and back-up buildings. All the building types involved cannot be covered in one volume but the Bibliography on page 147 lists a wide range of books in related fields. Also *Design for Leisure Entertainment* by Anthony Wylson deals specifically with the design of holiday resorts, entertainment centres, theme parks and a vary wide range of leisure facilities that attracts many holidaymakers and tourists.

For detailed planning data, *Planning*, published by Butterworths, covers all the buildings that relate to tourism and holidays, including residential accommodation, sport and entertainment, shopping, airports, garages and transport facilities. *Planning*, however, does not deal with aesthetic or architectural design, but provides essential information and technical data, contributed by experts in each field.

In this chapter it is intended to paint a broader picture and discuss certain buildings for holidays and tourism against a wider background. The subjects covered are residential accommodation in both temporary and permanent structures, essential buildings relating to the infrastructure of a tourist area, and the problem of buildings in wild and remote places or areas of special significance because of their historic importance or natural beauty.

Camping accommodation and caravans

The growth of the popularity of tents and caravans of varying kinds has developed enormously in the last twenty-five years. Before the 1939–45 war camping was largely associated with the international Scout Movement and other organisations for young people.

In recent years the increasing number of students with long summer vacations and limited budgets but an insatiable desire to see the world has led to a world-wide expansion in tented camping. Walkers, hitch-hikers and cyclists equipped with a lightweight tent and the minimum of camping equipment are able to cross continents and enjoy a wide variety of new holiday and leisure experience. In addition, families using a private car as transport with more sophisticated tentage and equipment can tour in their own and foreign countries at minimal cost and with complete freedom of movement across at least some national frontiers.

The development of the touring caravan, one towed by a car, and the motorised caravan has greatly widened the horizons of tourists addicted to this form of holiday. It is estimated that no less than 19 million holiday nights were spent in tents by British residents in England in 1977, and in the same year 13 million holiday nights were spent in touring and motorised caravans.

Overseas visitors to Britain also find this type of holiday attractive, and although accurate statistics are not available, the English Tourist Board estimates that in 1976 at least 650 000 holiday nights were spent in Britain by foreign visitors in touring caravans and nearly 2 500 000 holiday nights in tents. Projected world-wide these figures suggest that each year an enormous number of people, for a variety of reasons, choose this form of holiday accommodation.

This type of mobile holidaymaker can be classified as 'self-reliant' for there is no dependence on hotels or similar establishments and less dependence on restaurants and entertainment centres than other tourists. However, there is a greater need for local food supplies, camp sites and the infrastructure of roads and associated services.

Campers and carvanners can now visit 'far-away places', either on organised tours or independently. It is possible to trek through the jungles of Thailand, or the Nubian desert of Egypt, visit Katmandu and camp in the foothills of the Himalayas in view of Mount Everest or in Ambroseli National Park in Kenya at the foot of Mount Kilimanjaro. These are but a few of the world-wide options available.

From the tourist point of view, this type of holiday offers mobility, flexibility and economy. From the host areas standpoint, there are however a number of disadvantages, the mobility of the visitor usually means a concentration at peak holiday periods and in already popular areas.

Control is difficult particularly when saturation point is reached, and unauthorised use of lay-bys on roads and car parks, private fields or woodlands can produce congestion or a rapid degradation of a natural beauty spot, beach or wild-life reserve. The resulting litter, damage to tracks, fouling through lack of sanitary facilities etc, can be extremely damaging. Where prepared sites exist these can be heavily over-used leading to health and safety hazards.

The trends seem to suggest that the popularity of this type of mobile, go-as-you-please, holiday will increase as greater leisure and shorter working weeks mean that people can take a few days camping or caravan holiday with little pre-planning or forward booking. It is possible that the figures given earlier for Great Britain could be increased by 30% by 1985. The Camping Club of Great Britain and Ireland, the oldest of its kind in the world (founded in 1901) now has a membership of nearly a quarter of a million and is growing each year.

The mobile tourist and his needs must therefore be carefully considered in any local, regional or national plan for tourism if the greatest benefit is to be derived by both host and guest, and if the destruction and degradation of the tourist attraction is to be avoided.

Camping sites

Although camping and caravanning are usually regarded as rural or countryside holiday exercises, the problem can be relevant to the urban situation because these holidaymakers are also attracted to cities and other centres of historic interest.

The provision of camp sites for mobile tourists around the periphery of a major conurbation is therefore important. London for example is served by some forty-seven sites in the Greater London Council area, on or near to the main routes into the capital, and the London Tourist Board operates an advisory service from their Victoria Station Tourist Information Centre. This pattern is one which is followed in many other developed tourist countries, for both urban and rural situations under the auspices of National Touring Clubs, motoring organisations, Tourist Ministeries or Tourist Boards, and private companies.

Location

The basic requirements of a camping site wherever it is located, must be considered from two angles: firstly the comfort, convenience and safety of the user and secondly, but just as important, preservation of the local environment and the protection of the natural inhabitant; people, wild-life and their habitat.

Advance planning must include a survey of existing facilities, if they exist, and an expansion forecast so that growth in demand can be catered for. This will help to avoid early saturation and over-population. Although some authorities recommend flat and grassed fields, some of the most attractive camping sites are in forest and woodland settings in Scandinavian countries; Switzerland; Scotland and the Rockie Mountains of Canada. A series of smaller well separated sites is preferable to large bleak areas and the objective should be to provide not only a pleasant aspect for the campers but also to screen them so that they are not a visual obtrusion in the local environment.

While flat, tree-less sites may be easy to manage, undulating areas with established trees, shrub planting and other forms of landscaping including earth mounding will increase individual privacy and help to overcome amenity objections. The chosen sites should be accessible from an adjacent highway but not immediately adjoining it, access from the highway is important, it must be of adequate width and construction and carefully signposted.

The question of signs in town and country is of great importance. The size of an individual site will vary with the expected use: some authorities recommend a minimum usable camping area of from 2 to 4 ha (5–10 acres) and a maximum density of 75 units per ha (30 per acre). Great Britain and most other developed countries have a licensing system for permanent camping sites and regulations set out under Town Planning Acts or similar legislation are designed to prevent haphazard and indiscriminate camping. It is difficult to control casual camping, but in some countries and in particularly sensitive areas such as locations of special natural beauty, protected wildlife areas, and woodland, unauthorised camping is strictly forbidden.

Facilities and services

Adequate services are essential and the minimum must include toilets (with special facilities for disabled), with drainage facilities, water supply, emptying point for chemical toilets, adequate provision for collection, storage and disposal of refuse. Fire precautions are necessary, especially in forest or heathland situations and details of first-aid facilities and emergency telephone numbers should be displayed with other site notices.

The range of facilities will vary with the size and population of the camp site, the distance to the nearest village or town, the local environment, and the scale of charges made to the visitor. A large camp site may have extensive permanent facilities including a permanently staffed reception centre, first-aid post, public telephone and electricity, camp shop, laundry, indoor and outdoor recreation facilities for adults and children, and visitors car parking

All these provisions require buildings that are well designed, constructed of materials sympathetic to the local surroundings, easily maintained and unobtrusive in character. The inevitable dilemma arises, however, as the camp site becomes larger and the amenities more sophisticated, so the primitive peace and quiet of the simple life originally sought by the mobile tourist inevitably disappears.

We are constantly being reminded that in some parts of the world over-grazing is causing rapid deterioration of an area resulting in a partial or total destruction of the ecosystem. In much the same way, 'over camping' can equally effectively create a landscape of dereliction.

To avoid such an end result, careful planning, design and management are essential for all such

Camping by one of the 96 000 lakes in Sweden. Informal camping of this kind is one of the most carefree forms of holiday, but can lead to problems of pollution if it is not carefully controlled (*Swedish National Travel Association*)

An attractive camp site at Tunnel Mountain in Banff National Park in the Canadian Rocky Mountains, Alberta (*Alberta Travel*)

A well organised semi-permanent camp site in the Ambroseli, Kenya game park within sight of Kilimanjaro (*Edward D. Mills*)

Well designed and carefully sited communal facilities in a forest setting in Alberta, Canada (*Alberta Travel*)

recreational and holiday areas. The case studies that form part of this chapter illustrate examples where a conscious effort has been made through good design in its broadest sense, to minimise the destructive results of the impact of people in areas used by mobile holiday and tourist visitors.

Static caravan sites

The rapid increase in self-catering holidays where holidaymakers do not depend on the services of hotels and other forms of serviced accomodation has been

due partly to the rising demand for a cheaper holiday option, and partly to the greater freedom of action that goes with such holidays.

The mobile camper and caravaner takes his accomodation with him and thus enjoys the maximum mobility. For tourists not wishing to be burdened with mobile accomodation, the static caravan site has become an economical alternative to serviced accomodation.

Many such sites started as areas where large caravans were permanently parked, the holidaymakers arriving by their own, or public transport. The static caravan site generally provided the minimum of

Bryn Morfa, Wales. Caravan sites are difficult to plan and organise and few reach the standard of this example (*Wales Tourist Board, R. Thompson*)

communal facilities apart from the essential management and safety needs. Such sites were seasonal, being primarily used during the popular peak holiday periods of the year, which varied according to the location of the site. In recent years the term 'caravan' has ceased to be accurate as, in many cases caravans have become elaborate and often luxuriously fitted out, and have acquired additions that have made them into immovable short life holiday homes.

Holiday cabins

The ultimate development has in this type of accomodation been the holiday cabin, virtually a permanent caravan. These have become very popular in many parts of the world and often fulfill the same function as small scale holiday apartment or villa. The log cabin of Scandinavian and Canadian origin has been the prototype of many such developements. In Britain the Forestry Commission has been responsible for a number of highly imaginative and environmentally attractive schemes, examples of which are included in the case studies.

The layout and siting of static accomodation of this kind whether it is in the form of caravans, cabins or chalets is of great importance for the structures remain on the site throughtout the whole year even if they are not occupied all the time. The static 'caravan or cabin' site has a number of special requirements in addition to those needed by sites for mobile campers and caravaners.

The access requirements are similar, but the static site requires a fixed layout of habitation units and an internal hard surfaced road system and mains services. Electricity, drainage, refuse disposal and water are needed according to the sophistication of the dwelling units provided. A management and information centre together with a shop able to supply basic needs is desirable and first-aid provisions and fire fighting equipment are essential.

British practice is regulated by Act of Parliament and distance between separate occupation units is specified together with other requirements such as maximum density, distance from and dimensions for

continued on page 44

Coylumbridge Highland lodges, Aviemore, Scotland. Well-designed permanent timber cabins that harmonise with the landscape. Communal facilities are provided in the adjoining hotel (*The Stakis Organisation Limited*)

Case Study 1

Holiday Cabins
Kernton forest, Herodsfoot, near Liskeard, Cornwall, England

Architects
Hird & Brooks

Client
Forestry Commission, Estate Management Division

Engineers
Chapman & Smart

The Site   The location of the Deerpark Forest Cabins is a steep wooded hillside overlooking the valley of a tributary of the West Looe River once the site of a 19th century powder mill. Riding, fishing and sailing are available nearby and there are many tourist attractions in the area. The Forestry Commission's brief required the development to 'impart a sense of adventure to the occupants and provide a contrast to their normal living conditions'. The cabin group is completely surrounded by the forest and there are attractive nature trails through the woodlands and an abundance of wildlife to be seen, birds, animals and wild flowers.

Design and layout   The scheme was developed in two stages, the first comprised twenty-nine pitched roof cabins and the second a further fifteen mono-pitched cabins. In addition, the old Powder Mill buildings have been reconstructed to provide communal facilities; other ruined buildings have been retained as landscape features on the site. Whenever possible existing woodland tracks have been reinstated: car parking has been carefully integrated in the layout. The old mill pond has been restored to form an attractive water feature around which some of the stage one cabins are grouped. The entrance to the site from the public highway includes the reception buildings and the Warden's house.

The cabins each have an open plan living area with kitchen, a double bedroom, a bunk room and a bathroom, and sleeps six people. The front and rear walls are largely glazed in order to enhance the feeling of living in the forest environment: each cabin has a large verandah and in the pitched roofed ones the 'loft' provides a magnificent viewing base and also acts as a playroom or studio.

Construction and materials   The cabins are built on old stone foundations or built into the hillside supported on heavy timbers. The architects designed a system of timber prefabrication, utilising standardised panels for walls and floors. The wall panels are of sandwich construction with external sawn boarding, insulated stud frame and inner plywood lining. A high standard of insulation is incorporated so that the cabins can be used in winter.

The design was developed to reduce site labour and four men can erect a cabin shell in a day and complete the internal partitions, lining and glazing in six days. Electrical and plumbing services are also prefabricated for speed of erection. The construction system has been used on another Forestry Commission development at Keldy Castle, North Yorkshire and is now available commercially.

Comment   Holiday chalet and cabin groups have ruined many attractive sites and the low standard of design of such schemes has given many such developments a poor image. The Herodsfoot Valley, a site of exceptional natural beauty could easily have been spoiled by an unsympathetic holiday development, but the imaginative approach employed by the architects has resulted in a design of outstanding quality far removed from the 'standard' log cabin originally investigated by the clients. The cabins have been very successfully integrated into the natural environment and sited in a manner that ensures good aspect and outlook for each unit. The use of the technique of prefabrication not only produced rapid and economical erection, but also caused minimum disturbance to the forest environment.

The scheme received a well deserved Civic Trust Award in 1978 and to quote the Trust's report, 'shows convincingly that quality is far from impossible in such chalet type developments'. The straightforward use of natural materials, timber and stone, have been far more effective than any attempt at 'vernacular' design and as a result a derelict valley has been transformed for the benefit of holidaymakers and tourists.

1 Aerial view of development, restored mill pond left centre of the picture
2 Deerpark cabins at the edge of the mill pond
3 Cabins built into the hillside: note the cantilevered verandah extension of the living area which also acts as a car port
4 Mono-pitched cabins (Stage 2) adjoining a forest track

(Photos: Hird & Brooks)

2

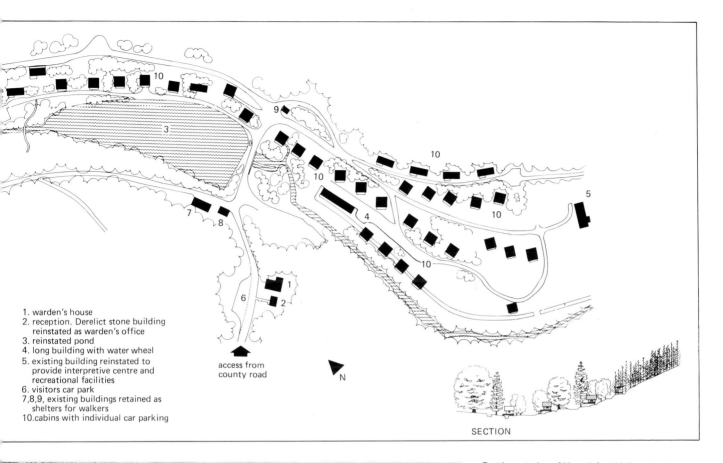

1. warden's house
2. reception. Derelict stone building reinstated as warden's office
3. reinstated pond
4. long building with water wheel
5. existing building reinstated to provide interpretive centre and recreational facilities
6. visitors car park
7,8,9, existing buildings retained as shelters for walkers
10. cabins with individual car parking

access from county road

N

SECTION

Part layout plan of Herodsfoot Valley development

3

4

roadways, size of hardstandings, and services and safety provisions.

Extensive sanitary facilities are not always necessary as the living units can be very spacious, and usually have their own bathroom accomodation built-in; only a minimum of communal toilet accomodation is needed for visitors.

As many holidaymakers bring their own cars ample well planned car parking is essential; the alternatives are individual parking bays attached to each accomodation unit or separated communal car parks away from the living areas. The latter solution is probably the most desirable visually, but is less popular with the visitors who expect to be able to drive up to their temporary 'front door'. In any case car parking for casual visitors is needed.

The extent of communal recreational facilities will vary with the size, location and character of the site, in particular its proximity to the local community.

Siting and landscaping

The fact that the 'static caravan' site is basically a permanent development, means that it can have a very considerable impact on the landscape. The choice of site is therefore of great importance; bleak, flat sites while easy to manage and service, are not to be encouraged.

Dwelling units should be planned in small groups, separated and screened by trees and planting and changes of level, small hillocks and similar landscape techniques must be employed to reduce the scale of the development and reduce its intrusion on the natural environment. Where the dwelling units are caravans or similar structures, the nature and colour of the materials used in their construction is of paramount importance.

The question of colours for caravans of all kinds has been the subject of much debate. White clearly is practical for maximum solar reflection, but in certain landscapes makes the units unduly prominent; green is seldom satisfactory as most manmade greens clash with the natural landscape of grass and trees. Neutral greys and browns tend to suit most locations and the Colour Code prepared by Sir Hugh Casson for the National Caravan Council should be carefully studied and followed in relation to any new developement.

Where the dwelling units are of a more permanent nature the range of materials available is wide and will be affected by local products and practices, for example, the thatched roofed 'bandas' found in East Africa which blend harmoniously with the local landscape. The question of structural forms and materials for both permanent and semi-permanent holiday buildings is one that needs very careful study, and

examples of good practice cas be seen in all of the selected case studies.

Self catering

Self-catering holidays occupy an important part of the total tourist accomodation. The facilities available vary world-wide, and include the most economical form, the static caravan; the chalet or cabin; the permanent holiday village; the apartment block and the individual house or villa.

While the importance of good planning and design of the permanent self-catering holiday accommodation is generally accepted, although not always achieved, many semi-permanent developments have lamentably low aesthetic standards and are often unplanned eyesores that destroy an attractive landscape because of the use of unsuitable colours or materials, poor layout and inadequate planting and screening.

Legislation and regulation can minimise environmental damage caused by any form of built development but only conscious design effort can produce a positive contribution to the environment rather than a negative one.

Permanent non-serviced accommodation

This type of holiday and tourist accommodation falls into three broad categories:

The tourist village or complex;
The apartment block;
The individual house or villa.

Developments vary in size and scale from the single villa to the large complex containing a considerable number of apartments. The common factor is the self-contained nature of the accomodation provided, which is planned to allow the occupants freedom to arrange their own catering for meals and other needs. Each unit consists of living space, sleeping space, bathroom and cooking facilities so that the occupants can be entirely independant of communal facilities if they wish.

In larger developments, particularly in isolated sites, provision is often made for communal recreation – swimming pool, golf course, yacht marina – together with restaurants, shops and petrol station. When facilities of this kind are incorporated, the complex assumes the proportions of a village or small town and the inevitable problems of a seasonal one-purpose community become apparent.

The holiday town of Vilamoura in the Algarve in Portugal (Architects, the Eric Lyons Cunningham

Partnership) on which construction started in 1978 and part of which is now in operation, is designed for an ultimate population of 50 000 people. At present some 273 apartments have been completed with 93 shop units and part of the yacht marina which will ultimately accommodate 1 000 boats. Further stages already planned include over 400 apartments and a range of community facilities.

On a smaller scale the Festaval Tourist Village at Mellieha, Malta (Architect, Richard England) comprises 31 apartments with from one to three bedrooms, a clubhouse, mini-supermarket, a playroom and both indoor and outdoor swimming pools.

At the other extreme, the small group of individual holiday homes in the maritime Provence in the South of France (Architect, Santa Raymond) consists of several self-contained family units grouped together

Holiday villas in Malta, an attractive site spoiled by haphazard unplanned development with no architectural character (*Edward D. Mills*)

on an attractive site. Included in the scheme is a 13 m high circular tower dwelling especially designed for solar heating. All three examples are the subject of case studies.

Most holidaymakers dream of a holiday escape to an environment that is completely different from their normal living conditions and the demand for holiday apartments and villas that can be rented or purchased is continually growing. The rapid rise in the standard of living in the Western world has resulted in a growing demand for a 'second home' which can be used for family holidays and perhaps later as a

retirement home. In recent years the holiday flat or villa in Spain, Malta, Majorca and other Mediteranean or Caribbean areas has become very popular. This has led to large developments of ill-designed apartment blocks and monotonous, repetitive, land consuming villas of indifferent architectural standards, sometimes poorly constructed of unsympathetic materials with little consideration for the local traditions or site features.

The fact that such accommodation is sometimes left unoccupied for considerable periods has led to justifiable concern, and in some cases obvious hostility. It can clearly become a source of friction where local inhabitants seeking accommodation find themselves in competition with outsiders who may have greater financial resources, and thus cause a local housing shortage and a rapid escalation in property values to the disadvantage of the native population. Events in Wales in recent years have emphasised the problem and illegal action against 'second homes' and their owners have created suspicion and hostility which has damaged the overall tourist industry.

The ownership of a holiday home is the ambition of many people, but unless this type of development is planned and managed with great care and imagination the benefits that can accrue to a holiday area can easily be placed in jeopardy. The economic benefits arising from second homes can be significant and include rates paid to the local authority, money spent in local shops, garages and entertainment facilities and employment to local people for the cleaning and maintenance of the properties. One of the recent innovations in this field has been that of time-sharing or multi-ownership which is discussed later.

The provision of self-catering accommodation either let for short-term stays or sold freehold or on a long lease, whether it is a single house or villa, an apartment in a holiday complex or a flat in a multistorey block makes considerable demands on the locality in which it is sited. The obvious needs are proper access, adequate services in the form of electricity, water and drainage, and back-up services such as fire prevention, medical facilities and shops for food and other essentials. In return the visitors provide employment, and contribute to the economic growth of the local community.

The first essential is therefore a Master Plan that envisages the ultimate extent of the development in outline. Whether the plan is for a large or small complex, it must take into account not only the physical requirements of the visiting tourist and the well-being of the local inhabitants, but must respect the existing natural environment; the existing features of the site on which buildings are to be erected and the
continued on page 64

Case Study 2

Holiday Town Marina
Vilamoura, Algarve Coast, Portugal

Architects
Eric Lyons Cunningham Partnership
In association with GEFEL
Gabinete de Estudos el Empreedimentos
TecNICOS Sarl, Lisbon

Clients
Lusotor
Sociedade Financeira de Tourismo, Sarl

The site   Vilamoura is on the Algarve coast near Quarteira, 10 km from Albufeira, and 20 km from Faro International Airport. The total site is 10 square kilometres in area surrounded by pine forests, agricultural land and golf courses. The land is generally level with no outstanding physical features apart from 3 km of sandy beaches. The climate of the Algarve is semi-tropical and in the neighbourhood a wide variety of holiday attractions are already available with future plans for other developments.

Design and layout   In 1972 the Eric Lyons Cunningham Partnership shared the highest award in an international competition promoted by Lusotor, their design was placed equal with a Portugese firm of architects. In 1978 the ELCP was commissioned to design the Vilamoura Marina surrounded by mixed housing and shopping for holiday visitors as the heart of the tourist development; they prepared the Master Plan for the down town area. The new tourist town is planned for an eventual population of 50 000, and the marina will ultimately accommodate 1000 boats.

The first phase of the development around the Marina, which has been excavated inshore to avoid interference with the holiday beaches, has now been completed and includes 273 apartments, 93 small shops and part of the Marina facilities. Further phases will include community facilities and over 400 additional apartments.

Most of the buildings on the edge of the harbour are generally four storeys in height, grouped around a series of car parking courts and shopping lanes that slope down to the quayside from the loop road that will serve the future downtown Tivoli complex. The layout and design of the buildings have been developed to create picturesque settings and have been influenced by local

technology and tradition. Richard Lyons of ELCP has called the architectural style 'Modern Picturesque'.

Construction and materials   The construction follows the typical South European standards, *in situ* reinforced concrete structural frames, floors and flat roofs precast concrete ribs with hollow clay pot infill and concrete topping. Walls are concrete or clay blocks and external cavity walls are finished with a rough cement and sand render. Local clay pantiles in differing colours are used on pitched roofs and the white rendered walls have focal touches of earthy Algarve reds, browns and yellows.

Comment   This development designed specifically as non-serviced accommodation for holiday makers has suffered a number of setbacks, but the buildings completed so far fully justify the early enthusiasm of both the architects and the competition jury who said in their report "the future centre is well related to the existing road and the coast and it is very well placed in relation to the developing surrounding area." The grouping of the buildings around the harbour and the strong silhouette on a virtually featureless site, coupled with the use of bold shapes and colours makes a strong visual impact. The courtyard planning helps to create a feeling of intimacy and human scale. The completed buildings, while they employ local materials and techniques, are not a 'pastiche' of rural Algarve traditional building but a very successful application of these elements in a contemporary manner to a 20th century design problem. The popularity of the first stage of the Marina, among tourists and holiday makers, suggests that the architects and promoters have achieved their objective – the creation of a lively stimulating and enjoyable holiday centre.

5

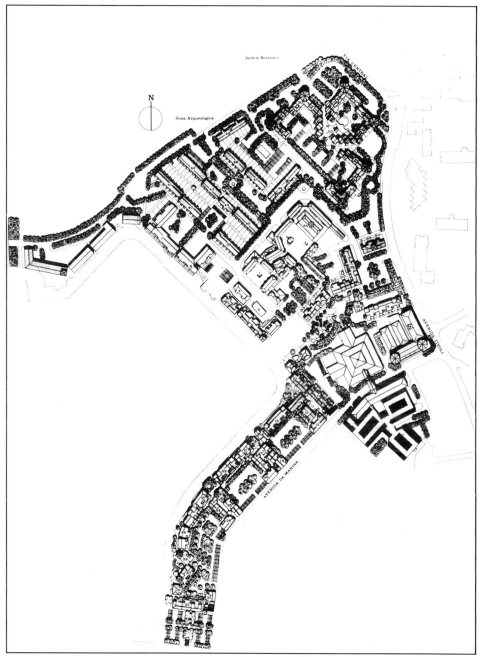

View of apartment blocks and shops across
harbour
Apartments with large balconies, tiled pitched
roofs and bright colours
Shopping arcade on quayside with apartments
over
Internal pedestrian precinct and access to
shops and apartments
Detail photograph showing the use of local roof
tiles, rendering and board marked concrete
*(Photos by courtesy of Eric Lyons Cunningham
Partnership)*

Layout plan of Marina, including Tivoli Centre and
future development

Case Study 3

Apartment Complex
Mellieha, Malta

Architects
England & England
Design:
Richard England
Site Supervision & Organisation:
Albert Borg Costanzl

Clients
Festa Limited

The site   The Festaval tourist village is situated on the north west part of the Island of Malta overlooking the small sandy beach of Mellieha Bay and beneath a historic 17th century defence tower. The site, just under a hectare in area, is steeply sloping and very rocky with fine panoramic views down to the sea. The architect has carefully integrated the building into the steep hillside in order to make it as unobtrusive as possible. On a nearby plateau is the larger Danish tourist village (Case Study No. 5) and at the foot of the hill is a very unfortunate semi-permanent holiday cabin site. Mellieha a short distance away is a typical Maltese village dominated by its Baroque church.

Design and layout   The complex provides a total of thirty-one non-serviced apartments: ten one-bedroom, fifteen two-bedroom and six three-bedroom units together with a clubhouse, lounge with indoor pool, a small supermarket and recreational facilities. The main terrace at entrance level adjacent to the clubroom, has a large open-air swimming pool with magnificent views to the sea and the village of Mellieha.

   All the accommodation provided has been contained in a single building that is entered at the highest level. The apartments are designed as a series of units planned between long, sloping spine walls that follow the slope of the site. The terraces formed by the roofs of the apartments at lower levels provide sheltered open-air living and sunbathing areas to each unit.

Construction and materials   The structure consists of masonry loadbearing walls on concrete foundations with *in situ* simply supported continuous reinforced concrete slab roofs and floors. Doors and windows are anodised aluminium and external walls are finished with lime wash on the natural Maltese limestone. The building structure and materials are those traditionally used on the island.

Comment   The Festaval complex is an excellent example of the architect's concern for what he has called 'the voices of the site'. By allowing the particular features of the Maltese terrain to dominate the design, a unique relationship of the building to the surrounding landscape has been achieved. What is virtually a six-storey building has been built into the landscape so that it is not the dominating feature but a complementa one carefully related to the adjacent histori building (sadly in need of restoration and repair).

   The building mirrors the pattern of the surrounding traditional man-made features such as the typical Maltese stone terraced field walls, and the use of local natural construction materials unites the building with the natural environment. The result is building of considerable architectural merit contemporary solution that has a genuine traditional pedigree.

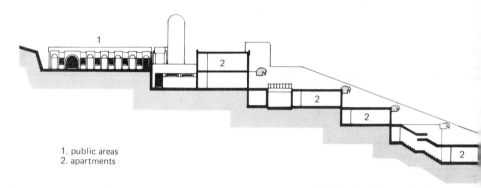

1. public areas
2. apartments

48

4

5

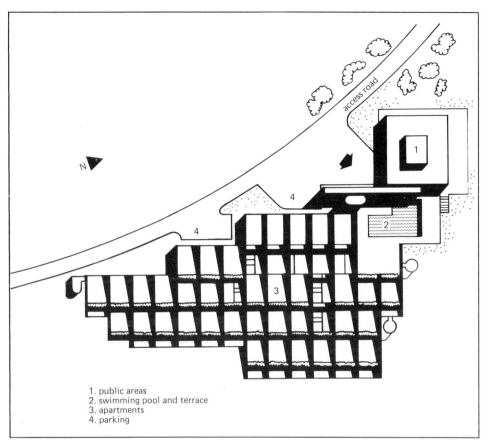

1. public areas
2. swimming pool and terrace
3. apartments
4. parking

Layout plan of complex

1 Section through the building showing the slope
  of the site
2 View of Festaval complex, the Danish village
  and the defence tower the unplanned camp site
  is between the two developments (*Photo:
  Edward D. Mills*)
3 Part of the Club accommodation at the highest
  level with the terrace and outdoor pool (*Photo:
  Edward D. Mills*)
4 The complex in relation to the Tower (*Photo:
  Edward D. Mills*)
5 Close-up view of the apartment units (*Photo:
  Edward D. Mills*)
6 The strong lines of the sloping structural spine
  walls contrasting with the natural rock outcrops
  on the site (*Photo: Richard England*)

6

Case Study 4

Villa Group
Provence, France

Architect
Santa Raymond

Energy consultant
Chris Branden of Solar Energy
Developments

Client
An English family

The site   This group of villas is built on a site of 2.5 ha about 10 km from the Mediterranean coast in the South of France, at the foot of a small mountain range. It is 1½ km from a large and ever expanding village. The lower southern part of the site consists of terraces with olive trees, and the upper northern part is pine forest and scrub. The area around is becoming increasingly popular with holidaymakers, but is still predominantly agricultural with some of the finest vineyards in France.

Design and layout   The town planning zoning for the area allowed two houses per hectare and the clients therefore decided to build four small villas and one 'Clubhouse' having a large living-dining-kitchen area and a minimum number of bedrooms. By this means guests and children would be independent and with four children in the family it is intended that each should have their own house. Unlike most of the property in the area this group of villas is designed to be used at any time of the year, and in particular during all school holidays. The four small dwellings are simple labour saving units separately sited and often used by different families. A swimming pool was built first followed by a two-roomed dwelling, next a three-room house, both with kitchen and bathroom.

   The Solar Tower is of particular interest as it is the first building of its kind in the neighbourhood. Planning approval was difficult to obtain as the building is 13 m high instead of the official 7 m ground to roof maximum.

   Considerable energies have been used to enhance the existing landscape by planting trees and shrubs around the houses and also as appropriate on the terraces. Mostly, indigenous plants existing naturally in the area, have been used. Eventually it is hoped that all houses and adjacent pergolas will be covered with greenery, vines and wisteria.

Construction and materials   The construction of all the villas is based on traditional local standards, walls are reinforced concrete with fibreglass insulation between the concrete block inner wall and the external skin. The walls are faced with a self-coloured rough surfaced rendering. Roofs, apart from the Tower, are local clay tiles. All houses have relatively small windows, all double glazed with two separate windows, the outer one being removable in the summer and replaced by fly screens. Shutters provide extra insulation and security.

   The ground floor living room of the Solar Tower has an open fire, also used for grilling food. The flue that is built into a thick external masonry wall radiates heat into the first floor bedroom.

   The solar installation is of particular interest; the solar energy is collected at roof level using a standard UK made solar collector, with the solar reservoir divided into three separate tanks one on each floor housed in a well-insulated cupboard. The heat output into each room can be controlled by insulated flaps. In winter the system heats the whole Tower and in summer all the heat is stored in the bathroom tank. The system is simple, effective and needs very little maintenance.

Comment   Great care has been taken in the grouping of these dwellings in a very attractive site in such a way as to cause the least disturbance to the natural environmen The landscape has been allowed to dominate. The use of local materials and construction methods have helped the integration of the development, while the use of a moder technique, solar energy, has proved most successful. This small and very individual group of holiday villas is a lesson to all developers of unspoiled sites and shows that new buildings for leisure use need not be an unwelcome intrusion in the landscape if they are designed with the same care and sensitivity as this group demonstrates.

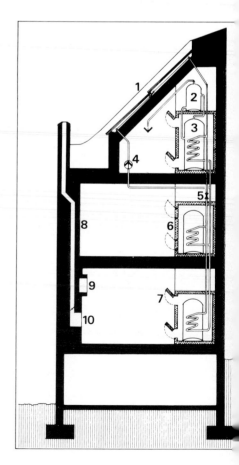

Section through Solar Tower showing the solar collection system (*Courtesy of RIBA Journal*)

1 solar collector
2 domestic hot water cylinder.
3 preheat tank for domestic hot water.
4 circulating pump.
5 isolating valve summer/winter operation.
6 insulated cupboards containing water tanks.
7 hand operated flaps control flow of warm air over hot water tank.
8 thinner internal wall radiates flue heat into bedroom.
9 wood store over hearth.
10 fireplace in ground floor living room.

1

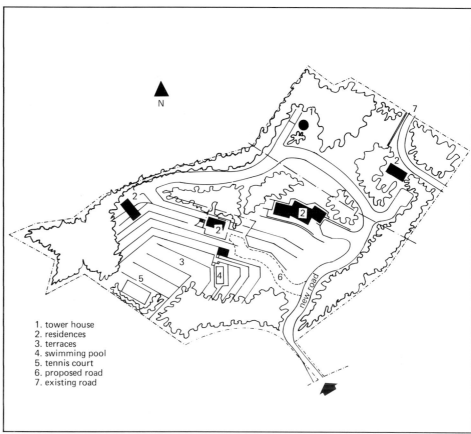

1. tower house
2. residences
3. terraces
4. swimming pool
5. tennis court
6. proposed road
7. existing road

Layout of site showing location of individual villas

2

1 The Solar Tower D, entrance door on the left, shuttered windows (*Photo: B & W*)
2 One of the small 'villas' on the West side of the site E (*Photo: Santa Raymond*)
3 One of the small villas in the centre of the site B (*Photo: Santa Raymond*)

3

Case Study 5

Danish Holiday Centre
Mellieha, Malta

Architect
Hans Munk Hansen

Client
Mellieha Holiday Centre Ltd
(Danish People's Holiday Assn and G.W.U)

Engineer
Carl Bros

The site The site is a 9 ha plateau which on its western and southern boundaries slopes steeply down to Mellieha Bay, nearby is the Festaval Tourist Village (Case Study No. 3) with which it shares the magnificent views of the village of Mellieha and the sea. The site is surrounded by agriculture, and with a large number of windmills, it is exposed and has little natural vegetation, with prevailing winds from the north-west. The Maltese climate is hot and dry with a long holiday season.

Design and layout The scheme is planned as two main elements, one hundred and fifty self-catering bungalows for families of six to eight people and a central complex that contains the general amenities which are available to the general public as well as the resident guests. The main entrance acts as the control centre for the whole complex and adjoins the large open-air swimming pool, with its self-service snack bar, the main self-service restaurant, lounge and bar, supermarket and other facilities including communal rooms which can be used for conferences during off peak periods.

The guests' village layout has been based on a study of Scandinavian holiday habits and priority has been given to sunbathing and outdoor activities. The individual units are planned in clusters, creating a series of enclosed and sheltered public spaces. These areas are densely planted with trees, shrubs and flowers to contrast with the bare surrounding landscape. All bungalows are the same size – L-shaped, with a combined living, kitchen and dining room and two bedrooms. There are ample cupboards and a well equipped bathroom. All rooms are planned around a protected courtyard for outdoor meals and a staircase leads to the roof terrace.

Architecturally, the Centre follows the pattern of the traditional Maltese village and

does not detract from the natural environment of the area. The individual buildings are planned at different levels to fit the natural site contours. Great care has been taken in the layout to maximise the attractive views and provide shelter from the wind.

Construction and materials The principle building material is Maltese limestone, walls are cavity construction both internal and external skins are of dressed stone, rubbed down and pointed. Stone is also used as the floor finish for guests' rooms with terrazo tiles in bathroom, kitchen, etc. Doors and windows are stained wood. Roofs are flat reinforced concrete slabs, insulated with polystyrene, with a butyl-rubber water-proofing membrane finished with an *in situ* concrete loading slab. The construction and materials are all traditional to Maltese building.

Comment The Mellieha Holiday Centre, already known locally as the Danish village, fits very happily into the strong, rugged Maltese landscape just as the older villages do in other parts of the island. The grouping of the units and their simple geometric shapes creates a pattern of light and shadow in the strong Mediterranean sunshine that varies throughout the day. The honey coloured local stone used throughout blends with the natural surroundings and weathers well.

While the Centre has been designed with Scandinavian holidaymakers in mind, the stated objective of the promoters is to 'facilitate the contact and the understanding between the Maltese and the Danish people'. To encourage this relationship between the host country and the holiday guests, the amenities complex is open to all visitors and special facilities are available particularly in the 'low' season for conferences and meetings open to Maltese and overseas visitors.

The Dansk Folke-ferie, the promoting organisation, is a co-operative social body that makes available inexpensive and enjoyable holidays, particularly to large families and those with limited means. The organisation has built many holiday villages in Denmark, and has developed the Mellieha site in conjunction with the Maltese General Workers Union.

1 Festeval Tourist Village from Mellieha Holiday Centre (*Photo: Edward D. Mills*)
2 Swimming pool, Mellieha church and village beyond (*Photo: Edward D. Mills*)
3 The central complex (*Photo: Hans Munk Hansen*)
4 Typical housing group (*Photo: Hans Munk Hansen*)

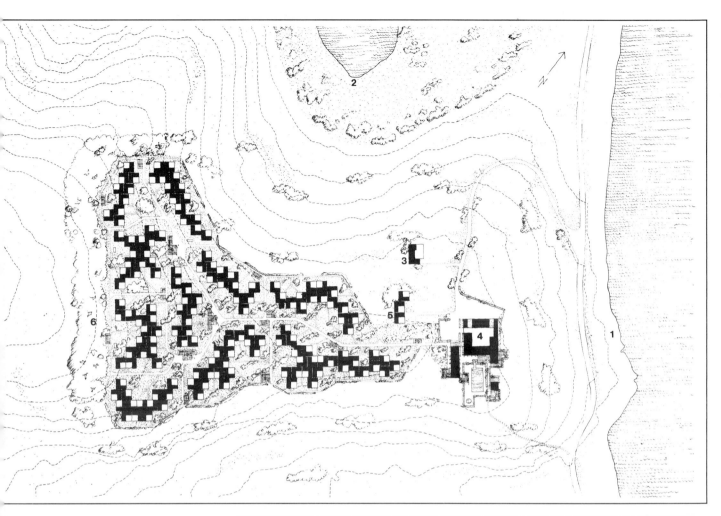

out plan

andy beach along the Mediteranean
ake and bird sanctuary
manager's residence
communal centre
staff quarters
planning for wind protection

4

Case Study 6

Holiday Cabins
Lochanhully, Carrbridge,
Inverness-shire, Scotland

Architects and Engineers
Shankland Cox Partnership

Clients
The Automobile Association of Great Britain

The site   The site covers 26 acres of un-dulating land, partly forested in the Highland region of Scotland, a mile outside Carrbridge with good access by road, rail and air. The neighbourhood offers a variety of outdoor activities such as fishing, sailing and ski-ing as well as pony trekking, birdwatching and grouse shooting. The centre of the site was originally a peat bog and the surrounding rocky hills are covered with heather and silver birch. The site falls South with fine views over the River Dulnain and the Spey Valley towards the Cairngorms. The winter Sports Centre at Aviemore is 7 miles away.

Design and layout   The original peat bog has been reformed into a 6 acre lochan lake fed by two streams around which the fifty self-catering lodges and amenity buildings are planned, with a footbridge linking the North and South sides. The development can accommodate up to three hundred visi-tors with special facilities provided for dis-abled guests, two of the lodges have been designed specifically for wheelchair users with wider doors, ramps, grab rails and easy reach power points. Special car parking is also provided.

The fifty lodges are grouped along the two roads on the site, eighteen are paired for parties or large families holidaying together. Each unit has a living area with cooking facilities, one double bedroom and a double bunkroom which together with sofa beds in the living room will sleep up to six people. There is a fully equipped bathroom and a large balcony for outdoor meals.

The communal facilities on the South side of the Lochan includes a bar and games room with a heated indoor swimming pool and a laundry. The reception building which adjoins the entrance includes a shop attached to the manager's house. The grouping of the buildings was dictated large-ly by the topography of the site, the lodges being oriented to obtain the best view from the balcony and provide South and West

aspect. The arrangement of the lodge units creates the feeling of a village in contrast to the large area of the site left in its natural state. The development is designed for use in both summer and winter.

Construction and materials   The lodges are built using a Finnish prefabricated timber system. The floors are raised above ground level and the walls are framed panels nailed together in 600 mm multiples delivered to the site as a sandwich of external vertical sawn boarding felt, 100 mm insulation, a vapour barrier and an internal lining of ton-gued and grooved boarding. A high standard of thermal insulation ensures comfortable internal conditions in winter weather. The roofs are covered with slate grey corrugated asbestos-cement sheeting over rafters and battens. A complete lodge shell can be erected within a day.

The bar, games room and swimming pool building are built using the same prefabri-cated system, but owing to considerable variations in site levels near the entrance, the reception buildings are built by traditional methods. Walls are loadbearing concrete blockwork with dark blue corrugated alumi-nium roof sheeting. Externally the blockwork walls are clad with vertical boarding to match the lodges. A bio-sewage treatment plant has been installed which produces an effluent suitable for discharge into the River Dulnain and because of the possibility of electricity power cuts during winter months a standby generator is available capable of supplying the electricity needed by the whole site.

Comment   The Lochanhully site is one of considerable natural beauty that has been enhanced by the creation of the Lochan from the peat bog and the careful siting of the holiday accommodation well back from the road. The existing landscape has been inter-fered with as little as possible and new planting has been confined to plants and trees that are indigenous to the locality. Where new paths have been created, parti-cularly around the Lochan, considerable use has been made of timber detailing; new roads are narrow, naturally drained without kerbs and follow the ground contours.

The use of stained vertical boarding for all external walls of buildings relates the various buildings to each other and the discreet use of colour adds to the character of the simple structures that sit very happily in a natural Highland environment.

1

2

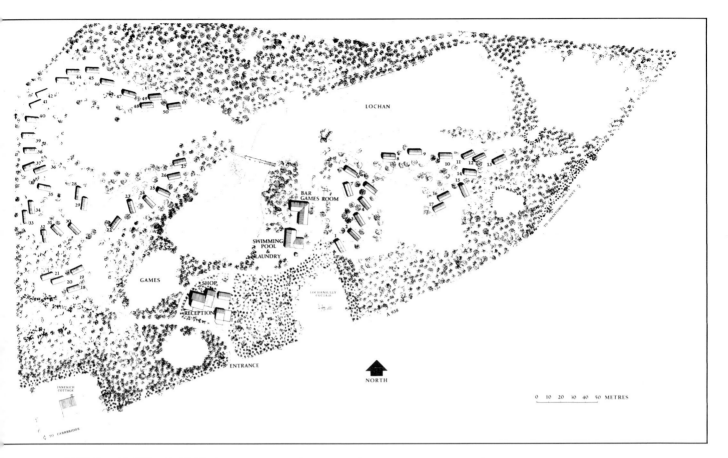

Layout plan of site

1 Typical timber cabin in natural landscape
2 Detail of timber construction
3 Cabins grouped around the reclaimed Lochan
4 The footbridge across the Lochan with cabins in
  the background

(*Photos: Shankland Cox*)

Case Study 7

Holiday Housing Complex
Stazzo Pulcheddu, Gallura, Sardinia

Architects
Alberto Ponis & Aldo E. Ponis

The site   The site of this holiday complex is about 30 ha in area, a few miles from the Gallurian Coast in natural, unspoilt surroundings; the first section slopes steeply down from the ridge of Mount Pulcheddu, the second is a central plateau and the third a series of minor hills linking with the surrounding plain. The area is covered by a dense network of dry stone walls. The land was originally grazing, its name means 'the beautiful fold' and there are existing two abandoned shepherds' cottages in the centre of the site and an oven and a well. The natural vegetation of the region is very varied including wild olives, myrtle and juniper. The prevailing winds are very frequent and strong from the North-west. The landscape is strong and rugged with extensive views across the coast to the sea.

Design and layout   A very detailed analysis of the site by the architects resulted in a layout for the development that concentrates the new buildings on the central plateau, adhering to the natural ground contours as far as possible and offering excellent views, protection from the strong winds and giving easy access. The two main groups of buildings consist of an apartment (self-catering) hotel, with clubhouse and swimming pool and a series of nuclei of large patio houses together with one of the old shepherd's cottages that has been restored and converted into a spacious villa with a studio.

Large communal green areas and a system of entrances to the development with parking spaces have been planned so as to minimise the impact of the motorcar. The central apartment block over 100 m long, in three blocks, is a series of dwellings some with individual gardens and the others with an intermediate floor so that the building follows the morphology of the site. Communal rooms link the individual blocks. The swimming pool and clubhouse are con-nected to the apartment block by a rising pedestrian path.

The individual patio houses contain large living areas including indoor and outdoor dining spaces, kitchen, two bedrooms with *en-suite* bathrooms and sheltered loggias, patios and internal walkways linking the various levels of the dwelling which closely follows the undulations of the land. Each dwelling unit consists of separate sleeping and living areas separated by a large open-air patio and enclosed by two parallel walls.

Other buildings also follow the pattern established by the main apartment block and the patio houses include groups of cluster houses to the North-west of the central complex.

Construction and materials   The materials used and the construction techniques employed are basically traditional to Sardinia, using loadbearing walls finished with rough plaster, colour washed to harmonise with the natural tones of the region. Large windows have anodised aluminium sliding frames, glazed with tinted glass to reduce glare. Pitched roofs of all buildings are covered with local clay Roman tiles. Pa

1

2

d terrace floors are paved with natural
racotta tiles, this finish is also used for all
e internal floor surfaces. Natural rock out-
ps and the natural landscape are inte-
ated into the building layout wherever
actical and the house patios have been
larged in some cases to include existing
cks and trees.

mment The Sardinian landscape has
en described as 'having a particular char-
teristic, an illusionary grandeur, being of
smaller dimensions than it appears at first
ght. Provided one scales even modest
ights the views are immense, in consequ-
ce just one building of the wrong size or
lour is enough to spoil kilometres of land.'
Because of the extremely sensitive nature
the landscape the architects of the Stazzo
lcheddu made a detailed analysis of the
gion and the morphological and visual
mponent in order to have as complete as
ssible picture of the natural environment,
special characteristics, disadvantages
d possible potential. This careful study has
sulted in a tourist development that com-
ements the natural environments and
oids the alien and ill-considered forms that
ve devastated so many areas of
eviously unspoiled countryside.
Although the buildings are of differing
es and functions, the final layout is inte-
ated with the form and shape of the land.
e use of traditional architectural forms,
cal materials and muted natural colours,
ves an unusually effective relationship be-
een the buildings and the site; making full
e of the existing natural features, the
anging views and the special character of
e region.

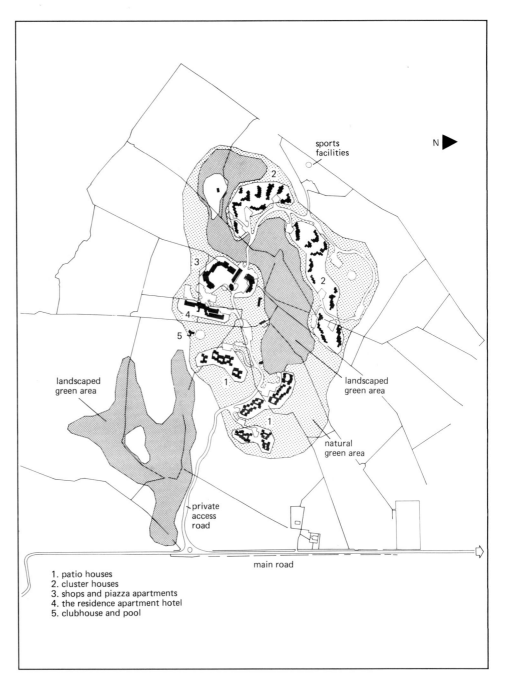

1. patio houses
2. cluster houses
3. shops and piazza apartments
4. the residence apartment hotel
5. clubhouse and pool

Layout plan showing grouping of houses

1 A group of patio houses
2 The clubhouse and swimming pool with an
   existing rock as a focal point
3 Internal view of one of the patio houses,
   sleeping area behind the camera, living area in
   front
4 The apartment block and to the left, the
   clubhouse and swimming pool with patio
   houses in the foreground

(*Photos: A Ponis*)

Case Study 8

Family Holiday Villa Group
Canakkale, Durdanelles, Turkey

Architect
Professor Sedat Gurel

The site   The site is on the West coast of Turkey near Alexandria-Troas. It slopes steeply to the south-west down to the Aegean Sea. Existing rock outcrops, pine, olive and oak trees form an attractive rugged terrain, which is situated in a historically rich area where settlements date back to the 4th century BC. The city of Alexandria reached its prime during the era of the Emperor Hadrianus, and the ruins of the necropolis, theatre and baths can still be seen today. The site is enclosed on the North-east boundary by a high stone wall which screens a footpath to the neighbouring village.

Design and layout   This vacation complex was designed for use by an extended family to provide for both family privacy and togetherness at the same time. The layout is a series of living and sleeping units for the members of the family; the units are grouped around two courtyards with as little disturbance as possible to existing trees and vegetation. There are four sleeping units, B, D, E and G, two living units C and F and one common service unit, A. The units vary in size, each living unit includes a kitchen and sleeping unit with bathroom and accommodates from one to five people. The climate allows outdoor living and the courtyards are designed as open-air living rooms.

   The complex has been conceived as a small scale village providing an opportunity for the owners to get away from the pressures of city life and enjoy a simple carefree existence closely related to nature with as little disturbance as possible to the natural environment.

Construction and materials   Indigenous materials, timber, stone and clay roofing tiles have been used throughout, with rough rendered loadbearing walls following the traditional architectural forms of the region. Timber windows are protected by wood shutters, and all the furniture for both indoor and outdoor spaces is built of local materials as an integral part of the structures.

Comment   Many holidaymakers wish to get away from their normal environment during their vacation, and holidays in simple village locations have therefore become very popular. This very attractive, modest complex with its intimate scale and careful detailing is an outstanding example of a small holiday complex that respects the natural environment and has become a natural extension of the nearby village and part of the fabric of the neighbourhood. The landscape, the sea and the sky are all regarded as essential elements in the architectural composition.

1

2

1 The N.E. boundary with the roofs of the units showing above the existing wall
2 One of the living units with balcony and outdoor living area
3 A sleeping unit overlooking a courtyard and space
   (*Photos: Reha Gunay*)

3

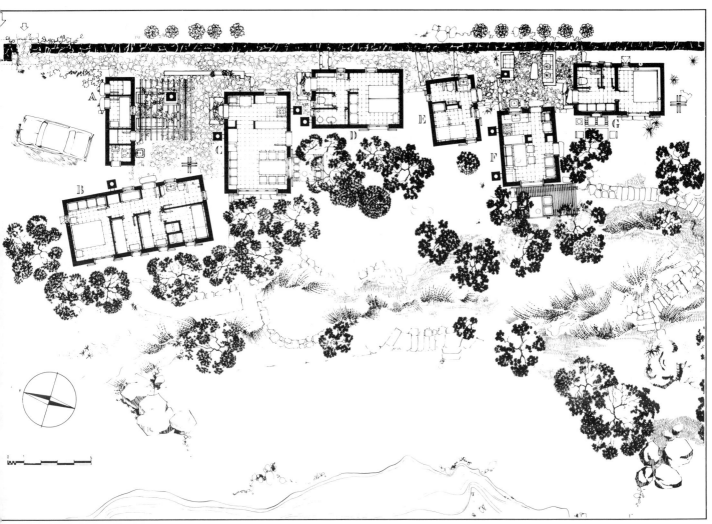

Plan and site layout

Section through the site and buildings

Case Study 9

Holiday Housing Complex
Portmadoc Harbour,
Caernarvonshire, N. Wales

Architects
Phillips, Cutler, Phillips, Troy
Clients
Portmadoc Holiday Development Co.
Engineers
Richards & Dumbleton

The site The site in Portmadoc on the north-east coast of Cardigan Bay is a narrow artificial tongue of land 1.55 ha in area, that originally served as a wharf for the slate from the slate quarries at Blaenau Ffestiniog. Before the holiday housing complex was built the site was occupied only by a deserted wartime pill-box and the Ffestiniog railway. The original harbour shared the decline of the Welsh slate industry. The famous holiday village of Portmerion, designed by the late Sir Clough Williams Ellis is three miles from Portmadoc, and three major conurbations, Birmingham, Manchester and Liverpool are within three hours driving distance.

Design and layout The layout is a simple grouping of dwellings around the perimeter of the narrow site in order to take full advantage of the views across the harbour and the sea. A central spine road contains parking courts, so that the cars cannot be seen outside the complex. The population density of the development is 314 people per hectare in 138 units, in two and three storey dwellings with living rooms on the first floor and bedrooms on the ground floor to achieve maximum privacy and the best views.

The dwellings vary in size and each includes a living/dining room with kitchen recess, bedrooms, and bathroom with open staircases and sloping ceilings to avoid box-like rooms. First and second floors have spacious sun decks with 'boatlike' access ladders or companionways. The dwellings have been designed as holiday homes for summer sailors or as permanent homes for retired people interested in sailing.

The architectural form of the complex echoes the traditional Welsh buildings of the town of Portmadoc with the informal mix of two and three storey houses grouped together to avoid long terrace-like roof runs. The arrangement of the pitched roofs is designed to emphasise the individual dwellings and the pedestrian walkways that break up the mass of the buildings.

Car parking within the layout is informal and cast iron bollards and mooring rings retained from the old quay fittings have been incorporated in the scheme wherever possible.

Construction and materials The houses have concrete blockwork cavity external walls with an inner skin of lightweight concrete blocks, precast concrete floor units, and natural Welsh slate roofs. Externally the walls are finished with a two coat cement rough cast and painted Tyrolean style with a sand-cement colour wash. The external wall colours are a mixture of pastel blues, greens and off-white.

Comment Sailing is one of the fastest growing leisure activities in the UK. It is estimated that nearly half a million people belong to coastal and inland sailing clubs. The development of tourist and holiday centres that have sailing facilities is becoming increasingly popular, both in Britain and in Europe. The Villamoura Marina (Case Study No. 2) in Portugal is a comparable European example.

Another development for sailing enthusiasts, designed by the same architects as the Portmadoc complex has been built at Port Dinorwic between Bangor and Caernarvon also in Wales. The Portmadoc site possessed no physical features but was set against the 19th century town consisting largely of terraced houses on the hillside that encircles the harbour. These houses differ in height and colour with slated roofs at various pitches creating interesting shapes and forms and creating a strong architectural character.

The new development 'remains within the confines of the traditional Welsh style, but at the same time uses selected modern materials, opulent forms and friendly colours. The houses, closely crowded together, arouse the total impression of close friendliness.'

The scheme has been accurately described as one that 'captures beautifully the atmosphere of holiday sailing'.

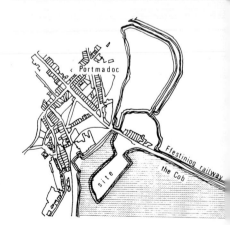

Location plan showing the Cob, an embankment across the River Estuary.

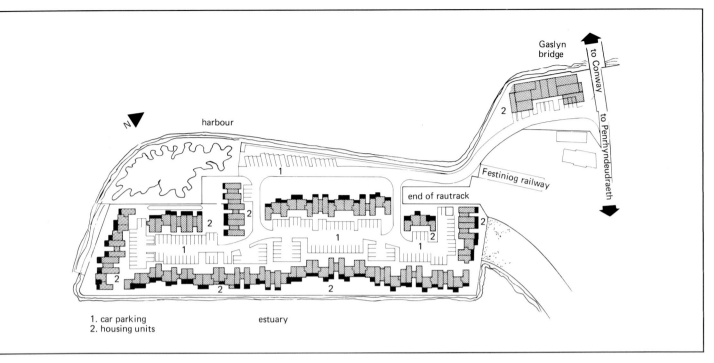

1. car parking
2. housing units

harbour

estuary

Gaslyn bridge

to Conway

to Penrhyndeudraeth

Festiniog railway

end of rautrack

te plan and location

1 General view from the south-west across the harbour
2 Close-up view of harbour site
3 View of internal access and parking spaces
4 Aerial view of the holiday complex with the mainland in the background
5 General view showing compact grouping of housing units

(*Courtesy of Phillips, Cutler, Phillips, Troy: Photos 2, 3, 4: Pearsons Studios Ltd*)

Case Study 10

Holiday Village
Belle-ile-en-mer, Morbihan,
Bretagne, France

Architect
Danielle Cler

Clients
Association Vacances Familles

The site The site is along the East coast of Belle-ile, between Le Palals and Port Collen. It has few physical features apart from the natural contours and the rough grassland with some trees, gorse and wild flowers. The area is 16 ha, overlooking the Atlantic Ocean, the coastline consists alternately of sandy beaches and rocky coves. The site is long and narrow and sloped down to the ocean on its northern boundary.

Design and layout The promoters are a non-profit making association that offers holidays that most people can afford. In the last twenty years they have developed 114 sites providing 50 000 bed spaces. The first developments were full-board holiday villages, followed by self-catering family 'camps' like the one at Belle-ile, now they are planning caravan sites as well. Because of the association's desire to make economical holidays available, the design and layout of the scheme is simple and direct. The eighty units which provide 492 bed spaces are located on a plateau with a slight slope and are planned along a central spine road in groups of ten units with a communal building at the end, nearest the site entrance. This central building comprises recreation rooms, restaurant, kitchen, activity rooms and toilets with showers together with a 'hostess' flat and reception unit. A large circular area provides 80 carparking places. Most of the housing units have two rooms, in addition to bathroom and kitchen recess, to sleep up to five people, some have three rooms. For large family groups a proportion of units have intercommunicating doors between adjacent dwellings.

Areas of the site are reserved for team games, children's play areas, picnics and other outdoor activities.

Construction and materials The construction adopted is simple and economical vertical gable walls are in concrete blockwork finished externally with white rendering. The steeply sloping roofs, that follow local tradition, are a prominent feature of the design and form the large proportion of the external walls, and are covered in dark grey fibre-cement slates on timber framework. A the buildings are centrally heated from a central boiler house adjacent to the central building.

Comment This holiday village shows that architectural character can be achieved by the use of strong building forms and the use of relatively low cost building materials used with imagination. The layout follows the contours of the site and the grouping of the unit ensures that the complex does not assume undue prominence. Great care has been taken to ensure integration with the local character and architectural tradition. The total impression is one of a well organised holiday community with a distinct local flavour.

1

2

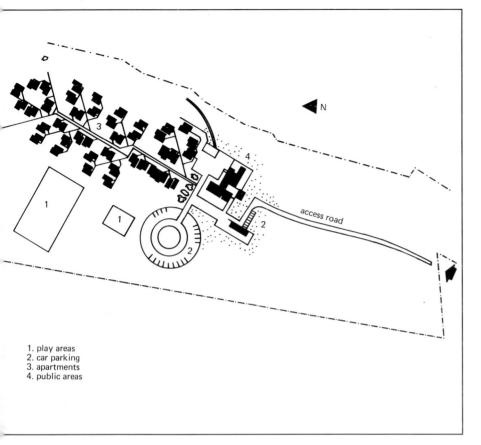

1. play areas
2. car parking
3. apartments
4. public areas

Layout plan of village

General view of complex
A cluster of 'tent' units
Gable ends of 'tent' units
Slate clad roofing to 'tent' units

Photos: Danielle Cler)

4

general background and tradition of the surrounding countryside.

The architect must play a dominant role and by his choice of layout, building forms and materials, produce architecture with which the people who use the buildings can identify. This does not mean a form of trendy 'peasant' architecture grafted on to a 20th century building technology, which only produces a 'pastiche' that looks as artificial as a stage set, it presupposes an understanding of tradition, scale and function in appropriate proportions.

In an article in the RIBA Journal (February 1980) the late Eric Lyons described his design approach to the Vilamoura holiday town, mentioned earlier, as follows:

'This was a different climate with different materials, but more significant was the acknowledgement that holidays are escapes, that holiday places are to be enjoyed by all. Of course, my twentieth century morality inhibited thoughts of pastiche but I set about producing buildings and places that responded to the locale. We behaved as theatrical or garden designers, creating diversified buildings to form places, seeking variety, contact, mystery, texture and so on . . . Then I found myself reasoning that people ought to enjoy their everyday architecture as well as their holiday escapes.'

Other examples of this approach to 'holiday' architecture can be seen in Port Grimaud on the South of France, designed by Francois Spoerry; Stazzo Pulcheddu Sardinia, designed by Alberto and Aldo E. Ponis and similar schemes illustrated throughout this book.

Serviced accommodation

The modern hotel has developed from the medieval inn and hostelry that provided accommodation for short stay travellers on their journeys from place to place. Many still exist in Europe and are popular with tourists for their quaint charm and the modern comforts that have been addded in more recent years. When they were originally built they provided basic bed and board and few additional amenities, for electricity, central heating, running water and reliable drainage, were all unknown.

The inn was usually situated in a town in the urban setting of the time, and it was not until the 19th century that travel for pleasure resulted in such accommodation being built in holiday resort areas. The great Victorian hotels in English seaside resorts like Brighton, Blackpool and Scarborough indicate their popularity, and in most English capitals and in

the early holiday regions like Lake Como in Italy, redundant palaces were converted or new hotels were built.

Tourist hotels

The modern tourist hotel is largely a post-war phenomenon, and the comparatively cheap package holiday to Spain and other popular countries with long hot summers resulted in a massive hotel building programme in the 1950s and 60s; it is estimated that in ten years more than one thousand new hotels were built on the island of Majorca. Such buildings were designed (if that is the appropriate term) for the

The Feathers Hotel, Ludlow, Salop. A medieval inn built in 1603, still offering hospitality to modern travellers (*The British Tourist Authority*)

tourist industry, and the main objective was to squeeze as many bedrooms as possible on to the smallest area of land. The result therefore was massive high-rise hotel buildings in an uncontrolled sprawl along the Mediterranean coast of Spain, and similar regions of Europe.

These new concrete jungles gave mass tourists what they sought, sea, sun and sand, and with them they brought drugstores, discotheques and other foreign imports which converted the area to a mirror image of the environment from which they sought to escape. Most of these developments were based on older fishing villages, which were rapidly engulfed.

A glance at any travel agent's brochure will show the crowded beaches and overpowering buildings. Yet the illusion is still retained, for the brochures still contain some photographs cropped to eliminate the high-rise hotels that overshadow the beaches or include the last remaining corner of the old original village. The advertising material often shows the suntanned bathing beauty on a deserted, seemingly endless stretch of sand. These once attractive places are destroyed forever by over-development, inadequate planning and poor design; they can never be reclaimed.

The tragedy for future generations lies in the fact that this disease is spreading. In places once considered too far away to be spoiled the same pattern is emerging as long haul jets make it possible to travel even further on a holiday trip. The high-rise hotel is logical in a high-rise urban environment, i.e. London, Copenhagen, Nairobi or New York, and with skill and imaginative design can provide a high standard of accommodation and convenience for the urban tourist, as the examples illustrated show.

The high rise hotel appropriate in a city setting. The Royal S.A.S. Hotel in Copenhagen, Denmark designed by Arne Jacobson is a good example of an urban hotel (*Edward D. Mills*)

There is, however, no logic in transferring the high-rise solution to a rural or remote location and the most architecturally and environmentally successful examples of modern hotel design are related to the site on which they are built and the environment of which they are a part. Many developing tourist areas now have strict zoning laws which limit the size and height of new hotel buildings. In Tunisia no building along the coastline is allowed to be built to a height greater than the neigbouring palm trees. However, trees grow upwards and sometimes there has been the temptation to add an extra storey when tree growth allows. This has, on occasions, led to disasterous building failures as the original structure was not designed to take an additional floor.

Some of the most successful recent hotels in developing tourist areas such as the Caribbean, East Africa, the Bahamas and elsewhere have been planned as loosely grouped one or two-storey bedroom

continued on page 78

A modern hotel. The Mughal Sheraton at Agra, India designed by Arcop Associates on an exceptionally sensitive site near to the Taj Mahal. Great care has been taken with the overall design, the landscaping and the choice of materials that were all produced locally (*Arcop Associates*)

Case Study 11

Hotel and Conference Centre
Kampala, Uganda, E. Africa

Architects
Robert C. W. Browning
in association with
Edward D. Mills & Partners

Clients
The Government of Uganda

The site   Kampala, the capital of Uganda, is like Rome, a city built on seven hills. In accordance with African tradition all the important buildings, the cathedral, the mosque and the International Hotel (originally called the Apolo Hotel) are built on hill tops. The site is in the centre of the city approached from Shimoni Road on Gun Hill adjoining a small, attractive public park and near to the principal commercial buildings and older hotels. All the important buildings of Kampala such as the Parliament, the National Theatre, the Central Post Office and the shopping area are within walking distance. Kampala is 24 miles from the international airport at Entebbe on the edge of Lake Victoria, the world's second largest lake. Although it is only 20 miles from the Equator, its altitude of nearly 4000 ft above sea level gives it a very pleasant year-round climate. Because of its location, the capital is an important centre for both businessmen and tourists; visitors to the famous Game Parks and other tourist attractions begin their 'safaris' in Kampala.

Design and layout   The facilities of the International Hotel have been designed to meet all the needs of visitors. The main provisions include a reception area, a conference centre with a banqueting room to seat 450 people and committee rooms, a shopping arcade, restaurant, grill room and bars, three hundred double bedrooms each with bathroom, swimming pool, a roof top night club, carpark, gardens and terraces. In addition, flats are provided for the senior management staff together with all the service and back-up accommodation.

The hotel building consists of two bedroom wings, both facing north and south with eleven floors of bedrooms on a three-floor podium that contains the principal public rooms and service areas. All the rooms have been orientated to take advantage of the magnificent views across the city and the surrounding countryside with Lake Victoria to the South. All bedrooms have large balconies and eleven V.I.P. suites are located on the 11th floor. Above the bedroom wings in the central tower is the roof garden night club with a birds eye view of Kampala on all sides and large roof terraces from which Lake Victoria can easily be seen.

The large elliptical swimming pool is situated on the Gun Hill together with changing rooms, outdoor restaurant and terraces. It has an island for cabaret shows, linked to artists' dressing rooms at a lower level and a childrens' pool.

The hotel grounds are landscaped, existing trees preserved and indigenous flowering trees and shrubs planted to link the gardens with the adjoining park.

Construction and materials   The seventeen-storey hotel has a reinforced concrete frame, with concrete floors and roofs. The infill walls are standard, locally made concrete blocks, rendered externally. Part of the lower service building is faced with local clay facing bricks. Windows, door and balcony balustrades are in natural anodised aluminium sections. All windows are protected from the direct rays of the sun, and glass louvres utilise the breezes that blow across the elevated site so that all the high ceilinged bedrooms and public rooms are naturally ventilated. Only the conference/banqueting area and the V.I.P. suites are air-conditioned.

The hotel has a central telephone exchange, electricity substations and boiler house. A service floor at second floor level beneath the bedroom wings contains all the hotel services; the staff flats and the hotel laundry with its independent ventilation are also at this level.

Local materials have been used wherever possible, particularly Ugandan hardwoods for joinery, locally made terrazzo flooring slabs and pavings, concrete blocks and facing bricks. The architects were also responsible for all the interior design of both guest and public rooms and much of the furniture and furnishings were specially designed and made by Ugandan craftsmen using African materials. Local craft products have been used decoratively in public rooms, particularly in the rooftop night club.

Comment   Kampala is a modern city of tall buildings and was founded less than 100 years ago. It has many open spaces with exotic trees and planting creating a green and colourful urban landscape. In a busy modern capital city of a country with a population of ten million people the International Hotel is a prominent landmark that provides a very high standard of accommodation and service. It has played an important part in the expansion of Uganda's tourist trade. At the present time, the country is still suffering from the effects of recent political upheaval, but it is hoped that more settled conditions will bring a revival of tourism to one of the most beautiful countries in the African continent, popularly known as the Pearl Africa.

The architecture of the hotel is urban in character, but the building has been designed specifically for the tropics taking advantage of the equitable climate of Uganda, and the special features of the site.

The hotel has become a popular meeting place for local people and tourists and has helped to foster genuine interest and friendship between hosts and guests.

2

1 Aerial view of architect's model
2 Main entrance and West bedroom wing
3 General view from Shimoni road – swimming
  pool complex to right
4 Detail of deep bedroom balconies (*Photo:
  Edward D. Mills*)
5 Swimming pool with the city of Kampala and
  surrounding hills in the background

Case Study 12

Beach Hotel
Jerba, Tunisia, N. Africa

Architect
Hans Munk Hansen

Clients
Societe Carthago, Tunis

Engineers
Larsen & Nielsen Consultor A/S

The site   The hotel site has an area of
10 ha with a 310 m sandy beach to the
south-east, and a main road on the north-
west boundary. The local terrain is a level
peaceful palm and olive grove bordering the
Mediterranean. The island of Jerba is a
popular holiday and tourist area of Tunisia
and is particularly popular with families with
children. Some existing traditional buildings
('menzels') on the site have been preserved.

Design and layout   The hotel, which can
house 500–700 guests, is built in two sections; a single storey communal central area
containing bars, restaurants, games rooms
and other guests' facilities, with a four storey
bedroom wing. A smaller separate bedroom
wing is grouped around a 'village' square
designed for outdoor activities. The bedrooms are in terrace form, to allow for variation in size and a sea view, and each room
has a spacious protected balcony. The variety of room sizes meets the needs of all
guests, from a single person to a large
family. The swimming pool adjoins the main
restaurant overlooking the sea. The main
attraction of the region is 'sun, sea and
sand'.

    The site is relatively isolated and a staff
village has been built to house all the hotel
employees together with a central laundry.
In the off-season months of January and
February, the hotel is used for conferences
and seminars to allow a year-round occupancy.

Construction and materials   The building
work was carried out by local craftsmen, and
consists of load bearing walls built of concrete blocks made on the site and finished
with a rough surfaced white plaster. All
rooms are roofed with brick vaults constructed without formwork. Roofs, balconies
and other areas are waterproofed with an

application of bitumenous emulsion. Windows and all other joinery are in Northern
Red Fir, and a traditional wooden grid,
known as a 'masharabiya' is used for sun-
shading and as a visual room divider in larger
rooms. All ironmongery is specially treated
to prevent corrosion due to the sea air. Local
handicrafts have been used extensively as
decoration throughout the complex.

Comment   The architectural design of the
hotel has been successfully related to the
Tunisian Islamic tradition of white cubic
houses with domed and vaulted roofs, and
although considerable use has been made
of traditional materials and construction
methods, the result is a modern building well
equipped to meet the needs of the holidaymaker. The building through its siting,
sculptural form and colour contributes interest to an otherwise featureless landscape,
and the strong building forms create a pattern of light and shade in the strong
Mediterranean sunshine against the cloud-
less blue sky.

    A high rise hotel would have been com-
pletely out of keeping with this long sandy
stretch of coastline. By keeping the height to
a maximum of four floors, a building with a
human scale has been created. The
architectural character has been maintained
in the design of the hotel staff quarters;
when these are provided they are often
regarded as second-class accommodation,
this is clearly not the case in this complex.

3

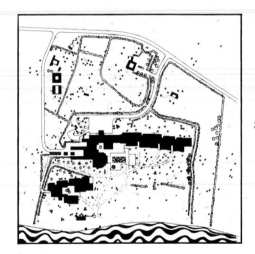

Site plan

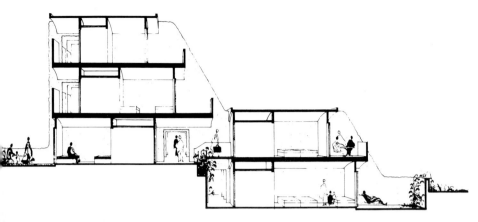

1 Cross section through bedroom wing
2 Communal area with bedroom terraces behind
3 Terraced bedrooms
4 General view from the beach of complete
  complex
5 Staff housing square

(*Photos: Hans Munk Hansen*)

4

5

Case Study 13

Beach Hotel
Camino Real, Cancun, Quintana
Roo, Mexico

Architects
Legoretta

Client
Western International Hotels

The site The Camino Real is a sandy
promontory almost completely surrounded
by water, the Caribbean and a salt water
lagoon. The hotel is situated on the beach
and the only physical feature of the site is the
expanse of flat, white, coral sand with palm
trees with clear warm sea water and mild sea
breezes. Cancun has many miles of sandy
beaches, and is situated at the tip of the
Yucatan Peninsula in the Mexican Caribbean. Centuries ago the Mayan Kings win-
tered here, and today the climate attracts
tourists all the year round. The region is
largely devoted to the tourist industry and
the ancient archaeological area of el Rey is a
short distance from Cancun. All the usual
typical holiday attractions including fishing,
sailing and golf are available in the area.

Design and layout The hotel consists of
two main elements, a guest block with 256
air-conditioned bedrooms, and suites each
with bathroom, balcony and sea view. The
section shows the relationship of the rooms
with a central courtyard or atrium. The
second element is the public zone which
accommodates the main restaurants, bars
and disco. The two areas are linked by a
covered way with an outdoor restaurant and
a very large swimming pool with its own
natural beach. Tennis courts adjoin the pool
and there is ample space for sunbathing on
beaches and terraces.

Construction and materials A modern
reinforced concrete structure with high quality finishes and contemporary decor and
furnishings. The hotel is completely air-
conditioned.

Comment The Camino Real is an unashamed contemporary holiday hotel for
tourists who wish to enjoy the location and
the climate in a relaxed atmosphere. The site
makes no demands – unlimited flat sand and
sea with the inevitable palm trees. This bold

architectural statement is ideal for such a
location and makes the most of the bright
sunshine and the open nature of the area, it
makes no concessions to local tradition in
either form or detail, but is very successful
as a holiday centre.

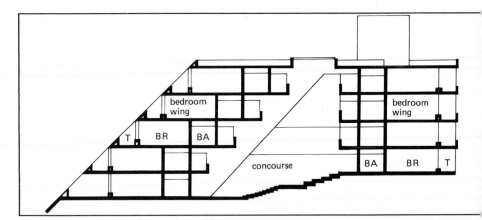

1. public areas
2. bedroom wing
3. lagoon
4. restaurant
5. main entrance
6. service entrance
7. tennis courts

beach

N

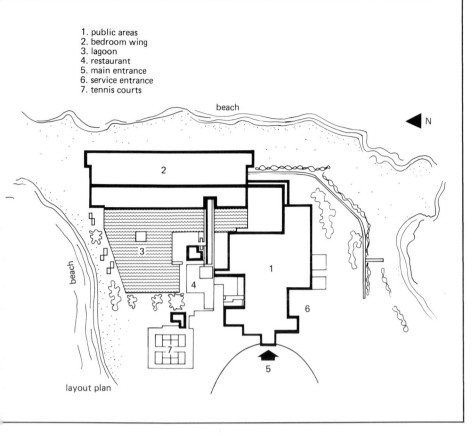

beach

beach

layout plan

1 Cross section thru' bedroom block
2 Bedroom block across the pool from the covered way
3 The covered way adjoining the main complex leading to the pool and open-air restaurant
4 Sunbathing island on the lagoon
5 Entrance and covered ways

(*Photos: Julius Schulman*)

3

4

5

Case Study 14

Borgaf Jall Ski Hotel
South Lappland, Sweden

Architects
Ralph Erskine

Client
The Dorothea Community

Engineer
K. Ritzen

The site   The site is a very dramatic one on the edge of a mountain region with lakes, rivers and ski slopes. To the east are forested hills with scattered small farms and timber camps. To the west are mountains with bears, reindeer, wolves and wolverine. The winter is cold with eight months of snow; the summer is short and intensive. Nearby is a small village of about ten families with a chapel and co-operative also designed by Ralph Erskine.

Design and layout   The hotel was placed on the edge of a gravel pit and forms a giant ground sculpture, windscreens have been built to gouge out and build up the snow in sculptural form. The adoption of this form provides home ski slopes that do not exist naturally; these ski runs start on the hotel roof. The layout of the building follows the site contours, the lowest level contains the dining room with kitchen, boiler etc, in a separate unit. On the top of this, as a balcony, is the lounge reached by a ramp of stairs winding like a mountain road. In the basement is a dance and meeting room, and a small shop is located halfway up the stairs.

The single-storey bedroom zone is planned over and around a central corridor; each bedroom has three levels, the lowest at corridor level (below ground level) with wardrobes and washing space. The next level is a sitting area, and above the corridor is the sleeping space with wardrobes.

The hotel accommodates 70–80 guests, and sites for private cottages in small groups are allocated amongst the trees around the hotel.

Construction and materials   Costs had to be kept low and as the nearest small town and railway are 120 km away the hotel is built in materials of the district. Wood came from the forest, sawn into boards on the spot; gravel and sand from the foundation excavations for concrete and concrete bricks and slate stone from a quarry 5 km away from the site. Steeply sloping roofs are covered with mats of wooden poles to give harmony with the environment in the summer as the snow does in the winter. At a practical level this also protects the roof covering from ski stick points.

Comment   To quote the architect 'it has been interesting to attempt to use rustic materials without sentimentalising them with "sport hotel" character and to obtain the "sport" feeling by choice of constructional forms'.

Considerable use of colour has given this small and intimate hotel a strong character. 'Under the turf covered roof the wooden building is painted in slightly dissonating primary colours to give, like the Lapps dress, a splash of intensive colour in the almost colourless winter landscape, and to express the hotel as the wooden toy that it is'.

The total design is a remarkably successful example of concern for the natural environment, the use of local materials, but firm design control by a skilful architect. It is not without interest that the building cost was half that of corresponding hotels.

1

2

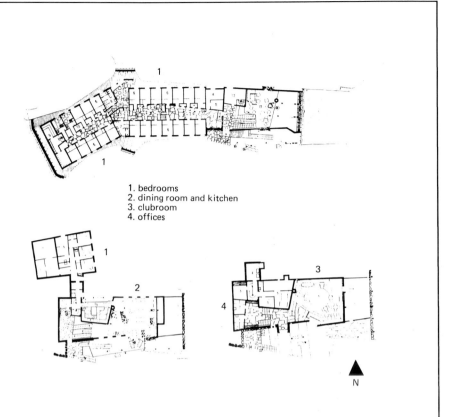

Plans at the three floor levels

1. bedrooms
2. dining room and kitchen
3. clubroom
4. offices

N

1 General view of hotel and surrounding landscape
2 The main roof slope designed as a practice ski run
3 Dining room interior with mezzanine sitting area
4 Robust detailing using locally available materials

(*Photos: Ralph Erskine*)

Case Study 15

Amathus Beach Hotel
Limassol, Cyprus

Architects
The Architects Collaborative Inc
& Fotis J. Colakides & Associates

Clients
Amathus Navigation Co. Ltd.

Engineer
Frank E. Basil

The site   The hotel is located in a popular holiday area of Limassol on a small typical steeply sloping site among existing olive and cyprus groves facing south to the sea; it is one of a chain of four hotels owned by the same client. The north boundary is formed by a road that provides access to the site, the difference in level between the road and the sea is some 11 m. Service access is located on the eastern boundary.

The neighbourhood is rugged with rocks and the remains of old stone agricultural buildings, the long sandy beach is much used for sailing, swimming and water sports; the hotel has its own marina and 200 m of private beach. Larnacu Airport is approximately 44 miles from Limassol. The history of Cyprus goes back to Greek and Roman times, there are extensive archaeological remains and the climate permits a year-round holiday season.

Design and layout   Owing to the limited area of the site, the hotel is planned as a compact block running east and west parallel to the seashore, with a separate thirty-two unit luxury suite addition to the west added after the main building was completed.

Although the building has seven floors, the careful exploitation of the slope of the land and the sloping silhouette of the building reduces the apparent height of the block.

The lowest level (7 m above sea level) contains the breakfast room/coffee shop, swimming pools, 'cabanas', terraces, etc that directly adjoin the beach which is Government property. At this level is the plant and service areas of the hotel. The ground floor and mezzanine levels include a two storey lounge, restaurants, shops, terraces and main entrance, with parking for one hundred and twenty-five cars. The four upper floors contain two hundred and twenty guest rooms, each with bathroom and a large balcony. The rooms are planned on

either side of a central corridor and have been staggered one above the other to create a sense of privacy and perspective. Other public areas include convention/conference rooms for 200 people and a discotheque and floodlit games areas are located on the site.

Construction and materials   The building is constructed of *in situ* reinforced concrete with a sandblasted finish externally. Internally local brick, plaster and wood is used for wall surfaces, with local marble and terrazzo flooring. Brightly coloured tiles are used to contrast with the off-white external walls. All materials have been chosen for ease of maintenance, and the architects were responsible for the interior design and landscape design. Most of the furniture designed by the architects was made locally.

Comment   The building is frankly contemporary in design but because of the careful use of the site contours, it fits into the landscape more successfully than the unimaginative tower block hotels further along the coast. The principal objectives of the architects were to maintain the natural qualities of the local environment, to encourage the circulation of the visitors to and from the

beach and to preserve the visual continuity in the meeting of land and sea. These objectives have been achieved with considerable success and the building blends with the natural characteristics of the rugged and sloping terrain creating a cheerful holiday atmosphere that takes full advantage of the attractive views of the sea and the surrounding landscape.

2

General view across the bay
View of main terrace with dining room
General view of the beach

Layout plan

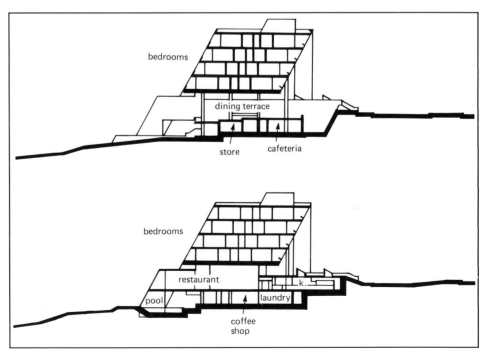

Cross-sections

Case Study 16

Hotel Oberoi
Bogmalo Beach, Goa, India

Architect
Uttam C. Jain

Clients
Tradewinds Ltd

Engineers (Structural and Services)
Techconsultants

The site   The hotel is situated on a narrow strip of land 15–30 m wide on one of the most picturesque stretches of Goa's coastline, with steep hill slopes on the eastern side and the palm fringed Arabian sea on the west. The site is 10 km from the port of Vasco De Gama and five minutes drive from Dabolim Airport, which is one hour's flight from Bombay.

The village of Bogmalo adjoins the site to the north. The history of Goa goes back to antiquity, it has a warm tropical climate, covers 3610 sq km with a population of some 626 000. The area has a wealth of archaeological remains and architectural monuments. The site is one of exceptional natural beauty and the wide sandy bay with the background of rocky hills covered with exotic vegetation is a unique setting for a beach holiday resort.

Design and layout   A series of design solutions for the hotel were considered, the three main alternatives were

1 a series of units cascading down the hill slope,
2 vertically stacked units,
3 a building with a 'contra-slope' in section with the upper floors projecting over the lower ones.

The latter solution was finally adopted.

To quote the architect 'we got the final clue from the palm trees on the site itself, the palm's bending trunk rising contra-slope holds the top mass while allowing free flow of the breeze in between'. The clients required 120 guest rooms, these are arranged on six upper floors paired in six sets of twenty. There are 114 twin bedded or studio type rooms and six suites, one on each floor, all with bathrooms.

The ground floor contains reception, lounge, restaurants, shops, health club and other public amenities. The administration offices, conference rooms, etc are at mezza-

nine level. Storage, staff facilities, plant and other service accommodation is at basement level. The outdoor swimming pool and terraces overlook the beach and the Arabian sea to the west.

Construction and materials   The main structure is shutter finished *in situ* reinforced concrete, with low height wings built of local clay bricks. Other finishing materials were chosen for their natural colour and texture which required little maintenance. Similar materials are used to the interiors to echo the regional flavour of the Konkan coast, of which Goa is part, and to create an open and casual atmosphere.

Comment   The unusual design of this hotel is a bold attempt to build in a positive style on an exceptional site. The solution adopted does the least damage to the challenging tropical landscape. Any building on this site would have been an intrusion but the completed building using the contemporary idiom and its original cross-section adjusts surprisingly well to the natural environment.

The overhanging bedroom floors facing the sea are also very practical as they provide much needed shade to bedroom win-

dows and the broad balconies have exceptionally fine views. The design makes use of even the mildest sea breeze and allows it to flow through the building. The architects conceived the hotel not only as one with all the normal comforts but also as a place where visitors closely relate to the natural environment.

While the west facade of the building is very successful as an architectural composition, the east elevation is spoiled by the heavy stair tower. The open shaded gallery access to the bedrooms with wide planted flower boxes is a pleasant feature well detailed and practical.

1

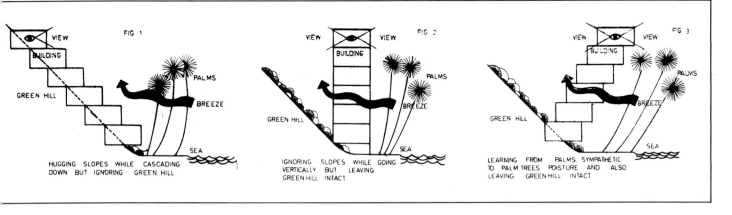

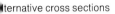

Alternative cross sections

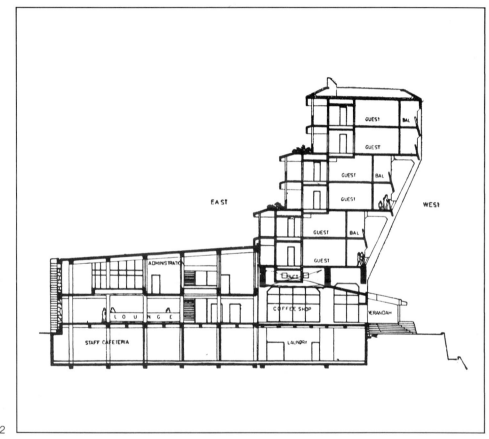

Cross section

1 Swimming pool, terrace and bedrooms (*Photo: Uttam C. Jain*)
2 Access gallery to bedrooms (*Photo: Uttam C. Jain*)
3 The general landscape of Bogmalo Beach (*Photos: Mitter Bedi*)

An attractive modern hotel on a rocky site at Paradise Bay, Malta designed to fit into its natural setting by Richard England. Sadly this building has now been completely swamped by a large and insensitive extension, out of scale with its surroundings (*Edward D. Mills*)

accommodation in landscaped gardens adjoining the beach with central dining rooms and other communal facilities as a focal point together with the inevitable swimming pool. This plan form not only creates a more pleasant and relaxed atmosphere, but also ensures that the buildings merge with the surrounding landscape and become less intrusive. In locations where sudden rain can be expected, simple covered ways can be incorporated linking the buildings.

The Case Studies illustrate a wide range of hotel buildings as far apart as Mexico and Lapland. Each example shows a different approach to the problem but in every case the architect has given serious consideration to the nature of the site, the materials available and the character of the surrounding area.

Motels

The tourist hotel in popular resorts was designed for the medium stay visitor – two or three weeks – but in the USA the Motel or Motor Hotel was originated. This was more akin to the medieval inn, as it catered for the motorist passing through an area on a long journey wishing to stop overnight.

The true motel is probably peculiar to the USA with its excellent highway network and long distances from coast to coast. The essence of the motor hotel is comfort and convenience, the facilities of the long stay hotel are not necessary, but car parking – one space for each room – meals available at all hours and bedroom with bathroom *en suite* are essential.

Because the motel is designed for the motorist it must be near to a main highway with well-designed advance signing, planned landscaping to provide separation from the road traffic and a good access layout to allow safe and easy entrance and exit. Cafeteria-type catering is usually acceptable, although waitress service is also available in the larger restaurants.

A wide variety of food and drink is generally available on a 24-hour basis from a light snack to a full meal. This means that food preparation and kitchen space need a considerable area, the total area of kitchen space and all the ancillary accommodation can be as much as the total dining or restaurant area. Public rooms, toilets and other amenities are required but the scale of them will be related to the location of the motel and the level of demand. These facilities should be available to passing travellers who need a meal and a short break.

The most important factor is the layout of the individual bedroom accommodation, usually one or two storeys in height. The section of *Planning*, dealing with motels shows some of the more usual arrangements, the essential feature being the accessibility of the bedroom unit from the visitors' car which is usually parked immediately adjacent. Insulation from the noise of passing traffic is of particular importance, and carefully planned landscaping not only helps to solve this problem, but also helps to reduce the visual impact of the large number of parked cars.

Planning for disabled people

Many holiday hotels are daunting enough to the able bodied visitor, the fact that disabled sportsmen now have their own Olympic Games, take part in motor racing, climb mountains and enjoy swimming and horse-riding, is no reason why a holiday hotel should be designed as an obstacle race for disabled visitors.

The first point at which a disabled person feels disadvantage is on arrival at a building. Many will arrive by car, and separate car parking spaces should be provided; the disabled can be either drivers or passengers. Reserved car parking bays should be clearly marked with the disabled driver's sign and should be located as near as possible to the entrance to the building. The spaces should be wider than normal, to allow adequate room for manoeuvring a wheelchair from the car. Steps of any sort are a hazard; kerbs should include a ramped section and entrances to buildings should be level or ramped. Existing steps can be modified by the use of prefabricated metal ramps, and for walking visitors a sturdy handrail is of great assistance. a level area at the top of a ramp is essential. Entrance doors should be wide enough to permit easy entry for a wheelchair; doors with self-closing mechanism must have a built-in delayed action and any glazing must be unbreakable.

Within the building, circulation corridors should be wide enough for a wheelchair and any change of level must be in the form of a ramp; steps are very dangerous. Handrails on one wall are much appreciated by the partially sighted or semi-ambulant who need some form of walking aid. Staircases cannot be negotiated by the non-ambulant (wheelchair visitors), but for others the steps must all be the same in any

Disabled people can now enjoy most of the leisure pursuits available to able bodied people (*C. Wycliffe Noble*)

flight with non-slip nosings to treads and rigid hand-rails. Where children or old people use the stairs frequently, an extra handrail is an added convenience.

Internal doors, lifts and lift doors should be designed to admit a wheelchair with lift controls within reach of the seated passenger.

Toilets for the disabled must be clearly marked and designed to permit use by wheelchair visitors. The door must be wide enough to permit access and the compartment large enough to allow for manoeuvrability. A variety of arrangements are possible and many manufacturers now produce such essential accessories as grab rails, special door fittings, specially designed cantilevered WC pans, hand basins and single lever action taps. The inclusion of a special toilet in plans for a new building presents few problems, but the inclusion of such special features in an existing building will require special consideration and consultation with an architect is strongly recommended.

Bedrooms need special consideration as cluttered rooms can cause accidents and damage; wheelchair occupants need room to manoeuvre. The bathroom also needs extra space, with aids and handrails particularly adjacent to the WC. Showers are easier to use than normal baths, and easily-reached controls to the water supply and hand grips are essential. Bearing in mind that wheelchair visitors are permanently in a seated position, such essential items as toilet roll holders, mirrors, lavatory basins etc should be at a suitable level. Lower than normal window sills, telephone points, light switches are desirable, and electric plug points should be above floor level for greater safety. Even the hotel reception desk can be made more inviting to a wheelchair guest by the addition of a specially lowered section.

Certain interior finishes such as doors which may be subject to damage by wheelchairs have already been mentioned. The most important internal finish however is the floor. Whether the user is confined to a wheelchair, semi-ambulant, partially sighted, a high spirited youngster with a broken leg or a careful octogenarian, the floor finish of any public or private building can make all the difference between a safe journey and a hazardous one.

Bathroom specially designed for use by disabled people. British Polio Fellowship hotel. Lantern hotel, Worthing (*C. Wycliffe Noble*)

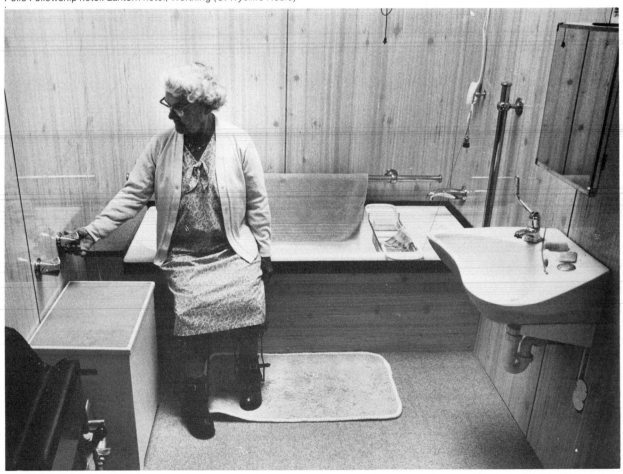

Floor finishes must be non-slip and must be maintained in such a way as to ensure that they remain so; they must also not look slippery. Flooring materials that mark or dent easily are to be avoided and for those users who can walk, a slightly resilient material is appreciated. The requirements of differing types of disabled users are sometimes contradictory and therefore special care must be taken in choosing a flooring material where considerable use of a space by disabled or elderly people is anticipated.

Provision for the disabled in any type of holiday situation can no longer be regarded as an optional extra. Any building which has been conscientiously designed for disabled users, will in fact be more convenient and attractive to able-bodied users and will make the holiday break for those travelling with disabled holidaymakers more restful and beneficial.

Remote places

The growing world interest in the conservation of wildlife and the protection of endangered species has helped to create a new dimension for tourists seeking an entirely different holiday experience. The creation of nature reserves and game parks like Serengeti in East Africa, the National Parks in the USA and the UK, extending over vast areas have proved not only to be of benefit to the native wildlife, but also a powerful attraction to tourists who come with cameras to photograph the animals where big game hunters once came to kill.

East Africa is unique in the world for its abundant wildlife and this has been enormous encouragement to the tourist industry. To quote a Kenya Government official:

'Wildlife in Kenya has proved that is has a right to exist not only as part of the aesthetic inheritance of the country but also because it is an economic proposition. Through attracting visitors, it has contributed financially to the welfare of the nation. It forms one of the biggest pillars of tourism, which is the third industry after agriculture and manufacturing. Some people may think it selfish for Western nations to conserve wildlife in Kenya in order for their people to come and see it. But, in fact, it has been proved here that this contributes tremendously to the economy, and therefore to the development of the country. So the selfish attitude may well be positive to the national development programme'.

Other developing countries of the world are also beginning to realise that local wildlife and other natural elements can attract both tourists and currency that can help a poor economy area. These countries, therefore are developing tourist industries based on their natural assets.

The inevitable dilemma arises once more, tourists need accommodation even in the most remote parts of the world. Accommodation means buildings and building means disturbance of the settled ways of life of the native human and animal population. Too many tourists, badly organised or careless, can cause as much destruction as the hunters of old.

Sir Peter Scott, now Chairman of the World Wildlife Fund, said in 1972 that tourists could be the salvation of many seriously endangered animals and wild places. But however good the scientific or ethical reasons for conservation, it is unlikely to succeed in the poorer countries unless it can be shown to have a direct economic value. Tourists, on the other hand, can be, he said, dangerous. They drive away wild animals or denude areas of vital fauna. They are also behind the increase of holiday development.

The World Wildlife Fund and its sister organisation, the International Union for Conservation and Natural Resources, are working on a code of conduct for the travel business. To quote Sir Peter Scott: 'We hope that all sections of the business, airlines, tour operators, steamship companies, hotel chains and so on, will adhere to the principles we shall be laying down' (*The Architect*, February 1972).

The legendary 'Treetops' in Kenya near Nyeri and at the edge of the Mt. Kenya was built as a two-room tree house over fifty years ago; it was enlarged in 1952 for the Royal visit. Here Princess Elizabeth became Queen Elizabeth II on the death of her father: this structure was burned down in 1954. Today 'Treetops

The animals in the world's game reserves and national parks are still undisturbed by building development, but their future often depends on the tourist industry (*Edward D. Mills*)

Treetops in Kenya, the famous hotel where the visitors are confined while the animals are free (*Block Hotels Ltd. D. K. Jones*)

Hotel' can accommodate forty people in comfortable bedrooms for overnight game viewing and is probably the most famous Game Park building in the world. It has done much to foster the world-wide interest in Kenya's wildlife. Over 20 000 people have enjoyed the unforgettable experience of night-time game watching from this elevated look-out.

The local environment

In the developed countries of the world, the scale of the tourist influx into areas of great natural beauty, and the natural habitat of wildlife of all kinds, has become enormous in recent years. Estimates show that in Japan, nearly 300 million visits are made annually to the twenty-six National Parks which cover 1.9 million ha. In the USA 95 million visits were made to the 81 million km^2 of National Parks.

In the UK the ten National Parks extend over 1.4 million ha but no records of the numbers of visitors are available. The Wildfowl Trust established by Sir Peter Scott at Slimbridge in 1946 now has six other Centres in the UK, where over half a million visitors each year go to view the vast numbers of wildfowl in their natural habitat. The work of the Trust has brought to the attention of visiting public the need for conservation and has emphasised the fact that man and his environment are mutually dependant.

By careful planning and development the Trust has enabled people to enjoy living wildfowl as part of our natural heritage; special facilities are available for disabled visitors and Slimbridge is equipped so that even blind people can derive considerable pleasure and interest from a visit.

Once again the work of conservation depends upon the support of visitors, and visitors need built facilities; the balance is a delicate one for in March 1979 the Trust welcomed its 6 millionth visitor. Clearly the reception and catering for such large numbers of visitors throughout the year is a major task and the Case Studies show that the Trust is very much alive to the importance of appropriate design for the buildings that are an esential part of their Centres.

Any building in a conservation area, whether it is a vast Game Reserve, a National Park, or a bird sanctuary, is a manmade intrusion into a natural environment and while it must provide the tourist with essential amenities, it must at the same time be as unobtrusive as possible. The preservation of the natural environment must be an essential element in the building design, for if this is not achieved the main purpose of the exercise will have been defeated.

One of the principal problems that arises with building in virgin areas is the fact that access is often difficult; if it were not so, much of the attraction would disappear. Essential services are usually non-existent, and the availability of materials for building is very limited. A detailed preliminary feasibility study is therefore vital and careful estimation of physical resources is of great importance.

One example can be quoted, that of waste disposal. In the USA and elsewhere, the indiscriminate construction of buildings in remote areas without proper means of waste disposal has caused the entrophication of nearby lakes through the seepage or direct disposal of sewage into them. Such damage to the environment is irreversible, and once again the advent of human intervention is destroying the natural environment that attracted the visitors in the first place.

Services

In any building project in an undeveloped area, therefore, the question of waste disposal must be given priority. Other essential services are equally important, electricity will need to be generated on site; in many parts of the world the use of solar energy can not only save fossil fuel but also provide power without atmospheric pollution. The radio telephone eliminates the need for expensive and disfiguring overland telephone lines.

Road access is often a major problem; hard all-weather roads not only disfigure the landscape but are expensive and difficult to maintain. In developed countries and where distances are relatively small, sympathetic road design is possible, but in the wide open spaces of the world, access by light aircraft to a simple landing strip together with consolidated access tracks is probably the most satisfactory compromise for the transfer of both people and supplies.

Sympathetic building construction

In all natural and unspoiled areas the problem of actual building construction is one which needs considerable study. The most successful results have been achieved by two opposite approaches. In the case of Chobe Lodge in Botswana the architects made use of materials on the site to construct the new buildings using traditional barrel vault construction to create an attractive and practical group of buildings. By using local craft skills and traditional building techniques, the problem of transporting large quantities of building materials was avoided and the completed building achieved a genuine harmony with the natural surroundings.

An alternative is the use of one of the most modern building techniques, that of industrialised building, in the form of prefabrication whereby much of the building fabric is made away from the site and transported in sections for rapid assembly *in situ*. The Deerpark cabins in Cornwall were built in this way, using prefabricated modular timber panels, a technique that has much to commend it, for building in remote areas where local building materials are nonexistent and both labour and materials have to be transported over long distances and difficult terrain.

Where tourist facilities are needed in rural and wilderness areas the result is bound to mean environmental change, for even the simplest provisions will include means of access, accommodation of various kinds and essential services.

> 'These must be provided in such a way as to conserve the natural environment and its inhabitants and provide enjoyment for the visitor by such means as will leave them unimpaired for the enjoyment of future generations.'

This paraphrase of a part of the US National Parks Act of 1916 underlines the essential objective of any building in a natural conservation area – the environment must dominate and the manmade contribution must be subservient. The Case Studies that are part of this chapter show that imaginative design, the choice of appropriate materials and structural techniques and above all, a sympathetic understanding of the problems can together result in architecture that enhances the environment and does not degrade or destroy it.

Vilalara on the Algarve, Portugal. A mixed holiday development of apartments, clubhouse and recreational facilities on a dramatic rocky site where the buildings accept the discipline of the natural surroundings (*Proalgarve Holding, S.A.*)

Other buildings for tourists

In one sense many buildings serve both the needs of the tourist and the occasional visitor; for example, airports, garages, service stations, restaurants etc. Many other buildings fall into this dual category and are, therefore, outside the scope of this book unless they are specifically linked with a particular tourist attraction. The excellent restaurant at the Windsor Safari Park being a particular example (see p. 100).

Information is always needed by visitors both at home and abroad and the provision of information about a particular holiday resort, tourist attraction, conservation area or historic building can be a valuable way of directing and controlling the number and flow of visitors at any particular time, thus helping to avoid the overload mentioned previously that can cause so much damage.

Many of the buildings in the Wildfowl Trust Reserves and similar conservation areas include an information centre which not only provides data useful to the casual visitor but often forms the basis of educational material for school parties and special interest groups. A high standard of exhibition display is required if such a centre is to be of maximum value to visitors. The information presented can often be live, not only through the medium of films and the cinema but by the use of live exhibits.

The Nairobi National Park animal orphanage is a well-known example; here immediately adjacent to

continued on page 100

Case Study 17

Nature Reserve Visitors Centre
Arundel Refuge, South Stoke,
Arundel, W. Sussex, England

Architect
Neil Holland
Client
The Wildfowl Trust
Engineers
Campbell Reith & Partners

The site In 1972/3 The Wildfowl Trust established a refuge for wildfowl which extends over 68 acres of protected water-meadows east of Arundel between Swanbourne Lake and the Black Rabbit Inn. The site is flat, with very poor bearing pressure and is susceptible to flooding (up to a recorded height of 600 mm). It lies in an area of flat watermeadows flanked to the North and West by high densely wooded land known locally as 'The Hanger'.

From the site, Arundel Castle can be clearly seen to the south-west and the Black Rabbit Inn is just visible to the east.

Design and layout The client's brief asked for several distinct spaces i.e. viewing gallery-cum-exhibition space, lecture hall, school room, bookshop, a curator's office and public lavatories, including provision for disabled. In putting these spaces together the following points had to be considered and evaluated:

1 Possible flooding of the surrounding area and poor bearing pressure.
2 A strong and well defined circulation pattern for visitors.
3 Local conditions and vernacular buildings in the area.
4 The scale of the development.
5 For economic reasons, the phasing of the building had to be possible with all the attendant problems of differential settlement due to bad ground conditions.

It has been attempted to resolve the above problems and satisfy the requirements in the following way:

Each main space has been defined as a separate structure i.e. the lecture hall, school room, bookshop, viewing gallery and exhibition etc, with circulation routes defined by lower flat roofs, except the main route which is defined initially by a low roof at the entrance doors and then by a glazed roof over into the viewing area and exhibition. It is intended that this strongly defined circulation route is expressed externally and internally.

In breaking down the building into separate units the architects feel that the scale becomes acceptable. The octagonal form of the units and the pitched roofs with central fanlights above produce a changing and irregular skyline sympathetic to the Castle which dominates the scene. Also by pitching the main roofs, screen walls and grass banking, the building 'sits' down on the site as gently as possible.

From the Centre, visitors gain access to hides overlooking ponds and reed beds where wildfowl can be viewed. There are pathways around the lake, and a special entrance for visiting parties of school children and ramps for disabled visitors. The south elevation which overlooks the largest of the twelve lakes in the Arundel Refuge is fully glazed beneath which is a feeding path which attracts large numbers of wildfowl. The Arun flood plain in which the refuge is situated is the breeding ground for Greenshank, Redshank, Teal, Snipe and Water Rail; the collection consists of over 1000 wildfowl from all over the world.

Construction and materials The building is raised 900 mm above ground level on a cellular concrete raft which prevents flooding and also spreads the load evenly over the ground on which the superstructure is bearing. Grass banking at 30° and ponds have been created round the scheme to visually integrate building and site.

The main buildings in the locality are The Castle, The Farm, The Lodge at Swanbourne Lake and the Black Rabbit Inn. Roofs are in the main slate or lead and external walls are stone, flint and colour wash. The materials for the buildings are Welsh slate roofs with lead hips and upstands and brick walls, the brick matching as closely as possible the general colour of the facades of the surrounding buildings.

The general policy of defining each space has structural relevance in as much that the interlocking pieces could have been placed on separate rafts with any settlement that may have arisen being taken up at clear changes of circulation i.e. at doors into different spaces, where they might be expected and anticipated. In the event, the finances were available for building the entire raft and building in one operation.

Comment The aim of The Wildfowl Trust is to protect wildfowl native to the UK as well as rare visiting species, and to educate and encourage the general public to understand and appreciate native wildlife. The Trust has seven centres throughout Britain of which Arundel is the latest. Although the Arun flood plains are a natural habitat for waterbirds of all kinds, considerable landscaping has been carried out including the excavation and improvement of the natural lakes. This has provided an ideal habitat with excellent observation points in as natural an environment as possible.

Such a setting is a challenge to anyone erecting a new building in such surroundings. At Arundel, the architects have produced a structure that is technically ingenious, and architecturally suited to its dramatic landscape. Two choices were open to the designer, a building that disappeared into its background or one that had a positive character. The latter alternative was chosen and the result is a cluster of octagonal pavilions whose shapes echo those of Arundel Castle, which can be seen on the ridge in the distance, when approaching the Visitors Centre. The materials used, slate roofs, light brown bricks and hardwood windows blend happily with the surrounding landscape.

1 Canada goose and chicks (*The Wildfowl Trust* Photo: A. C. Fletcher)
2 View from the North-west (*Photo: Neil Holland*)
3 View of centre across the lake (*Photo: Neil Holland*)

Layout plan

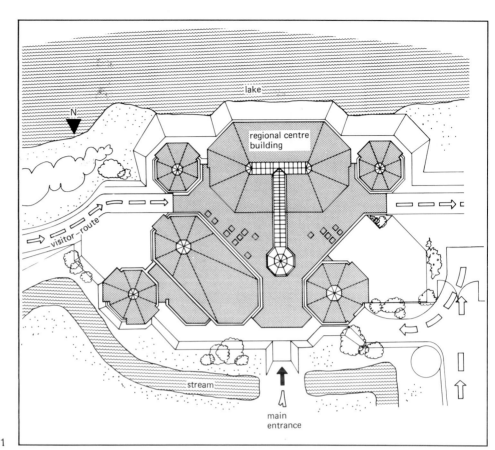

Case Study 18

Wildfowl Refuge
Martin Mere, Burscough, Lancashire

Architects
Building Design Partnership

Client
The Wildfowl Trust

Engineers
Building Design Partnership

The site   Martin Mere is five miles from the Lancashire coast at Southport and covers 120 ha of marshland on the site of what was once the largest mere in Lancashire. It is now one of the finest nature reserves in the UK. Each year it is visited by thousands of wild geese, ducks and waders, including the annual visit of some 14 000 pink-footed geese which come from Greenland each winter. The collection of 1200 birds includes wild fowl from all parts of the world with freeflying flocks of many European species.

Design and layout   The architects were given a brief to design a visitor complex to include an education centre with lecture theatre and exhibition area, together with a concourse, souvenir shop, field laboratories, offices and toilets. The plans allow for future extensions to include a staff hostel, visitors' suite, curator's house and observation tower. The plan developed on a grid at 45° to the axis of the mere overlooking both Swan Lake and the adjacent and smaller flamingo pool. The concourse which is the focal area of the complex and is the entrance to the building allows visitors to view the water areas through large panoramic windows. The concourse is two storeys high with a gallery that contains exhibition space and a curator's office, with an observation window that provides views over the entire marsh.

The buildings are basically single storied with gently sloping roofs with wide overhanging eaves; the buildings separate the refuge from the main access road Fish Lane to the North; the car park is adjacent to this road.

The budget for the scheme was strictly limited but was assisted by money from various bodies, including the Lancashire County council, who financed the educational section of the complex for use by groups of visiting school children.

Construction and materials   The complex has a reinforced concrete raft foundation, and a superstructure based on a Norwegian system which uses 150 mm thick logs, tongued and grooved together with a special interlocking joint. There is no internal lining to the walls, which have a very high insulation value. An unusual feature is the roof construction which consists of timber joists, purlins, tongued and grooved boarding and cork insulation covered with built-up felt and a top layer of a slow growing, drought resistant turf, which is kept in trim by the resident geese. Windows are horizontal sliding sashes, doors are timber framed and glazed with georgian wired polished plate glass.

Comment   In contrast to the Wildfowl Centre at Arundel, Sir Peter Scott of The Wildfowl Trust was anxious that the buildings should not obtrude into the landscape, but would blend into the large areas of flat land of the surrounding area. The horizontal emphasis of the log walling helps to reduce the mass of the building and the grass-covered roof means that the buildings merge with the landscape and become part of the natural environment. The only focal point, which helps to locate the complex for visitors, is the spire-like rooflight over the centre of the concourse.

1   Disabled child with Cape Barren goose. Spec[?] facilities are available for disabled visitors at al[?] Wildfowl Trust Centres (*Photo: Brian Gadsby*)
2   General view of the buildings, across the wate[?]
3   Interior of exhibition with pyramid rooflight
4   Norwegian log construction helps the building to blend with the landscape; note the grass covered roof. The pyramid rooflight acts as a landmark for visitors

(*Photos 2 and 3: Building Design Partnership, Roger W. Park*)

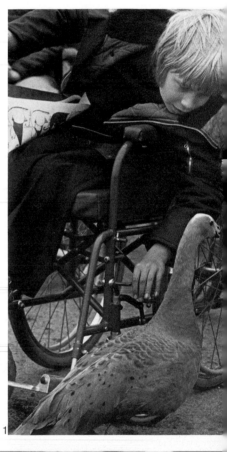

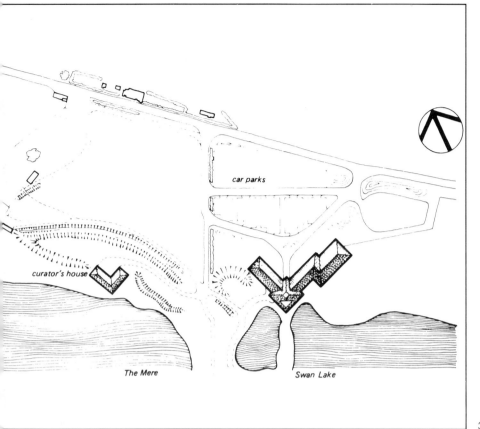

curator's house

car parks

The Mere

Swan Lake

3

Case Study 19

Safari Lodge
Semliki Game Reserve, Uganda,
E. Africa

Architects
Hans Munk Hansen

Clients
Uganda Development Corporation

The site Semliki Safari Lodge is set on the bank of the Wasa river in one of Uganda's Game Reserves in wild unspoiled game country; the area abounds in wildlife and access is by murrum tracks which are sometimes impassable in the rainy seasons. The Reserve is in the Western Region of the country and the lodge is 50–60 km by road to Fort Portal which is halfway between Lake Albert and Lake Edward.

Design and layout The Lodge consists of a central complex containing the reception area, lounge, restaurant and bar overlooking a large swimming pool. Adjoining this block is the service area, kitchen, staffrooms, etc in three blocks around a central courtyard. The guest accommodation is in eleven detached 'bandas', nine with four separate double bedrooms with WC and shower and two with three rooms. These 'bandas' are grouped informally to each side of the main block in a pattern reminiscent of the traditional African village. The total accommodation can cater for eighty-four visitors. The 'bandas' are approached by simple paths and a small carparking area is screened by a clump of trees near the main entrance.

Construction and materials The main problem encountered with building in isolated sites in game reserves and similar locations is that of transporting labour and materials; buildings must be as simple as possible. This safari lodge is constructed primarily of local materials, the most important element being roofs with their deep overhangs to provide shade. All roofs are of timber construction with ceilings only in guests bedrooms and the main kitchen, the roofs are covered with cedar shingles and the supporting structure consists of timber logs. The lower part of the walls are built of random stone masonry, using stone obtained from the vicinity of the site.

The upper parts of the walls are of vertical boarding on a timber frame lined internally with chipboard or asbestos cement sheets. All timber is pressure impregnated.

Doors and windows are timber, and windows have no glazing, openings are closed with wooden doors or top hung wooden shutters, with horizontal wooden louvres for ventilation above door height.

Comment The area in which the lodge is situated has been left as natural as possible with minimum disturbance to existing trees and shrubs. The long low line of buildings and their extended layout makes them almost invisible from a distance, and the illusion is heightened by the colour and texture of the materials used. Here the wildlife is the natural population of the area and animals are free to wander round the lodge for there are no boundary walls or fences, the human visitors are the intruders and these buildings by their design and layout minimise the feeling of intrusion.

1

1 Interior of dining room
2 General view
3 Two adjoining 'bandas'
4 Bandas and main building

(*Photos: Hans Munk Hansen*)

Layout plan

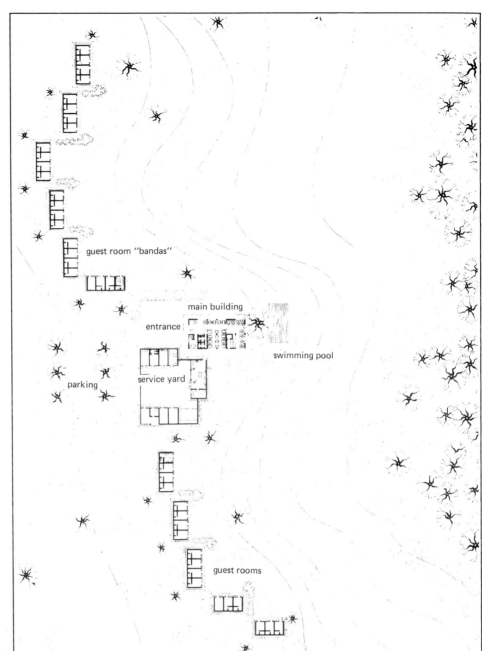

guest room "bandas"

main building

entrance

swimming pool

service yard

parking

guest rooms

3

4

Case Study 20

Safari Lodge
Nile Falls National Park, Uganda, E. Africa

Architects
Hans Munk Hansen

Client
Uganda Development Corporation

The site Pabuka lodge is situated on a hill on the bank of the river Nile in Uganda's largest game park originally known as The Murchison Falls National Park which covers an area of 1200 square miles and is bisected by the Victoria Nile. The Park is on a direct road, 54 miles from Masindi which is 140 miles from Kampala, the capital city of Uganda; there is also an airstrip.

There are large numbers of animals in the Park including elephants, buffalo, lion, giraffe and many varieties of antelope, with an abundance of bird life and thousands of crocodile and hippo can be seen in the Nile. The lodge is in the north-western area of the Park and the site offers splendid views across the river and surrounding plains.

Design and layout The layout of the lodge has been dictated by the size and configuration of the hill on which it is built and the demand for a view of the River Nile from both the main building and the guest rooms. The centre of the complex is the reception area with direct connection to the lounge, bar and restaurant with two large viewing terraces, a swimming pool and a separate service zone. The guest rooms consist of seven two storey blocks containing a total of sixty-four double bedrooms and twelve triple bedrooms with WC and shower and large balconies with extensive views.

The buildings follow the natural contours of the site. Deep roof overhangs have been designed to give protection from the sun and occasional heavy rain showers, with maximum cross ventilation to provide cool interiors without air-conditioning. Car parking is located near the main entrance.

Construction and materials The lower walls and gable ends are built of local stone laid in random fashion, and the supporting structure for the roofs is in uncut eucalyptus logs, exposed internally. The guest rooms have open access balconies with balus-

trades infilled with bamboo which is also used for screens and sun shades. Roofs are covered with cedar shingles and all joinery is in local wrought Mumyama with a natural finish; ceilings are wood boards.

Comment Unlike Semliki lodge, this complex is not hidden in the landscape, but blends with the natural surroundings which have been disturbed as little as possible. Because of the contours of the site and the two-storey guest room units, the buildings can be seen from a distance but the serpentine layout and the natural materials used soften the impact and ensure that the lodge fits into the landscape.

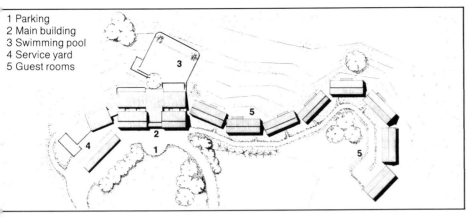

1 Parking
2 Main building
3 Swimming pool
4 Service yard
5 Guest rooms

Layout plan

1 Guests' bedroom block
2 Detail of timber structure with bamboo infill
3 Guest room access, close-up showing construction using timber poles and bamboo
4 Guest rooms, stone gable walls and protected balconies

(*Photos: Hans Munk Hansen*)

Case Study 21

Visitors Centre
Risley Moss Nature Reserve,
Warrington New Town, Cheshire,
England

Architects
Building Design Partnership

Client
Warrington New Town Development
Corporation

*Structural Engineers and Landscape
Architects*
Warrington New Town Development
Corporation

The site Risley Moss has an area of about
83 ha. It lies in the north-east of the Warrington New Town designated area with a railway
line on the south boundary and farmland to
the east. When the new Birchwood District is
completed, housing and a district park will
adjoin the north and west boundaries. The
Moss is largely enclosed by a perimeter
fence with public access at one point only,
halfway along the northern boundary off the
District Distributor road.

The site is mostly flat; half the area is peat
moss covered by grassland and scrub cros-
sed by drains and dykes. The rest of the area
woodland, with birches on the peak and
mature oak, elm, and ash on the clay soil.
The Moss is within easy reach of a large
number of people including local residents.
A new expressway road links with the motorway system, and the new Birchwood railway
station will be only a mile away.

Design and layout The location chosen
for the visitors centre is near to the entrance
to the reserve, close to the tree screened
carparking 'pods' for ninety-six cars and four
coaches hidden by trees. The building is a
simple timber structure consisting of a large
entrance foyer, two exhibition areas, with a
visual aid room, a lecture room, lavatories
and accommodation for the 'rangers'. The
various areas are roughly octagonal in shape
because the exhibition designers required
spaces that were free of 90° corners.

The Moss has a series of nature trails,
picnic areas, bird watching hides and an
observation tower (designed by Warrington
Development Corporation Architects). The
development of this new nature reserve has
been financed jointly by the Countryside
Commission and the Development Corporation.

Construction and materials The structure is built in a grid of concrete beams that
sit on piles driven into the clay and peat
subsoil. The concrete beams cantilever from
the piles on the perimeter of the building and
this separates the ground floor from the
ground so that it appears to float. The building itself is entirely of timber, apart from the
blockwork walls to the lavatories. The timber
frame is sheathed with plywood with horizontal battens to take lapped vertical sawn
redwood boarding as an external finish.

The simple pitched roofs are covered with
mineral faced felt strip slating, blue grey in
colour. Rigid glass fibre panels provide the
insulation for roofs and walls. The walkways,
bridges, eaves and windows, all in timber,
have been detailed with great care and
finished with a red stain.

Comment Unlike the buildings in the vast
nature reserves in Africa, this building is in a
recently created reserve almost in the middle of a new town in England. An abandoned
peat bog, part of a post-glacial mossland
system of great antiquity has been rescued
because of its ecological importance and is
now a nature reserve where visitors, local
residents, holidaymakers and school children can learn more about the history of the
area, and enjoy the flora and fauna, particularly the bird life of the area. The Centre is an
excellent example of a building of simple and
direct architectural character that compli-
ments its natural surroundings. Buildings
designed with this degree of care would
meet the needs of many holiday and tourist
situations.

1

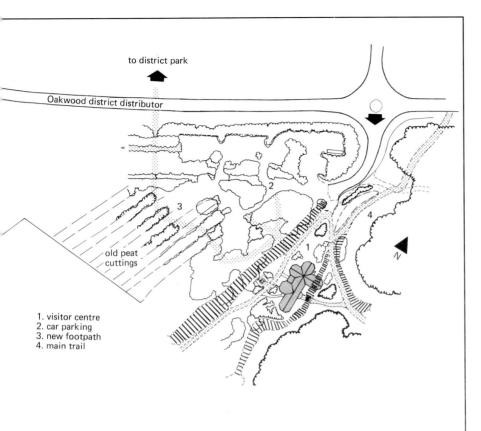

Layout plan

to district park

Oakwood district distributor

old peat
cuttings

1. visitor centre
2. car parking
3. new footpath
4. main trail

1 The building supported on concrete beams is
  half hidden in a woodland clearing
2 The all-timber building has been detailed with
  great care
3 The attention to detail is continued in the
  walkways and outdoor seating

(*Photos: John Mills*)

Case Study 22

Café and Tourist Centre
Tollymore, Newcastle, County
Down, N. Ireland

Architects
Ian Campbell & Partners

Clients
Tourism Branch Department of Commerce
for Northern Ireland & Department of
Agriculture for Northern Ireland

Engineers
Blythe & Blythe Associates in Association
with Dr. J. R. Gilfillin

The site   The Café is located on a flat area
between two car parks in the Forest Park at
Tollymore on the northern foothills of the
Mountains of Mourne near to the coastal
town of Newcastle. The site itself has no
distinctive physical features, but the views
from the area of mountain forest and the
distant sea are exceptionally fine. The adjoining car parks are at different levels and
the tea room was required to be accessible
from both levels, with facilities for disabled
visitors at one level.

Design and layout   The building is planned at two levels to correspond with the car
park levels, the lower floor consists of a shop
for the sale of supplies to campers and
caravanners on a nearby site, with an ice
cream kiosk, lavatories and stores for the tea
room over with a small goods hoist. A staircase gives access to the first floor which
overhangs the ground floor and provides
covered queuing space. The tea room has a
central preparation area with washup and
staff lavatories with two self-service coun-
ters. Seating accommodation is provided for
one hundred and twenty-four people at
tables for four arranged around the perimeter of the tea room to gain maximum
advantage of the views across the Park.
Direct access from the upper car park is by a
bridge that meets the North tip of the diagonal plan.
   Because of the exposed position, the
building has been made as vandal proof as
possible. The toilets and stores have no
windows and the shop doors and ice cream
kiosk window are protected by large timber
shutters at night. Beneath the access bridge
is an ornamental pool.

Construction and materials   The lower
structure consists of *in situ* reinforced concrete column and ring beams, with loadbearing concrete brick cavity walls and piers in
local granite carrying the reinforced concrete
first floor. A separate timber structure of
Douglas fir columns with pine pole windbracing carries the timber framed partly
pitched roof which is covered with tongued
and grooved boarding, fibreglass insulation
with a vapour barrier and asbestos cement
slates on timber battens. The first floor clad-
ding is Redwood V jointed boarding and all
the joinery including the tea room sliding
windows is in red stained timber. Blockwalls
are pebble dashed externally and plastered
internally and exposed concrete surfaces
are untreated. The first floor timber pole
windbracing that also forms the basis of the
access bridge construction is stained blue
black with a red stained plank walkway.
Materials have been chosen for their robust
character and maintenance free qualities.

Comment   Tourist restaurants and tea
rooms are often among the most untidy
buildings in the contryside; they are seldom
designed for their purpose and are usually
singularly unattractive. The Tollymore teahouse demonstrates very clearly that this
state of affairs need not exist and that in the
hands of a sensitive and imaginative designer such buildings can make a positive
contribution to the landscape of which they
form part. In this example there were no
immediately neighbouring buildings which
could be used as a design reference, the si
chosen, between two car parks would not
normally appear to be the most promising,
but the views from the location were exceptionally attractive.
   Fortunately the site is encircled by matur
trees and the architect has taken full advantage of these by careful siting. By using
carefully chosen materials and bold colours
he has produced a delightful building that
meets the clients brief and is both aesthetically pleasing and at the same time has a ga
holiday air.

Layout plan (*opposi*

2

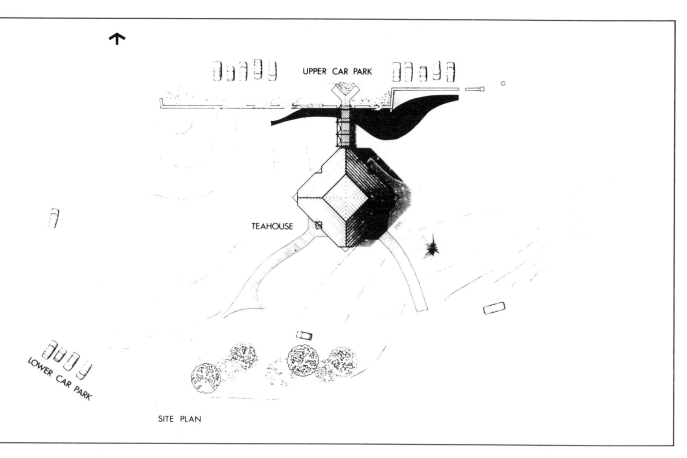

SITE PLAN

The approach to the teahouse from the upper
car park (*Photo: Crispin Boyle*)
The bridge with its pole construction from the
upper car park to the tea room (*Photo: Crispin
Boyle, Henk Snook & Associates*)
View from the upper car park, the exposed pole
windbracing forms a practical and decorative
feature (*Photo: Fabienne de Backer, Henk
Snook & Associates*)
General view from the lower level including the
bridge, pool and existing stone car park
retaining walls (*Photo: Anderson and
McMeekin*)

4

Case Study 23

Day Study and Information Centre

Witley Common, Witley, Surrey, England

Architect
Michael Cain of Casson, Condor & Partners

Client
The National Trust

Engineers
Jenkins & Potter

The site The Centre has been built in a woodland clearing on a plot of land bordering Witley Common approximately one mile south-west of the village of Milford. Access is by footpath only from a car park situated some distance away. The wildlife of the common therefore comes right up to the building and only the minimum amount of site works have been carried out.

Design and layout The Information Centre is the first of its kind to be built by the National Trust in order to give visitors to the common an appreciation of the management problems resulting from the increasing use of the countryside and a better understanding of countryside conservation. The ground floor accommodates exhibition and inquiry areas, externally accessible lavatories and substantial covered areas for shelter in wet weather. A workroom and a discussion room equipped for audio/visual displays has been provided within the steeply pitched roof space.

Construction and materials Loadbearing brick walls support the *in situ* concrete floor slab and the two laminated timber roof purlins running the length of the building. Timber rafters are covered with black asbestos cement tiles and clad internally with plasterboard. Electric underfloor coils give low background heating supplemented by industrial fan heaters.

Comment The Witley Common Day Study and Information Centre was a National Trust experimental project of great interest. The site was originally two wartime Army camps that had reverted to a wild natural environment with a wide variety of flowers, birds and butterflys in great abundance. The Centre attracts large numbers of visitors, both chil-dren and adults, individuals and school groups.

Great care has been taken to ensure that the building causes as little disturbance to the natural surroundings as possible and for this reason the approach is by foot, the nearest building being the Warden's cottage a short distance away. This Information Centre designed with great sensitivity proves that a new building can harmonise with a unique natural environment and by the use of appropriate materials and building forms it can become a positive asset to the area.

1 The side view of the building. The rooflights provide daylight to the first workroom, etc
2 View of the approach to the centre through the trees
3 Detail of the ground floor sheltered area and the bookshop display window (*Photo: Brecht-Einzig Ltd*)

1

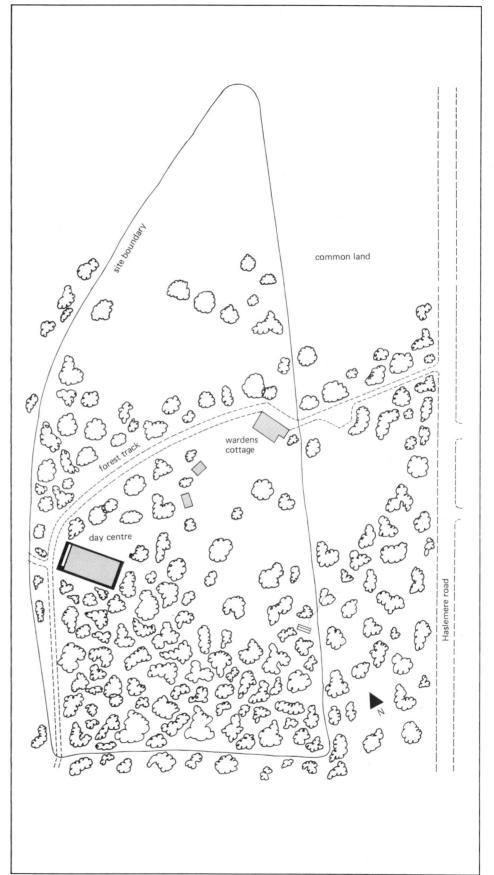

Site plan

common land

site boundary

wardens cottage

forest track

day centre

Haslemere road

N

Case Study 24

Tourist Information Centre
Brodick, Island of Arran, Scotland

Architects
Baxter, Paul & Clark

Clients
Highlands & Islands Development Board

Engineers
C. M. Lochrie

The site This Information Centre for tourists is located near to the pier at Brodick adjoining the harbourmaster's house, with a road running to one side and a car park and the sea in front to the north. The only limitation made by the Planning Department was the requirement to give consideration to public safety for both pedestrians using the Centre and the heavy traffic using the adjacent car parks and roadways.

Design and layout The original tourist centre was a temporary wooden building. The permanent replacement, for which only approximately 70 square metres of site area was available, provides a public enquiry counter with working space for two administration assistants and three counter staff, with lavatory and tea-making facilities together with storage facilities and a room for the tourist officer, large enough to hold meetings of up to six people. The need for maximum display space was of great importance.

Construction and materials The structure was designed to allow for prefabrication of the main elements, as it was anticipated that the location of the site might make it difficult to obtain competitive tenders. The contract was, however, carried out using local labour by a contractor who chose not to prefabricate.

The building is of traditional construction and utilises a composite construction for external walls, of Forticrete concrete blockwork external skin, and timber framing with dryboard lining in the interior. The north entrance facade combines glazed walls with timber-framed walls lined with Douglas Fir which has been stained to blend with the adjacent red sandstone harbourmaster's house. The roof over the main area is carried on a light tubular frame; it is lined internally with red pine and is clad externally with second-hand slates. The roof over the tour-

ist officer's room is clad in high-performance felt and stone chips. The public counter is of laminated elm.

Comment The Centre received a Scotland commendation in the RIBA Architecture Award 1980, and is an interesting example of a small building for the tourist industry designed by experienced architects unhampered by planning restrictions. The building is modest but handsome, and by its shape and form invites tourists on arrival in Arran to use it. The RIBA Award's jury picked up this point in their report; they said

'the cocked rooflight to the octagonal slate roof acts as a beacon'. The site levels resulted in the building being raised above the carpark level, and the three steps would be deterrent to disabled visitors, the inclusion of a ramped approach would have undoubtedly been welcomed. The general impression is of a building that is practical and attractive.

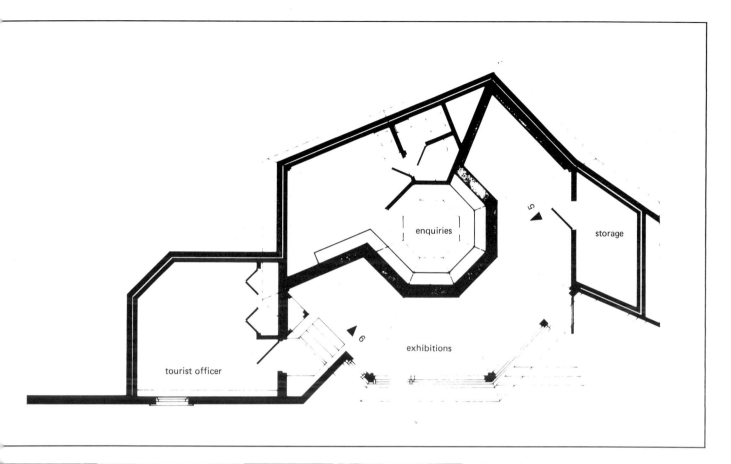

Layout plan

1 General view across car park
2 Main elevation close-up
3 Interior of exhibition, enquiry area

3   (*Photos: Spanphoto, Dundee*)

The restaurant at Windsor Safari Park designed to cater for 400 visitors with views over the Park toward Windsor Castle. The design based on a Kenyan game lodge is constructed of materials that blend with the landscape, with timber walling and cedar shingle roofs; the large terrace takes full advantage of the views and the ramped access is convenient for elderly and disabled visitors (*Garnett Cloughley Blakemore & Associates, Architects*)

the National Park with its population of wild animals, are orphaned animals which can be seen at close quarters as an introduction to those in the wild. In several of the Wildfowl Trust Centres, tame and wild birds mix together particularly in winter.

The information centre in a less selective area than a nature reserve needs a more robust treatment for it has inevitably to compete visually with other buildings. It must therefore be easily recognisable and readily accessible. The tourist information at Brodick on the Isle of Arran in Scotland fulfils all these requirements and by its design and location catches the eye of the tourist leaving the ferry from Adrossan nearby.

The design of all buildings ought to be influenced by the characteristics of the site on which they are built whether it is a remote area of special importance that requires a low key modest building, or an urban location where a dominant design is essential. Richard England, who has always held very strong views on this issue summed up the situation very clearly in a recent article, as follows:

'In experiencing and listening to what I have elsewhere referred to as "the voices of the site" perhaps lies the secret of future building, belonging to that place and becoming an integral part of an overall totality concerned with an ideology of identity. Natural features and architecture must unite into overall entities as individual solutions to particular problems generated by the general process of tourism. The voices will tell the Architect (if he is a sensitive one) whether the environment is weak and this in turn requires him to be strong and dominant: or perhaps that the environment is strong, and that he, in turn, should be docile and subservient. Only after this spiritual contact has been established can the wheels of the rest of the architectural creative process begin to turn.'

Chapter 7
Tourism and building conservation

In an earlier chapter we have seen that tourism and mass travel in its early days was not greatly concerned with the modern craze for 'sun, sea and sand'. The main interest was in visiting foreign lands and their historic places, scenery and differing culture.

Thus the cultural centres of Europe have maintained their attraction for millions of visitors; London is of course no exception for each year more tourists visit the capital in order to see the museums, art galleries, historic buildings and traditional customs. London is still top of the list for all tourists to the UK, with Edinburgh in second place. Cathedral towns, ancient universities and locations of special interest – the obvious ones in the UK being Windsor and Stratford-on-Avon – also attract tourists.

In other parts of the world, ancient monuments and historic buildings have also for centuries been a major source of tourist attraction: Paris, Rome, Vienna, Venice, Moscow, the list is almost endless. In many other places which were once the centre of ancient civilisations, such as Egypt, India, Pakistan and the Far East, the attraction of historic sites, cultures and the fascination of the past is as strong as ever.

Tourism and increased leisure time coupled with the increased availability of rapid and comparatively cheap travel should inevitably encourage the conservation of historic buildings as an essential part of the tourist industry worldwide. The cost of maintaining such buildings increases year by year and unless some means can be found of encouraging financial support in this work many are doomed for, in present day reckoning, the maintenance of such buildings is uneconomical.

In many eastern European countries the State has taken over the responsibility of restoring and maintaining the major architectural monuments. In the USSR enormous sums of money are spent annually on the preservation of the Russian architectural heritage as a visit to Moscow or Leningrad will show. Tourists are encouraged, often because they bring much needed hard currency. Whatever the reason, the result is building conservation of a very high standard. In France, Spain and Germany the adaptation of historic chateaux, country houses and castles into hotels and other forms of tourist accommodation has opened up new areas of interest for holiday visitors and tourists.

1975 was designated European Architectural Heritage Year and interested groups devoted considerable energy and expertise to the problems of the preservation of the architectural heritage of the world. In Britain, the Working Party on *Alternative uses of historic buildings* was established in 1979 under the chairmanship of Lord Montagu of Beaulieu who is

The 11th century cathedral, Baptistry and campanile at Pisa, Italy which together form one of the most famous building groups in the world; visited by thousands of tourists each year. The famous leaning tower, where the upper part overhangs the base by over 4 m (*Edward D. Mills*)

Petridvorets, near Leningrad, USSR severely damaged during the war (1944). Known as the city of fountains this Palace and the great cascade of fountains has been carefully restored by the Russian Government (*Novosti Press Agency*)

himself the owner of a famous historic house. The Working Party produced an excellent report *Britain's historic buildings: A policy for their future use*, which is essential reading for anyone concerned about the future of our architectural heritage.

The changing economic and social climate in most developed countries of the world has resulted in many fine buildings of the past being destroyed or abandoned and allowed to fall into disrepair. This is particularly true of the large country mansions in England and it is estimated that over 1500 important country houses have been lost in the last hundred years. The reason for this destruction is not difficult to find. In most cases the buildings were too large and inconvenient for present-day, single-family occupation, large numbers of relatively low paid servants were no longer available, the cost of maintenance and upkeep has become increasingly costly, and traditionally skilled building craftsmen have decreased in numbers.

In the case of non-domestic buildings, the shift of population has, for example, made many fine churches redundant as the congregations on whom they depended for financial support moved away. Historic industrial buildings such as watermills, oast houses and maltings no longer fulfilled the needs of modern industry or were sited in inconvenient areas and have thus also become deserted and often derelict. Similar examples can be found all over the world, and as the egalitarian society of the present age spreads still further, the problems will increase as more people seek the comfort and convenience of modern buildings for both living and working.

It is however imperative that the architectural heritage of the world should be preserved not in 'museum' form but as a living element in our modern society for within this heritage are the roots of our civilisation. When discussing the rebuilding of Warsaw after the destruction during the 1939–45 war, Polish architects and planners were insistent that the city must be restored to its former glory as it was an essential part of the Polish heritage and represented Polish history in visible form for all to see. Thus, the world's architectural heritage must be preserved and used for its historic value, its beauty and its character.

It is widely recognised that historic buildings are very important to the tourist industry. Ancient monuments, churches and cathedrals, castles, country houses and chateaux are visited by vast numbers of tourists in all countries of the world each year. The 1980 accounts of the National Trust of Great Britain reveal that more than six and a half million people paid to visit their two hundred buildings and gardens, and that of the Society's income of over £20 million, 75% was accounted for by the maintenance and management of their properties.

Historic buildings are equally important as a means of providing accommodation and services to holidaymakers and tourists after conversion or adaption. Because of this dual interest, tourism can be a valuable ally to architectural conservation.

Castles, chateaux and country houses

Buildings of this kind, that have been used for residential purposes for generations, are always popular with the tourists, either as living museums where they can see a historic house and its contents in their original setting or as places where they can find accommodation that provides them with the atmosphere of the past.

In the first case the 'tourist dilemma' once more becomes apparent for the inevitable high cost of maintaining an historic building requires ever more visitors to provide the necessary funds for the continual repair and reconditioning work. These extra visitors, as we have already seen, increase wear and tear on floors and staircases, furniture and other items on display and even the fabric of the building.

At Knole in Kent, for example, one stonemason firm has been employed continuously for over twenty years on the repair and restoration of the stonework. Large numbers of visitors create other problems, the vast number of tourists at peak periods can overload floors and staircases originally built for use by comparatively few users. Many people in a relatively small space, particularly in the summer months, can cause ventilation problems which are difficult to overcome, and even wall coverings that have survived for centuries break down rapidly as shoulders rub them or fingers inspect them.

Tourists arrive in groups and car parking is essential. Provision must also be made for prams and wheelchairs. Planned access, circulation routes, toilet facilities and, in many cases, refreshment facilities are all part of the provision needed by tourists and the provision and staffing of these needs to be very carefully considered.

In order to ease the pressure of over-visiting and to spread the load on the more vulnerable parts of their properties, the National Trust has developed what has been called 'honey potting' or diversionary attractions which are designed to siphon off and regulate the visitor flow. This interesting technique will be discussed in the next chapter.

Where historic buildings are available for conversion to other tourist uses, residential use has a high priority. A brief glance at many holiday guides will reveal the fact that many hotels, and other tourist attractions, register themselves as being of architectural or historic interest. One of the most successful tourist organisations that has a special concern for historic buildings is 'Gast-Im-Schloss' which covers castles, chateaux, hostelries and country houses in Germany, Austria, Switzerland and France. All of these buildings have been adapted for use as hotels with modern facilities in a traditional atmosphere.

The task of restoring and converting an historic building for tourist accommodation is both fascinating and time consuming. It can also be very costly, but the final outcome can be very worthwhile. Professional advice is absolutely essential both in assessing the potential of the property and the design and execution of the necessary work. The fact that many such buildings in Britain often originally in a very bad state of repair, are being restored and converted to flats or similar residential accommodation on a commercial basis, indicates the possibilities. A recent example of this kind of 're-birth' can be seen at Thorndon Hall in Essex, a Grade I Listed building, until recently a burnt out shell of the original Palladian mansion designed by Thomas Paine in 1764 and destroyed by fire nearly one hundred years ago. Today it comprises eighty luxury apartments for sale on long leases with a restaurant planned in the brick vaulted wine cellars. The grounds, originally laid out by Capability Brown, now accommodate a golf course.

Another similar case is that of a magnificent Charles I mansion built in 1635, Broome Park, near Canterbury, Kent, once the home of Lord Kitchener which has recently been divided into nineteen self-contained units with a wide range of communal facilities for second home or holiday accommodation on a weekly occupancy 'time sharing' basis. The theory of 'time sharing' for holiday accommodation will be discussed in the next chapter. Broome Park also has extensive grounds and a golf course.

The choice of a redundant country house, mansion or castle for conversion for holiday and tourist use needs a great deal of careful preliminary investigation.

Broome Park, near Canterbury, Kent. Another Grade 1 Listed building restored and converted into 'time-share' holiday apartments, with extensive recreational facilities (*Gulf Leisure Developments*)

For one hundred years this Grade 1 Listed building, Thorndon Hall near Brentwood, Essex stood as a burnt out shell. It has now been restored and converted into thirty-seven apartments surrounded by over 350 acres of woodland park, golf courses and gardens (*Thomas Bates & Son Ltd*)

The location, availability of special features that will appeal to the visitors, accessibility, and the structural condition of the building are all important factors. The support and co-operation of the Planning Authority, in the case of the UK, and other relevant bodies is of the greatest importance and early consultation can be a vital element in the success of the project.

Some buildings which may have much to commend them as structures that can be economically restored, may by their layout and construction be unsuitable for conversion to short term tourist accommodation. In such cases the main building has been adapted for communal use, restaurant, conference centre, museum, craft centre or similar purpose, and the outbuildings such as stables have been adapted for tourist and holiday self-catering units.

Alternatively such units have been successfully located adjacent to the main building. A good example being the Loch Rannoch, Perthshire development in Scotland where attractive, modern units (another 'time sharing' scheme) carefully sited along the Loch side, are served by the original building, once an elegant Edwardian hotel.

In North England the Telford Development Corporation in conjunction with the Historic Buildings Council have recently restored Madeley Court, a fine Elizabethan house, once the home of Abraham Derby, the ironfounder. The Gate House is now being restored for use as a restaurant for tourists visiting Madeley Court and the Ironbridge area.

The use of buildings of this kind for tourist purposes is not of course limited to the 'stately homes' of Europe. In other parts of the world existing buildings which no longer serve their original purpose effectively can be successfully adapted for holiday and tourist use. In Spain the 'paradores', or tourist hotels often originally feudal castles, have been converted into attractive tourist accommodation with assistance from the Spanish Tourist Authorities.

The 'Gast-Im-Schloss' organisation based in Germany, mentioned earlier, includes in its programme some fifty historic buildings providing tourist hotel and restaurant accommodation including Sababurg, the Sleeping Beauty Castle of the brothers Grimm fairy tale, the moated castle of Anholt which includes the Museum and Art Gallery of the Counts Salm-Salm, and Schloss Waldeck situated on Germany's largest reservoir. Some of the buildings available to tourists in this way, date from the 12th and 13th centuries and are still privately owned. For instance, the Burgschenke Burg Guttenburg, a medieval castle, has been in the family possession since 1449.

The opportunities for tourist development of this kind exists not only in developed countries of the world, but also in developing countries with ancient traditions and historic buildings of a past age which no longer serve their original purpose. These buildings could be profitably 're-cycled' as tourist accommodation as an alternative to the construction of new and often architecturally unsympathetic and intrusive buildings.

Henry Smith's village grocer's shop, c 1830, at Ironbridge. Now converted into the Ironbridge Gorge Museum Trust shop with the assistance of the Landmark Trust (*Telford Development Corporation*)

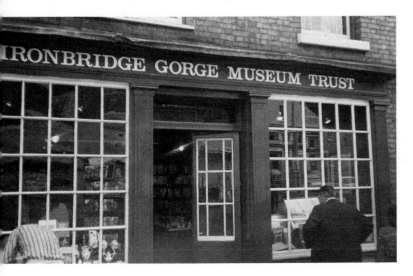

Wasserburg, Anholt, Germany. Originally a moated castle dating back to the 12th century it is now a tourist hotel with a fine museum and the picture gallery of the Counts Salm-Salm whose family still own the property. The hotel is part of the German 'Gast im Schloss' organisation (*Park Hotel, Anholt*)

Churches and religious buildings

Marcus Binney's book *Preservation Pays* (published by SAVE Britain's Heritage) refers to churches as the 'Cinderella of tourism' for, in Europe at least, they are most numerous of historic buildings open to the public. They usually contain much of historic and artistic value and are often the most important architectural feature in a village, town or city.

The great cathedrals, abbeys and monasteries attract enormous numbers of tourists and holidaymakers, the majority of whom seldom visit a church for the purpose of worship, but regard such buildings as an essential part of a holiday excursion. Few religious buildings make a charge for admission, relying upon voluntary gifts, the sale of souvenirs, postcards and guides to supplement their income.

In many European religious centres like Assissi in Italy, the home of St. Francis, the tourist facilities are very highly organised and it is evident that cathedrals, abbeys and historic church buildings not only attract tourists themselves but generate trade in the area. It is estimated, for example, that the preservation of Canterbury Cathedral is worth at least £5 million gross income each year to the local economy. This sort of figure can be repeated in most other cathedral cities in Europe.

Recently the Archbishop of York, Dr. Stuart Blanch said that tourism has been the greatest single change in the life of York Minster in 500 years. The Archbishop regarded the 2 million visitors to the Minster each year as a challenge to the Church and an opportunity for useful service.

Many churches and cathedrals have considerable treasures in the form of vestments, manuscripts, silver, paintings and other items of great historic and monetary value and these are often inadequately and even insecurely displayed. The proper display of such treasures can be a valuable source of income and can help to siphon off visitors from the more vulnerable parts of the building. It is important however that such treasures should be displayed with skill and

The Treasury of Norwich Cathedral is sited on the Reliquary Arch within the north Ambulatory. This arch was built around 1424 to house relics and to form an ante-chapel to the Reliquary Chapel, which was subsequently destroyed. (*Architects: Stefan Buzas and Alan Irvine*)

The site of the Treasury of Christ Church Oxford is the 12th century Chapter House. This is a room of great architectural distinction, and was extensively restored in 1968, as far as possible to its original design. The entrance is from the cloisters reached from a corner of the main quadrangle of Christ Church. (*Architects: Stefan Buzas and Alan Irvine*)

understanding using the best modern exhibition techniques.

Well-designed lighting is essential and in many cases carefully designed ventilation or even air conditioning may be necessary to ensure that the exhibits do not deteriorate. High security standards are regrettably essential, as valuable objects in a church are as vulnerable to vandalism and theft as those in any other location. Well planned display facilities can be a considerable attraction to visiting tourists and the advice and collaboration of experienced exhibtion designers can be of enormous value.

Once more the 'tourist dilemma' arises, for increased numbers of visitors accelerate the wear and tear on the ancient building fabrics, and can even interfere in the day-to-day religious work of the clergy and worshipping congregation who bear the burden of the maintenance and upkeep of the building.

Because the community at large benefits from the tourist interest in such buildings it would appear logical and reasonable that Government finance should be available for the maintenance and preservation of historic church buildings. This is of course the case in some European countries, and surprisingly in the USSR where historic churches and cathedrals and monasteries are carefully preserved and maintained as museums and cultural centres.

The ever rising cost of maintaining many historic buildings is a matter of concern in all parts of the world and the tourist industry can play an important role in helping to alleviate this financial burden. In Britain the shifting population has led to many churches and similar buildings being declared redundant and each year many are demolished. Such buildings can often be converted to other uses and examples can be found of redundant churches that have been successfully used for student housing, studios and concert halls, e.g. St. Paul's Church, Queensgate, Huddersfield. Some of these new uses involve tourists – in particular, music and drama centres.

St. Mary's Church, Castlegate in York is now a Heritage information centre and permanent

St. Mary's Church, Castlegate, York. Founded in the 11th century became redundant in 1958 was purchased by the City of York in 1972 (for 5 pence) and converted into an Exhibition Centre known as the York Story by James Gardner in association with architects George Pace and Ronald Sims. It was opened in 1975 and contains the work of many contemporary artists and craftsmen (*Castle Museum, York. Photo: Richard Stanford*)

exhibition for tourists visiting the Minster City of York. It not only gives information and help to the thousands of tourists who annually visit the historic city and Minster, but also displays an exhibition illustrating the history and places of interest in the region.

In Germany, the Hotel Klostergut Jacobsberg at Boppard am Rhein was originally a monastery founded by Barbarossa in 1157. This building and the former estate of Amorbach Benedictine Abbey in the Bavarian Oden Forest have both been successfully converted into holiday and conference centres.

Other buildings

Many historic buildings, other than those originally built for residential and religious use, have become unsuitable for their original purpose for political, social or economic reasons; they have become redundant and in danger of demolition unless an alternative use for them can be found.

The use of castles and country mansions and similar buildings as museums, craft centres and art galleries has already been mentioned, but other disused buildings previously used for agriculture, industry or commerce are especially vulnerable. The use of such buildings for tourist and holiday purposes is worth serious consideration bearing in mind that many modern tourists seek spiritual as well as physical recreation during their holidays; and seek to enjoy music, drama and ballet.

One of the outstanding examples in England of the re-use of what was basically a redundant 18th century industrial building is the Maltings at Snape in Suffolk which has been converted into a fine concert hall and music school. The rejuvenated complex attracts large numbers of tourists and has helped the development of the annual Aldeburgh Festival.

An equally successful example in London has been the reclamation of two of the buildings in Covent Garden following the transfer of the famous market to modern premises at Nine Elms. The former Flower

The Maltings, Snape, Suffolk. Originally malthouses built about one hundred years ago, these were converted into a concert hall by architects, Arup Associates, who retained the original architectural character of this 19th century industrial building for the Aldeburgh Festival of Music and the Arts. The restored building seats over eight hundred people and is famous for its superb acoustic qualities (*John Donat Photography*)

Market, a listed Victorian glass and cast iron structure built in the 1870s, has been very successfully converted by London Transport to house their London Transport Museum of historic vehicles. The building was particularly suitable for this purpose because of the height of the halls, and the Museum has already become established as a major tourist attraction.

Facing the old Flower Hall is the Central Market Building that was in 1980 equally successfully restored and converted to a shopping and restaurant centre by the Greater London Council. By an ingenious use of the basement storage space the architects have created a lively and attractive shopping concourse on two levels, with space for stalls, street entertainers, shops and *al fresco* refreshment facilities; all protected from the weather by the elegant Victorian cast iron and glass roof structure. The two restorations complement and support each other, tourists visiting the Museum automatically visit the Market building for shopping or refreshment and vice

versa. The recent (1980) book *Saving old buildings* by Sherban Cantacuzino and Susan Brandt illustrates some seventy-five examples of old buildings of all kinds and from ten different countries being put to new uses; a number of these are related to touristic and holiday activities.

In the last hundred years the agricultural industry of the developed world has changed very dramatically from a labour intensive industry to a highly mechanised and productive one. This has resulted in many older farm buildings becoming redundant. One of the most interesting recent developments in the tourist industry has been the use of such buildings for tourist, holiday and educational purposes including the establishment of countryside museums. This interesting aspect of building conservation for tourist use will be considered in detail in the following chapter.

The fact that in many areas of life the finite nature of the world's resources of energy and materials is

continued on page 112

Case Study 25

The Market, Covent Garden
London, England

Architect
F. B. Pooley, architect to the Greater London
Council, Historic Buildings Division, G.L.C.
Department of Architecture and Civic Design

Client
The G.L.C. Covent Garden Committee

Engineers
The Greater London Council

The site Covent Garden is situated in the
centre of London near the Strand and the
Central Market Building has as its neigh-
bours the Floral Hall, now used as a Trans-
port Museum, The Royal Opera House and
St. Paul's Church designed by Inigo Jones.
A wide cobble-paved piazza separates the
Market Building from St. Paul's Church. The
area housed the famous Covent Garden
Market where fruit, vegetables and flowers
were sold for 300 years until 1974 when the
Markets moved to their new home at Nine
Elms. The name derived from the Covent
Garden held by the Abbey of Westminster
and the right to hold the market in the Piazza
was granted to William, Earl of Bedford in
1670 by Charles II.

Design and layout The Market Building
was designed by Charles Fowler and was
built between 1828 and 1830. It consists of
three parallel ranges of buildings joined by a
colonnade at the east end. A contemporary
account describes it as follows:

'Approaching from the east, the chief feature is the quadruple colonnade with the
conservatories over. In the central building is a passage 16 ft wide, open to the
roof, and on each side a range of fruit-
shops, forced articles, and the more
choice culinary vegetables and herbs.
Each shop has a cellar under and a room
over it, with a trap-door to the former and a
small staircase to the latter. There are two
exterior colonnades on the North and
South sides which serve as passages in
front of the shops. The shops on the North
side are different descriptions of culinary
vegetables and the commoner fruits, and
those on the South side are exclusively for
potatoes and commoner roots . . . The
open space under the quadruple colonnade is occupied at one end as a fruit-

market, and at the other with stands for
fruit and vegetables.'

The glazed cast iron roofs over the south
and north courtyards were added in 1875
and 1888 respectively. The whole building is
Listed as a 'building of historical and
architectural interest', and the entire area is
now being restored. Many suggestions for
the re-use of the buildings were considered
by the G.L.C. and it was finally decided that it
should be restored and adapted for commercial use in the form of small shops, studios
and restaurants.

The general form of the building has been
retained and the 19th and 20th century
additions removed. The shop fronts have
been restored to the original designs, but the
interiors were the responsibility of the new
tenants. One of the main problems, which
applies to many historic buildings when they
are restored for contemporary use, was that
of upgrading the entire structure to meet
present day standards. Regulations relating
to fire and means of escape exercised the
greatest influence on the basic planning of
the conversion.

'These regulations affected the use of the
two main halls and basement, where certain limitations have had to be accepted.
The end and clerestories of the two halls
remain open, and their use has been
restricted to activities which do not in
themselves present fire hazards. The
basement is not one clear space, but a
labyrinth of small, brick vaulted spaces,
and the use of these by the shops has
been made dependent on the provision of
adequate means of escape routes in case
of fire. This condition has been met in the
South Hall by opening up the basement
area to form two 'lower courtyards', readily
accessible from ground level by new staircases, and in the North Hall by linking the
basements of the Lettings on either side
of the Hall to provide alternative escape
routes.'

Construction and materials The original
structure was primarily of brick and stone
loadbearing walls with slated roofs, and cast
iron and glass roofs to the courtyards. Basically the structure was in a sound condition
and required little structural repair. Old electricity, gas and other services were stripped
out and numerous layers of paint were removed, brickwork and stonework was
cleaned and patched as necessary. The
original colour scheme included light brown
cast iron columns, pale blue ironwork with

other features picked out in cream or buff,
this colour scheme has been restored. The
pavings in and around the Market are York
Stone slabs and granite setts.

Comment The recycling of historic
buildings is always a difficult task with many
problems to overcome. Undoubtedly the fac
that the G.L.C. were both landlord and
architect in this instance was a great
advantage, and the resulting rehabilitation o
the Market Building has been generally
welcomed as a success. The Market in its
new form has attracted some four million
visits in its first year of operation. The varied
shops, craftsmen's stalls, open-air eating
and drinking places, and the visiting street
musicians and entertainers all combine to
create a lively atmosphere that has
contributed greatly to the revitalisation of the
Covent Garden area.

The care with which the Fowler building
has been restored and adapted is illustrated
by the obvious attention given to such items
as the excellent signing, the well-designed
lighting lanterns and the neatly detailed
handrails. One of the welcome features is
the lack of clutter. The banning of car parkin
as a G.L.C. policy coupled with the severely
limited delivery access and the refuse
storage and collection arrangements all help
to keep the building and its precincts tidy.
Many tourists visited the Covent Garden
Market Building when it was used for its
original purpose and it is fitting that it should
become in its new form, a major London
tourist attraction, and an example of how a
redundant historic building can be adapted
to new uses.

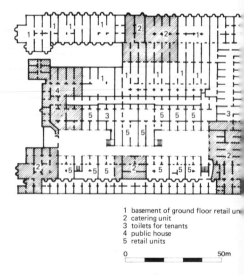

1 basement of ground floor retail un
2 catering unit
3 toilets for tenants
4 public house
5 retail units

0   50m

Basement plan

Layout plan of Covent Garden

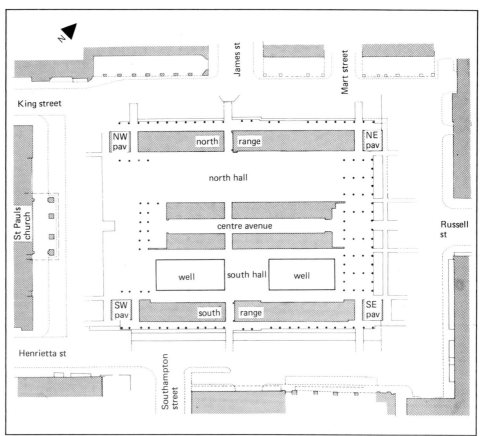

1 A porter of the original Covent Garden
2 One of the glazed Halls before restoration
3 The South Hall after restoration showing the new lower courtyards
4 The central avenue between the two Halls
5 The South colonnade, looking Westwards before restoration

(*Photos: GLC*)

Historic buildings have for centuries been a major source of tourist attraction. Venice has always been high on the tourist list: a view from campanile of the cathedral of St. Marks, Venice (*Edward D. Mills*)

becoming increasingly apparent, underlines the necessity for re-cycling not only wastepaper and tin cans but in some cases at least, buildings where these have an obvious historic or aesthetic value. This does not mean saving all old buildings just because they are old, but it does suggest a careful examination of each case on its merits. The creation of a new building is a very satisfying achievement for designer and user, but breathing new life into an old building can provide an equally worthwhile sense of fulfilment.

To quote Lord Montagu of Beaulieu in a recent lecture to the Royal Society of Arts:

'Historic buildings, it is increasingly widely recognised, are a prime resource of one of the nation's major industries – tourism . . . The potential for adaptive re-use of historic buildings in the broader interests of the community is enormous.'

Chapter 8
The developing pattern of holidays and tourism

In various periods of history, the proportion of work to leisure for the people in differing countries has varied according to religious and social customs and many other factors. In ancient Egypt, workers were entitled to only fifty-three rest days a year, later in Rome one-third of the year – the days known as Nefasti – were considered unpropitious for work.

A century ago the majority of working people in the industrial world worked a 72-hour week, while today the average working week is almost half of this figure; recent demands by Trade Unions and others envisaged a 35-hour working week, and some of the factors outlined in earlier chapters suggest that this may well be regarded as the norm before the end of the century. A simple calculation shows that throughout the modern industrial world the average worker enjoys 130–150 non-working days each year. (Approximately the same proportion as the ancient Romans.)

The result of this change in leisure patterns means greater opportunities for second holidays, long weekends and similar holiday and leisure breaks in the working life of the average man and woman of the developed contries. The populations of many developing countries may gradually follow the same trend.

As living standards improve throughout the world, the human life span has become prolonged. It is of interest to note that in Britain in the Middle Ages most people died before they were 30 years old, today the average life span is probably over 70 years; a recent announcement by the UK Registrar General recorded that the number of centenarians in Britain has risen from 300 in 1971 to over 1800 today.

This dramatic increase in healthy longevity has meant that more people of retirement age (there are now over 10 million pensioners in the UK) are able to enjoy increased leisure; today, tourism and holidays specially designed for the elderly is a rapidly expanding aspect of the tourist industry. These factors of increasing leisure time and longer life for millions of people, coupled with improved living standards, are helping to widen and enrich the concept of leisure both in content and purpose.

Clearly holidays and tourism can play an important part in this changing leisure pattern for it has been suggested that citizens throughout the world can choose from nearly 10000 leisure activities. While these have not been specified, there is an obvious trend for holidaymakers and tourists to seek a wide range of pursuits in addition to the inevitable 'sun, sea and sand' of the travel brochure. Tourism and cultural interests are rapidly becoming inter-related, and although attempts have been made to categorise tourists, they seldom fall easily into sharply defined groups. The sun seeker in Italy spends part of his holiday visiting the historic buildings of Florence and Pisa, or the museums and art galleries of Rome and Milan.

Holidays and tourism therefore embrace interests in art, culture and history, sport and recreation, natural beauty and wildlife conservation; crafts and hobbies and many other physical, educational and cultural activities. To choose one example, the use of leisure for educational purposes has resulted in many Universities and Colleges all over the world welcoming holiday visitors for special out-of-term courses in an ever widening range of subjects, and when new buildings have been erected this aspect of their use has often been borne in mind. The additional income thus generated assists in defraying increasing costs of upkeep and staffing and helps to broaden the educational aspects of the holiday market.

The growth in individual participation in sporting activities such as sailing, golf, winter sports, etc, which has developed since the turn of the century has also encouraged the increase of sport-based holidays. Throughout the world holiday facilities centred around such activities have become increasingly popular. For instance, the Algarve in Portugal is noted for its golfing facilities, Port Grimaud near St. Tropez in France and Vilamoura in Portugal are both

Many private educational establishments when erecting new buildings incorporate in their plans facilities that are suitable for holiday visitors during school vacations. At New Hall School, Boreham, Essex, summer schools and holiday courses use the buildings. The riding school is very popular with disabled riders – young and old (*Edward D. Mills*)

The International House of S. Wales, Penarth. This is a residential student hostel, and holiday visitors use the accommodation during vacations. The communal facilities were planned on a scale that could cater for both types of occupancy. Architects for both buildings: Edward D. Mills & Partners

tourist villages built in the last twenty years specifically for sailing enthusiasts, and the winter sports centre at Aviemore in Scotland was created to provide a base for winter sport enthusiasts.

All of these diversifications of the tourist industry require buildings and many of the examples included as Case Studies have been designed to cater for these diverse leisure interests. The companion book in the Butterworths Design series *Design for sport* by Gerald Perrin includes reference to buildings for leisure sporting activities in a holiday context.

Multi-ownership or time sharing

The world-wide phenomenon of greater leisure time for millions of people throughout the world, for reasons outlined in earlier chapters, has led to a greater interest in developed countries in 'second homes' for holiday purposes. In Sweden the ownership of a holiday house, usually a log cabin in the mountains or by a lake, is a well established tradition.

At the same time some of the problems of holiday home ownership have been highlighted in recent years: the rising cost of the maintenance of a property that is not in full-time occupation, rates and taxes and even vandalism of a frequently empty apartment or house. Time sharing is being offered world-wide as a viable and economic alternative to full-time normal ownership, with attractive sales slogans such as 'a lifetime of holidays for the cost of a car'.

The idea of multi-ownership started in a small way in France some fourteen years ago in an alpine ski resort. In 1973 the idea was developed in the USA as a way of selling holiday apartments during a period of recession. In the UK the idea is comparatively new, the Loch Rannoch lodges referred to earlier being the first such development. It is estimated that there are now over five hundred schemes in more than thirty countries (there were only about twenty in the world eight years ago) with over 500 000 time-sharing owners in the USA alone.

The system which is known as multi-ownership, interval ownership or time-sharing is simple in concept. A single capital payment purchases one or more weeks of fully furnished and equipped holiday accommodation, in perpetuity or for a stated period of years according to the legal requirements of the country in which the property is situated. For example, in England and Wales, ownership in perpetuity is not allowed in law but it is in Scotland and other parts of the world.

The cost of weeks purchased, varies with the time of the year and, in addition, an annual maintenance charge is levied for each week. It covers maintenance, repairs and replacements. The investment is claimed to be inflation proof, as hotel and normal apartment renting increases in cost year by year.

Multi-ownership properties are available in the UK, the USA, Canada, many European countries and, in the Caribbean, luxury yachts are available on a time-share basis. Two international organisations run an exchange scheme whereby time-sharing owners can 'swop' accommodation. Units can also be let, sold or bequeathed by the owner. The time-sharing industry has become very big business in a comparatively short space of time, particularly in the USA and

Loch Rannoch Estate on the shores of Loch Rannoch, Scotland. The carefully landscaped lodges in 250 acres of woodland was the first multi-ownership holiday development in Britain (*Multi-ownership & Hotels Ltd*)

Time-sharing holiday apartments. Part of the Plas Talgarth Estate in the Snowdonia National Park, Wales. Communal facilities are provided in the 18th century mansion in the centre of the development (*Multi-ownership & Hotels Ltd*)

is therefore a growing part of the holiday and leisure market.

Many of the time-sharing projects are carried out to a very high standard, most are built specially for the purpose but some like the Edwardian Hotel Osborne in Torquay, Broome Park in Kent, mentioned earlier, and a 17th century Chateau in France are all buildings of historic interest that have been specially converted. The fact that ownership is multiple, means that unless good quality materials are used in the construction, furnishing and equipping the units, the heavy wear and tear of constantly changing 'owners' will result in high maintenance and replacement costs. Clearly the small print of the purchase contract is of vital importance and legal advice is recommended, before entering into this type of investment.

Location is of great importance, with the inevitable diametrically opposed demands for peaceful solitude and accessibility; special features like golf courses, winter sports and sailing have a wide appeal and if the units which are usually 'self-catering' are related to some form of communal facilities this is a great advantage. Management standards must be high and maintained thus if a multi-ownership project is not to be a failure. Good design, good location, good management make up the rules for success in time-sharing.

Agriculture and tourism

Agriculture – the cultivation of the land – is one of mankind's oldest activities. In every country of the world countless generations have been engaged in the essential labour of food production through agriculture.

The pattern of agriculture has changed over the centuries, and today, while it is still practised in the developing countries as a labour intensive industry, in the industrialised areas of the world agriculture has also become industrialised and is now regarded as one of the most efficient industries; no longer depending upon hand crafts with a high labour content. In Britain two hundred years ago, 92% of the working population were employed on the land to feed the remaining 8%; today, the situation is completely reversed and agriculture requires only 2–3% of the labour force to feed the rest; similar figures could be produced for most other Western countries.

New farming techniques, greater efficiency and

higher production have all contributed to this change, and one result has been a greater separation between town dwellers and workers and country dwellers and workers. Another result has been the changing pattern of the tools, equipment and buildings used by the farming industry and the increase in the number of redundant farm buildings, those no longer needed for day-to-day agricultural purposes.

These two factors have a close link with the subject of this book, town dwellers have always regarded a country holiday as both enjoyable and economical. Many childhood farm holidays, often 'living-in' with the farmer and his family and joining in the farm activities during harvest time or some other season, has led to a life-long interest in the countryside and its conservation. As city life in the Western world becomes more artificial and leisure time increases, the opportunities for extending the link between agriculture and tourism also increases.

In Europe including Britain, the planning of farm holidays is assisted by various organisations; the Gites scheme in France, the UK Automobile Association (through its *Handbooks to farms throughout Europe*, and SEATER (*Service d'etudes d'amenagement touristique en espace rural*) are among the most prominent. In the USA holidays, on working cattle ranches are very popular. Special facilities are usually available with purpose-built accommodation and a wide variety of activities, riding, visits to local places of interest and participation in some of the everyday activities of the ranch.

Redundant farm buildings are often suitable for conversion to holiday accommodation as the accompanying illustrations show. Disused barns, often of considerable historic interest, make admirable subjects for conversion to such purposes as craft centres,

Redundant farm buildings on the former Cawdor Estate at Stackpole Quay, Pembrokeshire, Wales now owned by the National Trust, that have been successfully converted into holiday cottages. The buildings are in the Pembrokeshire Coast National Park and the income derived from holiday lettings helps to subsidise the opening of scenic parts of the estate to the public. The restoration work was carried out under the Government's Manpower Services Commission's job creation scheme (*Martyn Evans & Cedric Mitchell Architects*)

One of the redundant Cotswold stone farm buildings (1815) at Buckland Manor near Broadway, Worcestershire converted for holiday use (*P. M. Ansdell*)

museums, restaurants, information centres, etc. A good example is the Great Barn at Avebury, in Wiltshire which has been converted to a Folk Life Museum for the Wiltshire Folk Life Society by Architects Imrie, Porter and Wakefield.

Another example is the Working Farm Museum at Strongborough Hall, Staffordshire (Architect: S. Wyatt) run by the County Council, and an unusual conversion by the Cotswold District Council (Architect: Tim Moore) is Northleach House of Correction built in 1790 as a model prison, now redundant. It houses the Cotswold Countryside Collection

of ancient farm machinery and agricultural implements in a colourful and interesting way.

A novel development which could be a valuable contribution to the idea of agricultural tourism is the recreational farm. One, which is claimed to be the largest in the world, is at Flevohof in Holland.

This was originally started over twenty years ago by Herman Eschuss as a national permanent working agricultural centre with financial backing by farmers and commercial firms. However after two years of operation, when most of the visitors were connected with the farming industry and mainly concerned with the technical aspects of the exhibition, the attendance began to decline. It was decided to focus attention on non-farming visitors and to attract tourists and holidaymakers by including holiday chalets and leisure activities, as well as the exhibitions illustrating in graphic form the working of the agricultural industry.

The whole complex is built up around the centre's commercial farming enterprise, and visitors are able to circulate through working farm buildings; for example, there are signposted walks through greenhouses, and an overhead catwalk that runs through the dairy giving views of day-to-day work in progress. This enterprise which is now ten years old is so

continued on page 120

The Great Barn at Avebury converted to a folk-life Museum by Architects Imrie, Parker & Wakefield for the Wiltshire folk-life Society (*Imrie, Parker & Wakefield*)

Case Study 26

Recreational Farm Centre
Flevohof, Eastern Flevoland, Holland

The site   The site of the Flevohof recreational farm covers an area of some 150 ha of the Eastern Flevoland polder, near Lake Velurve. The land is flat, reclaimed from the sea and very fertile. The whole of the island of Flevoland has been developed as a recreational and tourist area; and the new town of Lelystad, which started in 1966, is about 20 km to the North-west. The nearest major city is Amsterdam.

Design and layout   There are four major elements that make up the farm complex, the exhibition circuit, the working farms, the childrens village and the holiday chalet group. In addition shops, toilets, restaurants and extensive car parking (free to visitors) make up the major facilities available to visitors. Throughout the complex special attention has been given to the requirements of disabled visitors.

The exhibition circuit consists of ten pavilions linked by enclosed covered ways, each pavilion displays by means of models, photographs, films and other means the story of modern agriculture and horticulture, including pavilions devoted to dairy farming, poultry, cattle and meat, potatoes, sugar, grain and baking. Greenhouses with an area of 6000 m^2 produce tomatoes and cucumbers and a further 1500 m^2 of glasshouses are devoted to cut flowers and pot plants. The smallest pavilion is devoted to bees.

The stock farm is a working unit with one hundred and thirty-eight head of cattle including seventy milking cows, sheep, pigs and poultry. The viewing facilities have been arranged so that they do not interfere with the day to day operation of the particular unit, and an elevated catwalk allows visitors to watch milking in progress. The stockfarm has 35 ha of grassland. The arable farm of 65 ha consisting of nine separate units each producing a different crop in rotation, and all the produce is sold.

The childrens village is partly educational with a childrens farm of small animals and partly recreational with play area. There is a series of small buildings where children can paint, make pancakes or pottery, or engage in other activities.

The most recent addition to the Centre has been seventy holiday chalets, with provision for disabled visitors. These provide self-catering accommodation and are located near to the main restaurant which also contains facilities for conferences and demonstrations.

Comment   Although Flevohof was originally conceived as a permanent agricultural exhibition for the farming industry, its transformation into a major tourist attraction has been a great success as it now receives nearly three-quarters of a million visitors annually. The flat site has been laid out with considerable skill and imagination, and the range of facilities available has been carefully planned to attract visitors of all ages. The fact that the farming complex is a practical commercial enterprise and that all its produce is for sale is a feature that appeals to visitors who are able to learn more about the way in which their food is produced and retailed.

Flevohof is run by a non-profit making society, and all the surplus income is ploughed back into the work of the Centre. This unique venture helps to explain the work of the agricultural industry to a wider public and has established a valuable link with the holiday and tourist industry that is of mutual benefit. Architecturally the complex is a balanced mixture of traditional farm buildings and modern exhibition and recreatonal buildings, linked by manmade lakes and water features, the combination is practical and effective.

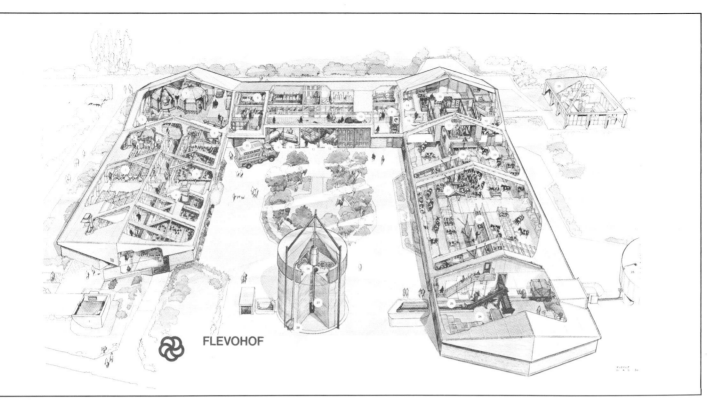

FLEVOHOF

...yout of Flevohof farm and exhibition centre

Key to main buildings
 1 dung pit for chicken house
 2 chicken house with flat-floored cage
 3 chicken house with wire grille
 4 egg sorting machine and packaging
 5 feed stuff silos
 6 pigsty and breeding pen
15 cow stalls
17 milking parlour for simultaneous milking of ten
   cows
18 stall for horned cattle
24 fodder storage
26 haystack
29 office

1 A glasshouse, where tourists can see work in progress and purchase produce
2 General view from the air
3 Air view of main entrance, shopping centre and restaurant (*Photos: Flevohof*)

4 Part of the childrens playground (*Photo: John Weller*)

4

Strongborough Hall, Staffordshire. Now a working farm museum run by the County Council. Architect S. Wyatt (*Photo: S. Wyatt*)

successful that it has to keep open all year round to cope with ever increasing numbers of visitors from Holland and further afield.

In Britain, Lightwater Valley near Ripon follows the Flevohof idea on a smaller scale. This comprises planned leisure facilities, refreshments, and other attractions all based on a working farm which produces poultry, fish and pigs on a commercial basis and open to view by the visitors.

The marriage of the agriculture and holiday industries can clearly be of value to both, and makes available in a convenient form a new holiday experience to many town dwellers. The principal possibilities, many of them illustrated in the accompanying illustrations, are the adaption of redundant farm buildings for holiday purposes, and the development of leisure and holiday centres based on working farms or similar enterprises.

The educational aspect of 'holiday farms' is also of considerable importance. In some city centres 'town farms' have been established as an educational service but these, however admirable, are no substitute for a real farm set in the countryside. The holiday industry can therefore play an important role in the educational field, in bringing rural and urban activities closer together.

Country parks

In the past, manmade country parks have been for the private enjoyment of the very rich; many are now owned by the National Trust in Great Britain and similar bodies or the State in other countries. The tradition of large scale landscaping largely developed in the late 18th century and famous landscape designers such as 'Capability' Brown established a pattern of the formal English Park that has never been surpassed. Today such parks once used by relatively few privileged people are now available to all.

Once again the problem of visitor saturation is a real one, and the consequent damage of over-visiting can be considerable. It is, therefore, essential that long term planning should aim at withstanding and controlling the impact of large numbers of tourists and by subtle means managing and directing the visitors in such a way that they are able to enjoy the facilities and attractions available and at the same time safeguard the quality of the established environment.

The 1965 Leonard Manasseh and Elizabeth Chesterton master plan for the twenty year development of

Beaulieu, the estate of Lord Montagu in Hampshire, is a model of its kind. This plan, prepared in conjunction with the County Planning Officer, was developed as a means of creating within the existing framework of the estate a pattern capable of withstanding the pressures of the increasing number of visitors seeking recreation without damaging the quality and character of the area. Beaulieu (the Motor Museum) and Bucklers Hard (the nearby boat building centre), all part of the estate attract three-quarters of a million tourists each year, and the numbers are bound to increase. Only by long term planning and careful management can the objectives be achieved and the interests of both residents and tourists visitors preserved (see layout plan on p. 33).

A similar development plan prepared also by Leonard Manasseh for Wellington Country Park also in Hampshire, for the owner, the Duke of Wellington, shows the same care and attention to management planning. In the 600 acres of the Stratfield Saye estate leisure and recreational facilities have been planned including picnicking, caravanning and camping, together with sailing on the lake, nature trails and other activities. Great care has been taken to preserve the natural environment; parking for 1000 cars, caravan and camping sites are all screened by existing trees and plants and tarmac has been avoided for hard areas. The buildings within the park have been strategically placed and designed to merge with the landscape, of which they naturally become a part.

Country and folk museums

At the end of the 19th century Arthur Hazelius founded the Nordiska Museet and Skansen in a parkland area of Stockholm thus establishing what can be called the 'international folk museum' movement which has now spread throughout the world. Skansen is probably still the greatest open-air folk museum in the world and attracts nearly 2 million tourist visitors every year.

The purpose of such a museum is to present a 'real life' view of the traditional way of life in the area concerned using actual buildings, often salvaged from other parts of the country and carefully rebuilt, furnished with original furniture and fittings. Very often, in the case of traditional workshops, mills and forges, these are operational, producing goods which are sold to help maintain the enterprise. Skansen, 75 acres in area, now contains about one hundred and

The 18th century Oktorp farmstead from the South of Sweden, now part of the Skansen Folk Museum in Stockholm (*The Skansen Foundation*)

fifty reclaimed buildings and a large collection of endangered Swedish animals. It is the centre for traditional festivals such as that of St. Lucia, Christmas church services and markets, folk music and dancing. Skansen is very much a live museum and Stockholm's most popular tourist attraction.

The Ulster Folk and Transport Museum is another good example; situated 8 miles from the centre of Belfast at Cubria Manor, Holywood, County Down. It covers some 70 acres and includes the Lismaclosky House built in 1717, the Ballyveridagh School, several other houses, the Lisrace Forge dating from the 1830s, and the Coalisland Spade Mill of about the same date. In this latter building, which was transferred to the folk museum in 1964, the great-great-grandson of the founder of an earlier spade mill has re-established the manufacture of Coalisland spades. Adjacent to the folk museum, a 30-acre transport museum is being developed and together they have become a popular attraction for both local and foreign tourists.

In Wales, the St. Fagan's Welsh Folk Museum was established when it was given St. Fagan's Castle and grounds near Cardiff where some seventeen traditional Welsh buildings have been re-erected and furnished. It is a policy of the Museum that no building is accepted (and they have all so far been gifts) unless they are in danger of destruction through demolition or decay. The stated object of St. Fagan's is to 'reconstruct the folk culture of the past'. The museum has its own team of craftsmen and the enterprise, which is funded by the Welsh Office, has become an important tourist centre.

In England, the Weald and Downland Open-air Museum at Singleton in Sussex was founded in 1969 by a group of enthusiasts who wanted to save historic buildings faced with destruction. It now consists of twenty buildings on a magnificent 40-acre site and in the 1980/81 season attracted nearly 150 000 visitors. Some 10 miles away at Amberley a new venture was stated in 1979 on a 36-acre site, the Chalk Pit Museum, with over 38 000 visitors in 1980, is devoted to the study, preservation and presentation of the physical remains of yesterday's industries.

The largest and perhaps the best known example of an historic educational institution is the Colonial capital of Virginia, USA, Williamsburg restored by the Rockefeller Family Trust. Since 1926 when the restoration commenced, Colonial Williamsburg has been visited by enormous numbers of tourists and students. Colonial Williamsburg was the capital of Virginia from 1699 to 1780, and is today restored to

continued on page 125

Stryd Lydan barn from Penley Clwyd (c. 1550–1600) (*National Museum of Wales*)

Case Study 27

Wellington Country Park
Heckfield, Near Basingstoke,
Hampshire, England

Architects
Leonard Manasseh Partnership

Clients
Stratfield Saye Estates Management Co.
Limited

Engineers
Felix Samuely & Partners

The site   The Country Park covers some 600 acres on the edge of the 10 000 acre Stratfield Saye estate owned by the Duke of Wellington and his family. The Park is bisected by a main road, the A32, and consists of large areas of thick woodland, a 30 acre lake, footpaths and nature trails. It is an area of great natural beauty.

Design and layout   The road running through the site allowed the two halves of the Park to be planned in different ways. On the west side the larger open spaces provide a golf course and a riding school, while the east side contains the main entrance with an information centre, management accommodation and toilets, the lake for sailing and fishing with a small restaurant, picnic, caravan and camping site, and car parking for 1000 cars. The nature trails run through a variety of differing natural settings.

Great skill has been exercised in locating the car parking, camping and caravan sites. These are situated in clearings in the woodland and broken down into small units with screens of trees between them, so that they are concealed from view. The children's play area also has a woodland setting where the play equipment such as swings, etc is constructed of timber from the woodlands.

The buildings have been designed as part of the natural landscape, using natural materials, planned as a series of pavilions with pitched roofs and large areas of glazing. The dark grey roofs blend with the distant hills in the background.

Construction and materials   All the buildings are planned on a 6 m^2 structural grid, with steel box columns and a roof structure of laminated timber beams. The roofs are lined internally with V-jointed timber decking and covered externally with blue-grey asbestos slates. Much of the

external walling is glazing in timber frames, solid walling is stained rough timber boarding fixed vertically. Rainwater pipes and gutters are concealed, and great care has been taken in the detailing throughout. Even the main entrance sign was designed by the architects.

Comment   The consistency of the design approach at the Wellington Country Park is a lesson to any developer of a tourist attraction. The buildings, their siting and the materials chosen, all harmonise perfectly well with the natural beauty of their surroundings; poor design and an unimaginative layout could easily have spoiled this attractive area of parkland. Particular attention has been paid to the location and landscaping of caravan/camping sites that are so often eyesores in similar situations. Car parking in separate units among trees with gravel surfacing instead of the usual tarmac is relatively inconspicuous but conveniently located near to the park entrance and information centre.

The architects have succeeded in producing an organised park that remains natural, where the essential buildings have very effectively become part of the natural environment in which they have been built.

2

View of information centre
View of lakeside restaurant

(*Photos: Leonard Manasseh and Partners*)

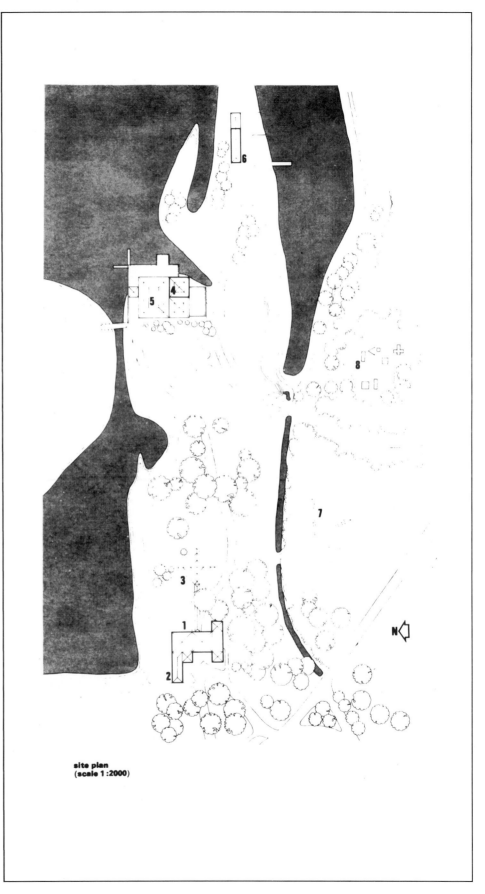

**site plan
(scale 1 : 2000)**

yout of buildings

information centre
offices
future museum
stage 1 restaurant and terrace
restaurant and terrace expansion
boat shed
nature trails
playground

Abernodwydd farmhouse interior, from Llangadfan, Powys
(c. 1600). This building together with Stryd Lydan barn (see p.121)
has been re-erected at the Welsh Folk Museum, St. Fagans,
Cardiff

A group of open air buildings re-erected in the Weald & Downland
Open-air Museum at Singleton, Sussex. (Left) Titchfield Market
Hall, 16th century; (centre) Crawley Hall, 15th Century; (right)
Lavant House, 17th century (*The Weald and Downland Open Air
Museum*)

The Hambrook Barn at the Weald & Downland Museum which has
been admirably adapted as an exhibition hall (*The Weald &
Downland Open Air Museum*)

Williamsburg, USA the colonial capital of Virginia. Street scene Duke of Gloucester Street (*The Colonial Williamsburg Foundation*)

its pre-Revolutionary appearance. It covers 173 acres and includes not only all the original major public buildings but also houses, shops and industries all of which are operated as a living history programme. Over 80 000 students take part in seminars, forums and other events each year, and the Foundation employs over 3000 people with an annual expenditure of some 20 million dollars. The Foundation also operates the Addy Aldrich Rockefeller Folk Art Centre, a museum housing one of America's outstanding collections of its kind.

Opinions differ about Williamsburg; to some it is akin to Disneyland, the fantasy world described by Anthony Wylson in *Design for Leisure Entertainment*. However, it is clearly enormously popular with tourists who undoubtedly regard it as a nostalgic reminder of the past and many visit it to escape from the harsh reality of their everyday surroundings.

Whatever the reasons for the popularity of country and folk museums, and similar exhibitions, it is clear that they have a place in the expanding pattern of modern tourism not only in developed countries but in developing areas as well. An East African Folk Museum 'The Bomas of Kenya' a Government developed cultural centre on the outskirts of Nairobi, Kenya, follows the pattern of European examples with examples of traditional Kenyan buildings, craftswork and concerts of African music and dance. The old Swahili town of Lamu on the Kenya coast, north of Mombasa has been declared a conservation area by the Government and is a fascinating example of a 'live exhibit' where the inhabitants carry on their traditional way of life but welcome tourists who see, not a staged event, but normal everyday activities in progress.

The development of new features of this kind is one

which needs great skill and understanding if the end result is to have a permanent cultural and educational value. Imitation, pastiche and fake must be avoided at all costs – the Tudor building with a steel frame structure and fibreglass beams is a worthless sham and has no value at all. The general pattern of re-erecting endangered buildings or saving them *in situ* is the only one that can be safely followed; in the Bucharest Folk Museum opened since the war, nearly 250 rescued buildings have been re-erected.

The work calls for skilled craftsmen and offers excellent opportunities for training to provide reinforcements for the rapidly diminishing skilled labour force. This, in turn, helps to create a new interest in handicrafts and many such museums supplement their income by the sale of the work of their resident craftsmen – a good example being the Coalisland Spade Mill mentioned earlier.

Developing countries with an expanding tourist industry are beginning to be aware of the interest of their visitors in their traditional way of life, traditional crafts and culture. This interest can be encouraged so that the heritage of the past is preserved and enriched not only for the present but for the future as well; the role that tourism can play in preserving and developing traditional and modern crafts will be considered later in this chapter.

'Honey potting' or diversionary attractions

The term 'honey potting' (allegedly invented by the National Trust) is an apt description of an important solution to one of the major problems that face everyone concerned with the future of the tourist industry. It means the creation of distracting or diversionary displays as part of an existing or new tourist attraction specifically designed to draw visitors away from the most sensitive areas, so that the tourist pressure can be spread more evenly. The problem has been referred to in earlier chapters, but it is important enough to be repeated.

The tourist industry, including the Stately Home owners, the National Trust and many others, need increased numbers of visitors to provide the finance to run and maintain these historic buildings. This also applies to areas of natural beauty and developing countries with economies relying heavily on holi-

continued on page 128

Case Study 28

Museum and Visitors Centre
Beaulieu, Hampshire, England

Architects
Leonard Manasseh Partnership

Clients
Montagu Ventures Ltd and the Trustees of the National Motor Museum

Engineers
Felix Samuely & Partners

The site The Beaulieu estate is a conservation area of considerable historic and architectural interest. It includes the village of Beaulieu, Beaulieu Abbey, the ruins of the Cistercian Monastery founded by King John in 1204, the refectory that has been restored and now used as the parish church, Palace House, a 14th century gatehouse converted into a private residence in 1538, and farms, woodland and parkland. Beaulieu River separates the old Abbey from the village and the visitor complex occupies an area of some 110 acres (46 ha) of wooded parkland.

Design and layout The complex, which consists of a Motor Museum, administrative facilities, library, restaurant and information centre, is part of the planned development of Beaulieu which has been carried out over a number of years. The main buildings are linked by a monorail system that runs through the museum building. The construction of a bypass road to relieve traffic through the village of Beaulieu allowed vehicular entry to the complex to the north of the Abbey and the village directly into carefully planned car parks in small units, surrounded by existing trees.

The principal buildings include the National Motor Museum. This is a square multilevel structure that houses over two hundred vehicles illustrating the history of motoring from the earliest days of the industry up to the present time.

The information centre is designed as the collecting point for visitors near to the car parks and the administration offices and library of motoring in the two storey John Montagu building are linked to the information centre. The restaurant, conference building which can seat some four hundred people adjoins the Museum, known as the Brabazon; it is cruciform in plan to provide for different types of catering. The sloping ground at this part of the site enabled public lavatories to be planned at a lower level.

Construction and materials The buildings are constructed with steel frames, exposed and painted, with high quality concrete blockwork walls and large areas of glazing. Flat roofs are built up felt with granite chippings on metal decking and sloping roofs are profiled aluminium sheeting. The Museum structure consists of two large diagonal steel girders formed by tubular steel members which carry the secondary steel lattice trusses. The supporting steel stanchions are uncased. The glazed roof and canopies are aluminium patent glazing, also used on the information centre.

In the John Montague building and the Brabazon restaurant, timber curtain walling vertical glazing is in the form of timber curtain walling with aluminium vertical sliding sashes. The concrete blockwork to all the buildings is fair faced externally and only plastered or tiled internally in the John Montague Building and the restaurant kitchens. The exposed structural steelwork is painted in bright colours.

Comment The Beaulieu complex is an excellent example of 'honey potting' in an historic setting of natural and architectural interest. By careful planning and design the huge number of tourist visitors are controlled and guided through the complex in a subtle way that avoids the use of blatant direction signs and organised routes. From the car parks discreetly planned in the woodland near the entrance through the reception centre and on to the Museum and restaurant, the buildings and their relationship on the site create flow lines that the visitor follows naturally without any feeling of coercion. At the same time this pre-planned routing protects the more sensitive areas of the site such as the Abbey, the Maze and the Palace House.

The architects' choice of large glass areas, particularly for the Museum, echoes the English Victorian tradition that associates glasshouses with country parks, of which the Crystal Palace built for the 1851 Exhibition in Hyde Park, the Palm House in Kew Gardens and the great glasshouses of Chatsworth were famous examples.

The use of patent glazing, exposed steelwork and fair faced concrete blockwork for all the buildings gives them visual unity in spite of their differing functions and sizes. The care with which the existing woodland environment has been preserved has helped to soften the inevitably hard lines of the buildings and integrate them with their natural surroundings.

The Beaulieu National Motor Museum and its complementary buildings is a showplace that attracts large numbers of tourist visitors without destroying the attractions that they came to see. The name Beaulieu means beautiful, and this tourist attraction is one of the few constructed in recent years that merits the name.

1

1 View looking South from woodland car park (*Photo: Leonard Manasseh and Partners*)
2 Brabazon restaurant/Conference building. Museum entrance canopy on left (*Photo: Leonard Manasseh and Partners*)
3 General view of museum from Test area (*Photo: Sam Lambert*)
4 Interior of motor museum from motor cycle gallery (*Photo: Sam Lambert*)

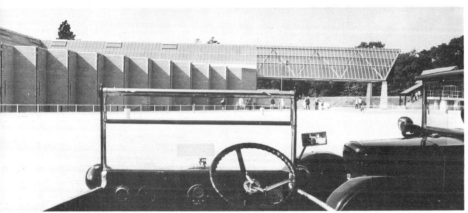

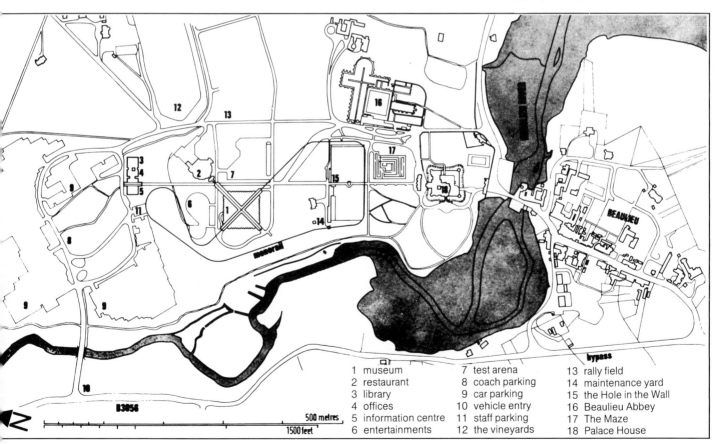

1 museum	7 test arena	13 rally field
2 restaurant	8 coach parking	14 maintenance yard
3 library	9 car parking	15 the Hole in the Wall
4 offices	10 vehicle entry	16 Beaulieu Abbey
5 information centre	11 staff parking	17 The Maze
6 entertainments	12 the vineyards	18 Palace House

500 metres

1500 feet

yout plan of Beaulieu. An overall plan of
aulieu Estate is shown on page 33

daymakers and tourists. At the same time it is clear that increased tourist pressure helps to destroy fragile buildings and their contents, sensitive natural environments and vulnerable ecosystems. 'Honey potting' can be one solution.

Lord Montagu of Beaulieu, owner of one of the great historic houses of England that attracts enormous numbers of tourists every year, appreciated the problem several years ago. He engaged architect Leonard Manasseh to prepare a master plan for Beaulieu which included the now famous Motor Museum, well designed caravan sites and other attractions that would not only encourage more people to visit Beaulieu but enable them to be more evenly spread over the estate. By this means oversaturation of the most vulnerable area – the historic Abbey and Palace House – was avoided.

Another example of the diversionary attraction is the Safari Park at Longleat – indeed many people are better acquainted with the lions at Longleat than with the magnificent 16th century Elizabethan house. The Safari Park has, without detracting from the principal attraction, increased the number of visitors to Longleat thus making more money available for the maintenance of the historic building.

Similar tactics have been employed by church and cathedral authorities, where specially planned exhibitions of vestments, plate and other treasures have been designed to control the flow of visitors through the main building fabric.

'Honey potting' is equally applicable to sensitive natural sites and scenery; planned nature trails and viewing points can direct visitors along a predetermined route and thus reduce wear and tear on over-used paths and tracks. The technique adopted by the Wildfowl Trust includes carefully sited 'hides' from which the birds can be viewed without causing disturbance. The wildlife conservation areas of Africa and elsewhere need a similar approach if the natural balance is not to be disturbed.

In many respects, 'Treetops' in Kenya, mentioned earlier, is an example where the animals are free to come and go as they please while the tourist is strictly controlled. Motor vehicles are forbidden in the area of 'Treetops' which can only be approached on foot in the company of a Park ranger.

The technique of diversionary planning to avoid over-visiting and excessive wear of building fabric or natural landscape is still in its infancy but it must be studied seriously if the destruction that is threatened is to be avoided. In the next chapter the question of positive planning for holidays and tourism includes consideration of this important subject.

Crafts and tourism

'Small is beautiful', a much repeated phrase that has become the motto of those in the developed countries who seek an alternative to the increasingly industrialised society of the twentieth century.

It is interesting to reflect that the micro-electronics revolution that has been mentioned earlier, has to some extent made possible the development of smaller units and even manufacturing industries on a more human scale. Large industrial conglomerates are giving serious consideration to reducing the size of their individual units, and this trend could well gain momentum as the full effect of the new technology is felt by traditional industries.

One of the developments that will clearly affect the way many people live and work in the future is the emergence of many craft industries producing a wide range of goods. Handicrafts have, like tourism, become a boom industry in developing and developed countries alike and the two can be mutually self-encouraging.

A recent directory of Craft Guilds and Societies issued in the UK lists no less than one hundred and forty-four National and Regional bodies in Great Britain concerned with arts and crafts at a practical level, including jewellery, pottery, leather work, toy-making and a host of others.

Many such activities are operated as cottage industries, others need special buildings, either specially designed or old ones adapted to their needs. The Spade Mill in the Ulster Folk Museum is one good example and the working smithy at the Chalk Pits Museum at Amberley, W. Sussex is another (both have already been described in this chapter). Many other examples can be quoted. The Notts County Council established in 1980 a craft centre in the Ruffold County Park, rehabilitating buildings around a ruined Abbey. The first building to be renovated was an old stable block which is now a display gallery and shop, and a series of craft workshops will follow. The funds generated by increased tourists and holidaymakers are to be used to finance the County's countryside conservation programme.

It is interesting to note that Ruffold Country Park is one of three in the region developed to relieve visitor pressure in other parts of the County. An excellent example of 'honey potting' referred to earlier in this chapter.

If tourism can be a benefit to craft industries in developed countries and experience shows that this is so, then it is essential in the countries of the Third world. The growth of tourism means that large numbers of visitors from the Western World are discovering the developing countries for the first time and

Local craft production, tie and dye fabric dying in the Gambia, W. Africa (*Edward D. Mills*)

returning home with souvenirs of their visit. Western shops now sell craft goods from many countries, tropical fruits are available in markets and shops, travel agencies display posters of distant lands, and TV programmes show the people and customs of 'far-away places'. All of these things help to familiarise the industrialised world with the arts and skills of the developing world.

Handicrafts, like tourism, is becoming a boom industry but few developing countries have exploited the boom wisely. Much of the rubbishy souvenir trade reflects badly on local craftsmanship and in some parts of the world the handicraft industry has almost become a mass production industry, with poor design and low quality as its trademark.

The International Labour Office has for some years been concerned with the development of rural crafts in the Third World because they tend to be labour intensive, utilise local skills and materials, employ large numbers of women and help to keep alive traditional skills. Many Third World Governments have recently become interested in the economic benefits of developing their local craft industries through tourism, and by this means they can provide local employment, earn much needed foreign currency and at the same time produce goods that make their economies less dependant on expensive imports.

The Federation for the Development of Utilitarian Handicrafts (FEDEAU) was established in 1977 with assistance from the EEC Commission to promote utilitarian handicrafts which would appeal to the European market and which can also be used in new buildings in their country of origin, such as holiday homes, tourist hotels and similar locations.

In another instance the Government of Benin, as part of its development plan, sees the growth of traditional craft work as an expression of the country's heritage. Through a specially established National Tourist Hotel Board (ONATHO) it is endeavouring not only to encourage the sale of handicrafts but also introduce tourists and foreign visitors to the life and culture of the country through its buildings, arts, foods, music and dance. A special centre in Cotonou is being developed with the aid of the EEC which will house not only a tourist information centre but also displays, exhibitions, music and dance performances, an African restaurant, and craft workshops. Such a centre will undoubtedly become a popular tourist attraction.

Unusually well designed local craft and souvenir shops in Malindi, Kenya where local materials have been used to create an attractive modern display ((*Edward D. Mills/MIM–DAN Ltd, Malindi, Kenya*)

Aerial view of model showing octagonal standard units. The Corris
Craft Centre set in the Welsh mountains on main tourist route to
the south of the Snowdonia National Park had been designed to
provide accommodation for Welsh craftsmen in a series of
workshops with a cafe and sales area. The Centre was built by the
Development Board for Rural Wales (*Architect: Gareth Evans*).

A group of workshops around the main courtyard with large
natural boulders as an integral part of the landscape. The simple
buildings with buff concrete brickwork, slate roofs and grey
precast concrete paving are fitted very carefully into the rugged
Welsh landscape (*Photographs by kind permission of the Cement
& Concrete Association*).

In Zambia, in the Livingstone and Victoria Falls area the Government have established the Maramba cultural centre to preserve the arts and crafts of old Africa. In typical dwellings from the main regions of Zambia native craftsmen work in the traditional manner as blacksmiths, wood carvers and mask makers. Traditional dances are performed for the entertainment of visitors.

This kind of enterprise is clearly of great importance not only in relation to the economic development of Third World countries, but also as a means by which tourists and other foreign visitors achieve a greater interest and a sympathy for the culture and history of the countries of which they are the short-term guests.

Buildings are necessary for many such enterprises as, although many local crafts start as cottage industries, they require proper display and sales locations and in some cases special facilities. The plan for an African craft complex incorporates workshops of various sizes, exhibition facilities with offices and reception areas, all planned on a modular basis to allow for future adaptation for location and growth in size as demand dictates.

If tourism is to play a constructive part in national development in the Third World then the future aim should be greater integration of the visitors with the everyday activities of the countries they visit and the promotion of their artistic and cultural heritage. Even

Plan for a craft workshop centre for an African village designed by the author. The units are modular and can be extended as the demand grows, the layout includes units of varying sizes as well as exhibition and reception facilities (*Edward D. Mills*)

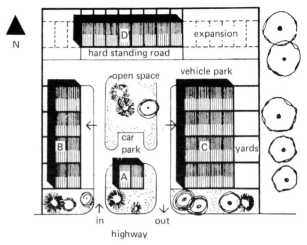

small rural industrial craft group based on a 30 × 15 ft module

A. administration and showroom
B. work shop units
C. nursery factory units
D. craft units

the Western tourist countries have realised the potential of this approach to tourism as the work of the Scottish Tourist Board shows through its Guides to Crafts in Scotland, the Burns Heritage Trail and Victorian Scotland (launched in 1978).

Chapter 9
Tourist planning for the future

The holiday and tourist industry is clearly a permanent feature of the 20th century and for a wide variety of reasons appears to be unaffected by many of the factors that influence other facets of contemporary life. World economic recession appears to have little affect on the growth of tourism; indeed it may help it grow as people seek to forget the everyday problems they face by taking a holiday in an entirely different environment to that in which they spend most of their lives. No longer is travel for the rich; mass tourism has opened up opportunities for all but the very poor.

Tourism is no longer a prerogative of the Western world, East and West can meet on holiday and the tourist traffic crosses most national and cultural barriers. The right to travel is one which cannot be denied to any who are able and willing to take advantage of the facilities available. The beaches of Brighton and the Caribbean Islands, or the deserts of North Africa and the foothills of the Himalayas are all readily accessible; the problem that has been reiterated in the pages of this book is that this accessibility can lead to the ultimate desolation and destruction of the attractions that the visitors enjoy, whether they are ancient cities, historic buildings or, as yet, unspoilt areas of natural beauty.

It cannot be denied that millions of people each year derive mental and physical refreshment and recreation, and spiritual enrichment through the medium of holidays and travel. If, however, these benefits are to be maintained for future generations, it is imperative that planning for holidays and tourism must be considered very seriously on a national and international basis.

In an article in the *Daily Telegraph* (21st August 1981) Elizabeth de Stroumillo discussed this problem and concluded with the following proposal:

'The simplest solution would seem to be to encourage big resorts to grow and even to create more of them in certain strategic places: Mexico's Ixtapa and Cancun, which keep the crowds away from more fragile areas, are cases in point. On other places "Stop" signs need to be put up. If some international system of cross-subsidisation were devised (surely not impossible?) then the inhabitants of areas earmarked for preservation could be compensated by their big-resort brothers and everybody, not least the genuinely discomfort-loving, solitude-seeking traveller, would benefit.'

The idea of developing and improving the already established tourist centres of the world, and conserving the endangered fragile regions is one that has much to commend it.

Fortunately, the international organisations, such as the intergovernmental World Tourist Organisation (WTO) an organ of United Nations, with its six Regional Commissions; the World Bank and UNESCO, together with National Tourist bodies in many countries both in the developed and developing countries are realising the importance of long-term planning and the formulation of a positive strategy for the controlled development of tourism.

Planning for the future

Comprehensive planning is essential for the preservation of the natural and physical assets of our planet. In the developed world, conservation of the environment must go hand in hand with the provision of tourist facilities. In the developing countries the opportunities for benefit to the community through the use of natural resources such as climate, scenery, wildlife and ancient cultures can be developed to generate employment, higher living standards and greater wealth for the local population.

If, however, such development is unplanned, haphazard and uncontrolled, the obvious benefits can rapidly deteriorate into positive disadvantages. Unplanned and inadequately conceived tourist development of any kind can place an unbearable strain on any national economy, in particular where the alternative growth areas are limited. The result can be a general worsening of the situation and the creation of an economic situation that is difficult to salvage. In the Caribbean region, for example, the dominant industry is tourism and a major employer of labour. In the Bahamas, tourism represents 70% of the Gross National Product and in other parts of the region 30–50%.

A comprehensive tourist plan that is to be effective at all levels must take into account both the environmental and economic problems and use the available resources physical and financial to the best advantage. Co-operation and collaboration must extend beyond national boundaries; it is of considerable interest to record that in 1981 the member countries of the Caribbean Tourism Association made a special presentation to the European Economic Community (EEC) in recognition of the Community's 'outstanding contribution to the advancement of the Caribbean countries through tourism', such international practical assistance is clearly a positive step in the right direction.

Unco-ordinated and random tourist projects whether national or regional can be counter-productive. The Shankland Cox Partnership, a UK-based planning consultancy that has undertaken over thirty projects in more than forty countries, and has been closely concerned with international tourism, has identified the four basic studies that are required in the preparation of a comprehensive tourist plan as follows:

(i) The tourist market: its origin, form, needs, rate of growth and competition for it.
(ii) The physical capacity of the area: its ability to absorb the requirements of tourism in terms of its natural attractions, infrastructure and economic resources.
(iii) The socio-economic impact on local communities migration, housing and social infrastructure for the support population.
(iv) The environmental capacity of the area: the limits imposed upon tourist development to protect the quality of the area in terms of landscape, townscape, tranquility and culture.

The development of such studies, to quote a recent publication by the Partnership:

'can then be integrated into a series of alternative development policies and the full social, economic and physical implications of each examined. The preferred alternative, decided by references to

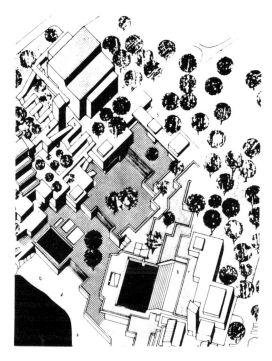

1. hotel rooms	7. shops
2. restaurants/bar	8. bowling
3. seashore path	9. hall
4. parking areas	10. childrens pool
5. excursion point	11. water polo pool
6. monument	12. squares
	13. beaches

A development plan prepared by Shankland Cox Partnership for the government of Yugoslavia for the expansion of the existing tourist centre of Crikvenica on the Bay of Jasenova (*Shankland Cox Partnership*)

agreed objectives, is then developed into a definitive plan appropriately phased in relation to the market demand and resources available.

In many cases it will need to be accompanied by recommendations for the machinery of implementation – its organisation and financing and its powers of co-ordination and control. The preparation of such a plan requires a closely integrated approach with contributions for experts of many disciplines – design, economics, market research, geography, finance and property administration.'

The role of the design team

Any large scale development requires the professional services of many different experts with experience in specialised areas of activity. Developments for tourism are no exception whether they are small groups of holiday villas, hotel complexes or complete holiday villages or towns such as Port Grimaud in France or Vilamoura in the Portuguese Algarve, or any other of the developments illustrated in earlier chapters.

Town planners, economists, architects, geographers, traffic and services engineers, civil engineers and even conservation experts all have a part to play which will vary in degree according to the size and location of the project. An important element in the plan is the role of the Government of the host country through a responsible Ministry or Department.

Many countries have very active tourist authorities, for example the Republic of Turkey established in 1963 a Ministry of Tourism and Information with an architect-director of Tourism Planning to formulate tourism development policies, and the application strategies to put the policies into practice. The Tourism Bank undertakes some of the investment on behalf of the Government and makes loans available to foreign investors to encourage other projects. The Turkish Ministry of Tourism, together with other appropriate Ministries is responsible for the provision of the essential basic infrastructure, such as roads, water, electricity and sewage systems, according to an agreed Master Plan. By this means the general strategy is co-ordinated and the possibility of uncontrolled development eliminated.

Variations of this procedure occur in other countries. In 1971, the Government of Morocco in conjunction with the Federal Republic of Germany produced a Moroccan Tourist development plan, referred to earlier, in which a detailed study was made of the tourist demand and potential.

In developed countries like the UK, the British Tourist Authority, the English Tourist Board and the Scottish Tourist Board have produced well-documented reports on tourist planning to 'encourage local authorities and similar bodies to adopt policies that will lead to orderly development of and management of tourism in their areas' (English Tourist Board. *Planning for Tourism in England. Planning Advisory Note 1978*). Such publications form a valuable basis for a planned approach to tourist development without which any project is bound to be less than satisfactory.

The list of possible members of the design team referred to earlier can never be entirely comprehensive. One specialisation that is often overlooked is that of landscape designer, whose role is of increasing importance as new areas of undeveloped landscape throughout the world are considered as potential areas for tourism. The importance of landscape conservation in wilderness and other unspoiled areas of the world is vital, and the value of landscape design in all forms of tourist development cannot be overstressed. Many of the case studies in this book show that imaginative landscape design can ensure that new buildings can be integrated with their natural surroundings thus becoming a positive benefit rather than an unwanted intrusion.

The role of the graphic designer is also often completely overlooked. The large movements of people and vehicles of every description that the growth of short stay holiday visitors engenders, the importance of well planned and clearly understandable direction and identification signing is often given less thought than it deserves. The importance of car parking and of adequate signing has already been stressed in earlier chapters. Whether the subject is that of traffic direction in an international airport, a capital city or a nature reserve, the subtle control of visitors can be achieved by good graphic design. The sign in a famous game reserve in East Africa that reads

| ELEPHANTS HAVE RIGHT OF WAY |

is well-known and makes clear to the tourist that he is the visitor and is expected to acknowledge the fact by his behaviour.

If the tourist industry is to grow in such a way as to ensure the preservation of the world-wide heritage of natural, and manmade resources, then the skills of a broadly based design team working in harmony with the national Governments and international authorities are of vital importance. Long-term planning in crowded cities or wild unspoiled places is essential, as Elizabeth de Stroumillo suggested in the paragraph quoted earlier, in the latter situation the planners major contribution may well be the locating of the STOP signs, hopefully designed by a good graphic designer.

Well designed signing that is informative and attractive for the Ironbridge Gorge Museum Trust (*Spel Products*)

Building materials and techniques

The internationalisation of commerce and industry has resulted in the growth of building development throughout the world, generated largely by the developed countries. Large-scale building projects usually originate from the Western world taking with them Western technology and ideas. This is not necessarily advantageous to the recipient country which may well have a tradition of building materials and construction techniques that have successfully withstood the test of time. There are obviously many examples of modern materials and techniques that are more satisfactory than their older counterparts, but a careful evaluation must be made before a design decision is made.

Where local materials and craft skills are available, their use should be given careful consideration as this does not only result in immediate economic advantage but also having long term benefits in the encouragement of local skills and the revitalisation of local employment opportunities.

An interesting example is the Chobe Safari Lodge in Botswana built in a remote area where the transport of building mterials was both difficult and expensive. Here locally produced materials were used to construct the buildings, using site fabricated hollow clay arches spanning 3.6 m supported by sand-cement brick cross walls on a modular layout, and surfaced with a rough plaster finish. This technique used at Chobe by architects, Mallows, Louw, Hoffe and Partners (Project architect: Bill Birren) and Joe de Beer (of Ove Arup and Partners, Engineers) was a logical development of an ancient form of construction used for centuries in Iran and Egypt.

The Chobe project resulted in the use of the technique for other buildings in the region thus employing local skills and materials and avoiding expensive imported products.

While this pattern may not have a universal application it serves to establish a principle that could well be applied to many buildings for tourist use. A number of the Case Studies in early chapters are evidence of similar successful experiments.

One of the principal attractions of many tourist development areas of the world is the climate. Vast

continued on page 140

The famous 'Elephants have right of way' sign in an East African game reserve. (*Edward D. Mills*)

Chobe National Park, Game Lodge, Botswana. Photograph showing prefabricated curved vault sections being manufactured on site by local craftsmen, using an ancient construction technique to solve a contemporary building problem (*Photo Malowes, Louw, Hoff & Partners*)

Case Study 29

Tourist Guest House
Yatri Nivas, Sevagram, Wardha,
Maharashtra, India

Architect
Uttam C. Jain
Clients
Ministry of Tourism, Government of India

The site Sevagram, or 'village of service'
is a small unpretentious village that symbol-
ises the Gandhian way of life. Here Mahatma
Gandhi made his home in later years and the
Ashram is now a national institution. In the
village in which he lived are preserved many
of his personal belongings and it has become a place of pilgrimage for many tourists
from all over the world. The village of Sevagram has a population of 2000 people and
about 500 people live in the Ashram. The
village has a railway station and Wardha is
6 km away. The nearest airport is Nagpur
72 km away, and Bombay is 765 km.

Design and layout The tourist rest house,
Yatri Nivas, is on the opposite side of the
road to the Ashram and its design has
therefore been strongly influenced by the
simple existing buildings, small in scale and
unpretentious in design. The plan is based
on a series of square modules for all units to
allow future expansion without changing the
basic character of the group. The communal
areas consist of a dormitory, dining room
with kitchen, a meeting hall and level two-
bedroom guest units clustered around covered courtyards. The architect's aim was to
create a community feeling that expressed
the Ashram way of life lived by Gandhi.

Construction and materials The
construction of Yatru Nivas employs building
materials and techniques available locally or
from the surrounding region. The simple
structures have walls of local brick,
unplastered both inside and out. Local
unwrought timber roofs in local timber with
terracotta tiled roofs. Window and door
openings, without glazing, have solid timber
shutters with bamboo security bars. Floors
and terrace pavings are of handmade brick
pavoirs. Ceilings have a teak frame to
support bamboo matting and natural
ventilation is assisted by a 'venturi' at the
apex of the pyramidal roof. The openness of
the layout and the courtyard plan ensures
comfortable living conditions in an area
where summer temperature can be high
(47.7°C).

Comment The design of this small group
of buildings as a guest house for tourists has
been conceived as being in complete
harmony with the buildings of the Ashram
with all its association with Gandhi, it is
simple and direct in its architectural
approach and displays many of the qualities
that could be usefully followed in other
unsophisticated locations to which the
tourist is often attracted.

1

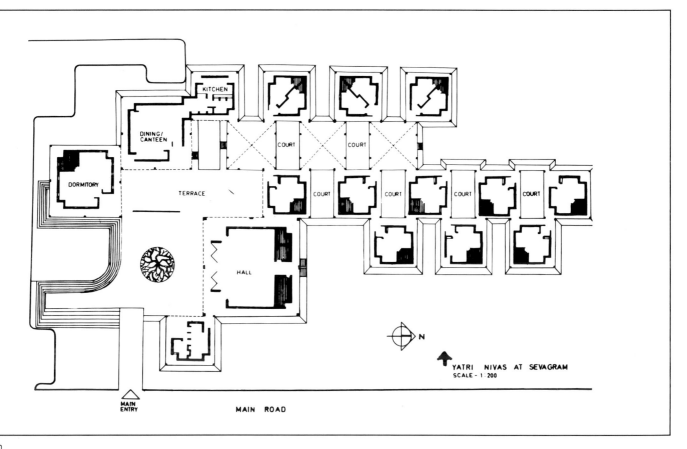

layout plan

Ba Kutur, the cottage in the Ashram built for
Mrs Kasturba Gandhi opposite Yatri Nivas
Typical guest room unit
General view of Yatri Nivas
Bamboo and teak ceiling to guest room

(*Photos: Uttam C. Jain*)

Case Study 30

Game Lodge
Chobe National Park, Botswana

Architect
Bill Birren of Mallows Louw & Hoffe

Clients
Southern Sun Hotel Corporation

Engineers
Michael Noyce of Ove Arup & Partners

The site   The Game Lodge is situated in the Chobe National Park on the south bank of the Chobe River, several miles upstream from the junction of the Chobe and Zambezi Rivers. The south river bank on which the Lodge is built is 40–50 ft high and faces northward across the Caprivi flood plains. The area is an undeveloped game area, with many wild animals particularly elephant.

At the time of construction the only overland access to the site was from Victoria Falls about 90 km away over a rough dirt road. Access by light aircraft is provided by a gravel landing strip on the south bank of the river. The site falls to the river and is very sandy and covered with trees and scrub.

Design and layout   The main lodge accommodation is stretched from east to west along the edge of the river bank, with a central building consisting of the reception area, lounge with bar and terrace overlooking the swimming pool, dining room and kichen together with other guest facilities and management accommodation. The guest bedrooms with *en suite* bathrooms form wings to the east and west; the rooms are in small blocks two storeys high, built into the slope of the site to eliminate staircases. To the south on the other side of the access road are the staff quarters, laundry, petrol kiosk, drainage septic tank. There is a small boat house and jetty by the riverside and existing trees have been preserved wherever possible.

Construction and materials   The method of construction is of particular interest. To have built with conventional materials in the conventional manner would have been an expensive and drawn out exercise. The architect decided to utilise the materials on site, the wind blown Kalahari sand which covers the area.

Sand and cement bricks would be made on site and the entire structure built of bricks

incuding the roof which would be vaulted. The only material to be transported in would be bags of cement. However, the Kalahari sand proved unsatisfactory by itself and had to be mixed with a small proportion of clean gritty river sand.

Hollow clay blocks were trucked in for the construction of the vaults.

To speed construction, the vaults were made of prefabricated curved sections laid against each other thus eliminating scaffolding and formwork. Inverted brick moulds were made to the curve of the vaults and when the blocks were placed in position, gravity pulled them tightly together. Light reinforcing rods were then grouted into the sides of the blocks and when dry, the curved sections were removed and stacked on their sides. Later they were turned over and carried manually onto the supporting walls which had been constructed by bricklayers whilst the prefabricated process continued nearby.

The entire building was completed in one operation by bricklayers who smeared the walls with a rough plaster by hand without straight edges or trowels. When the bricklayers left the site the structure was complete, including the quarry tile floor. The appearance of the building matched the surrounding sandy ground since the same sand had been used for the plaster. To avoid water penetration through the fairly porous plaster and bricks, the buildings were painted with a cement wash. Care was taken to ensure that the final colour matched the original plaster and surrounding ground.

Although air-conditioned, the interior of the building proved to be surprisingly cool in the hot African summer due to the massive masonry structure and generally unperforated walls on the east and west.

Comment   Mud brick vault and dome construction has been used for centuries in middle east countries. This developed out of the need for spanning materials in semi-arid regions where traditional materials like timber and reeds have become scarce. In Egypt the granary of Rameses built some 3500 years ago using this form of construction is still in existence. The use of this ancient building technique at Chobe Lodge has resulted in a tourist complex that has literally grown out of the ground and fits perfectly into its surroundings in one of Africa's unspoilt, natural locations.

In addition, the adoption of the prefabricated vaulted roofing system was a practical solution to the considerable problem of building in a remote area with very difficult access. It is of interest to note that the success of the design at Chobe has led to the technique being applied to low cost housing and other projects in the region. Chobe Lodge demonstrates the importance of traditional local building techniques in relation to tourist buildings in remote and wild areas where indigenous materials and local craft skills can be employed rather than relying upon imported techniques and materials that have no natural links with the region. Tourist buildings should ideally look as though they belong to the place in which they are built, this example meets this requirement with skill and imagination.

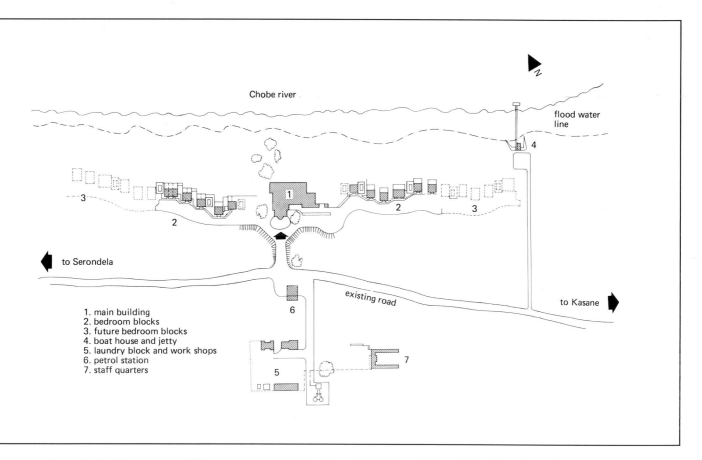

Chobe river

N

flood water line

3

2

1

2

3

4

to Serondela

existing road

to Kasane

6

5

7

1. main building
2. bedroom blocks
3. future bedroom blocks
4. boat house and jetty
5. laundry block and work shops
6. petrol station
7. staff quarters

Chobe Lodge layout plan

1 General view of bedroom units across the Chobe River
2 The main building, terraces and swimming pool
3 Detail of bedroom units

(*Photos: Mallows, Louw, Hoffe & Partners*)

Traditional methods of maintaining comfortable internal conditions in an old Egyptian building in Cairo. High rooms, shade and carefully designed louvred openings to encourage natural air movement (*Edward D. Mills*)

Fellowship conference centre hostel, Mbale cathedral, Uganda. Designed to eliminate air conditioning using shading, insulation and suitable orientation. Architects Edward D. Mills & Partners (*Photo: Edward D. Mills*)

numbers of holidaymakers from Northern Europe and similar regions seek the long hours of warm sunshine in the Mediterranean, Africa, the Caribbean and other 'sun spots' of the world. Early tourist hotels and other buildings following the European pattern with large unprotected window areas, poor roof insulation and thin external walls requiring expensive, and often badly maintained and therefore inefficient air-conditioning, to maintain a comfortable internal environment. There is much to be learned from traditional methods of keeping buildings cool in the hot/dry and hot/humid zones of the world.

Older buildings in Egypt and other Middle Eastern countries relied on high rooms, shaded windows and designed natural air movement (the masonry wind towers or BAADGEER on the old merchant houses in Dubai are a good example). Together with the thermal storage qualities of various forms of traditional wall and roof construction these features create comfortable internal conditions.

These techniques, coupled with modern technology can be adapted for modern use. For example, the International Hotel, Kampala, Uganda was designed to operate without air-conditioning in the major parts of the building. Carefully sited on a hill to catch the prevailing breezes, the principal rooms, including the bedrooms, have windows protected from the direct sun, with large balconies and sun breakers, with adjustable louvres to take advantage of the natural air movement. The resulting internal environment is entirely satisfactory. Ironically the VIP suites at roof level, largely used by Third World visitors, are the only ones that were air-conditioned at the clients' request.

There are many reasons why the adaptation of traditional building materials and techniques are particularly appropriate to buildings for the tourist industry, especially in developing countries. Imported materials are expensive and sometimes out of tune with the local scene; local skills and craftmanship need to be encouraged to increase employment opportunities, transport is often expensive over poor roads

Mulika Swamp game lodge in the Meru National Park, Kenya where the use of traditional building materials and techniques subjugates the architectural forms to the natural setting. The site was chosen by the architects, Archer Associates in consultation with the Park warden and much of the materials used in the construction were stone, timber and thatch collected from the Park (*Archer Associates*)

and long distances, energy in the form of oil and electricity is expensive and a diminishing asset and the maintenance and repair of sophisticated equipment is often invariably neglected. The holidaymaker often appreciates an environment, with buildings to match, that does not remind him too much of his normal surroundings from which he seeks to escape for a brief period.

This does not mean that copies of traditional buildings are appropriate or even the 'pastiche' that is a reminder of Disneyland, however successful they may be in a different context. The Case Studies show that an enlighted choice of materials old and new combined with an appropriate technology can result in an effective and efficient architecture for tourist purposes.

It is of interest to note that the Wildfowl Trust Information Centre at Martin Mere uses the very old technique of a turf covered roof which not only provides excellent thermal insulation, but also helps the structure to fit quietly into the landscape.

Technology has become the popular subject in the last decade; the high technology of space travel, low technology of windmills, and now intermediate technology somewhere between the two extremes. The design of buildings for tourism can make use of all three, and therefore, in practice requires 'appropriate technology', which the example of Chobe Lodge, previously mentioned, illustrates using an old technique in a new way.

The Tower House in Provence, is an interesting example of appropriate technology as solar energy is used to supply hot water; a technique that could well be adopted for countries with long hours of sunshine, popular with many tourists. In particular, the use of solar energy is particularly appropriate for tourist development in remote areas where electricity must be either generated locally or carried by land line over

long distances. Tiger Tops in Nepal has no electricity but relies on solar energy for the necessary hot water supply.

At the same time, the high technology approach to building through, for example, prefabrication can also play an important part. The timber holiday cabins at Kernow Forest in Cornwall were all built of factory-made standardised units easily transported to the sites and erected with local labour. The Moduli holiday cabins in Finlands are also built in the same way and this technique which has been successfully used for emergency housing following natural disasters could well be adopted for minimum buildings in nature reserves and remote areas of special significance.

Alternative ways of travel

While the motor car and aeroplane dominate the field of holiday travel, they also help in the destructive processes. Cars need reasonable roads and organised space to park to avoid congestion and pollution. Airports of international standards need large areas of land, create their own traffic problems and generate noise. Clearly, long distance air travel needs these temporary mechanical aids, and the developed tourist resorts of the world depend on them for their continuous existence. Developing areas could well consider less intrusive alternatives.

In sensitive and unspoiled areas, planners are taking a fresh look at communication alternatives to the motor car and the aeroplane. Cycle tracks, horse-drawn vehicles, mini-railways and organised bus services instead of the individual motor vehicle, are all possibilities which offer greater opportunities for avoiding uncontrolled visitor saturation. Traditional examples of this technique already exist in such places as the Island of Sark in the Channel Islands where motor cars are prohibited.

In conservation areas such as nature reserves and game parks the walking safari is already gaining considerable popularity. In Zambia, in the Luangwa National Park, an area the size of three English counties known as the Enchanted Valley, Norman Carr developed wilderness trails some twenty years ago. Small groups of visitors, accompanied by an

continued on page 146

A walking safari in the Luangwa National Park, Zambia (*Ian Murphy*)

Case Study 31

Serena Beach Hotel
Near Mombasa, Kenya, East Africa

Architects
Archer Associates

Clients
Serena Lodges & Hotels

The site   The hotel is on the Kenya coast of the Indian Ocean on Shanzu Beach 20 km north of Mombasa Island, with a tarmac road from the Malindi Road. The site is a flat sandy area of approximately 3.16 ha and a sea frontage of 163 m, with established palm trees. The nearest airport is Mombasa which is the chief port of Kenya; Nairobi, the capital, is some 300 miles distant.

Design and layout   The layout consists of a central building that contains the public areas, reception, shops and administration with two restaurants that overlook the swimming pool. The guest room accommodation is grouped in a series of two storey units arranged informally around courtyards and enclosed tropical gardens. The one hundred and twenty bedrooms are all air-conditioned, with bathrooms and balconies with a total accommodation for two hundred and fifty guests. Each unit contains four to eight rooms. The layout and design of the hotel is reminiscent of the old Swahali town of Lamu (now a protected conservation area) with narrow 'streets' linking the bedroom blocks, the architectural details, and the courtyards with fountains, a market square and exotic tropical plants. Car parking is sited away from the main building to the West adjoining the entrance road.

Construction and materials   The construction throughout is simple using mainly local materials, loadbearing walls are concrete block finished with a white colour washed rough rendering. Roofs are mainly traditional flat roofs. Timber is used extensively for windows, doors, balcony enclosures, etc. and ceilings to restaurants and other public areas are constructed using the traditional Lamu Boriti pole technique.

Comment   The design of Serena Beach Hotel has an attractive human scale largely due to the imaginative two storey courtyard planning of the guest accommodation. The influence of the Lamu tradition has resulted in an intimate atmosphere not found in the larger international style hotels in other similar holiday resorts. The site with all-season sea, sun and sand, together with the inevitable palm trees has been greatly enhanced by the landscaping. Critics may regard this as a 'pastiche' of Swahili architecture but it is nevertheless very successful as a tourist hotel. The modest scale ensures that it fits into the natural environment, and the materials, finishes and architectural detailing link it to the tradition of the Kenya coast.

1

2

Main public restaurant and reception building
across swimming pool
Bedroom blocks adjoining pool
Typical bedroom block courtyard
Bedrooms overlooking the beach and the sea
The market courtyard with open-air craft shop

(Photos: Edward D. Mills)

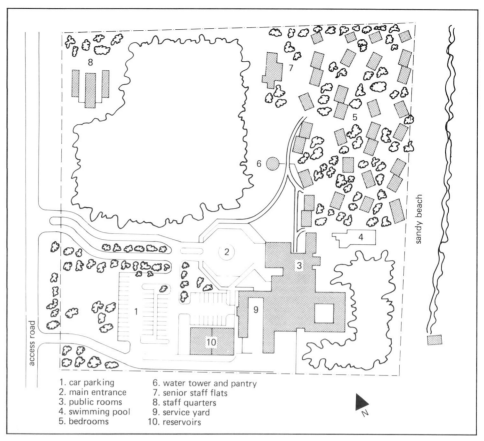

1. car parking
2. main entrance
3. public rooms
4. swimming pool
5. bedrooms
6. water tower and pantry
7. senior staff flats
8. staff quarters
9. service yard
10. reservoirs

Layout plan

Case Study 32

Prefabricated House Kit
Moduli 225, Finland

Architects
Kristian Gullichsen & Juhani Pallasmaa

Siting This prefabricated housing kit has been designed for d.i.y. assembly on any type of site to the purchaser's requirements for holiday houses and second homes.

Design and layout The modular basis of the design allows for an infinite variety of plans using the 2.25 m horizontal and vertical grid, and the completely interchangeable units do not exceed 50 kg in weight. A square metre of structure can be erected by four people in one hour.

Construction and materials The entire system consists of timber components. Walls are glazed or solid panels, incorporating single or double glazed horizontal or vertical windows, with insulation designed for both temperate and cold climates. The

flat roofs are waterproofed with plastic sheeting capable of carrying a snowload; rainwater is discharged by gargoyles. The timber structural frame, with standardised connectors, is supported on adjustable telescopic aluminium feet on concrete pads to accommodate variations in site levels.

Comment Moduli 225 is an ingenious, flexible system, which meets the need for holiday homes that can be erected by the owners using the prefabrication process and offering unlimited variation in plan form and arrangement. The result is a handsome

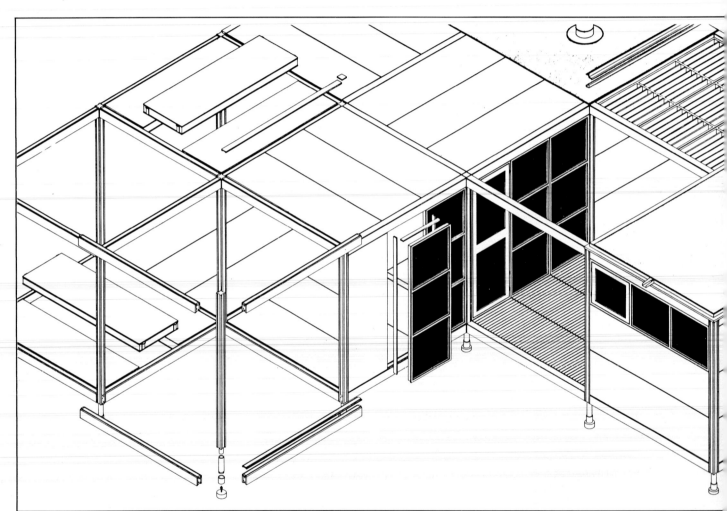

1 Isometric drawing of typical house layout
2 Drawing of structural frame and foundation
   assembly
3 Frame erected and packaged panels
4 Exterior/interior view
5 View of complete house – exterior

(*Photos: Arkkitehoit*)

cation house that will suit most site condi-
ns and for a reasonable cost. It provides a
elcome alternative to the static caravan
welling that is often an eyesore that spoils
any attractive holiday locations.

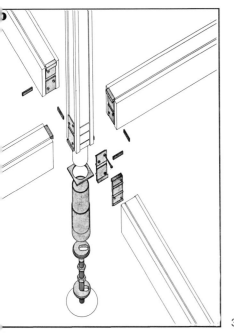

3

4

experienced guide, trek through the bush staying at semi-permanent camps en route. The camps are accepted by the resident wildlife, and animals can be observed in their natural habitat at close quarters. The Land Rover and safari minibus that often threatens the wildlife in other African reserves have been abandoned.

In Nepal, at Tiger Tops, a similar experiment has been highly successful; here, elephants, rafts and canoes are used for transport. In Pakistan the tourist authorities offer over one hundred organised trekking tours in the North of the country. It has been estimated that 50% of Kenya's export income is spent on imported oil, much of which is used as fuel for tourists' safari minibuses as well as air-conditioning tourist hotels.

As an alternative to the jumbo jet, light aircraft that do not need elaborate runways and airports have been in use for some years in island groups popular with tourists, such as the Seychelles and the Caribbean. Hovercraft and hydrofoils are other means of access to island resorts that could well be developed to minimise dependence on air transport.

If the destruction by over-use of recreational and tourist areas of the world is to be halted then careful management of such areas is essential and new and original solutions must be found to what is rapidly becoming a universal problem.

Conclusions

The fact that the numbers of tourists and holiday packages is likely to continue to grow in the foreseeable future means that both developed and developing countries must, as a matter of priority, formulate development plans – locally, nationally and internationally. The machinery for such planning already exists in both national and international form.

It is generally accepted that while tourism can bring considerable benefits to individuals who participate as visitors and the countries that act as hosts, it is also accepted that tourism poses a threat to many parts of the world in the form of congestion, environmental damage and ecological distress. If the benefits are to be maximised and the disadvantages of tourism are to be kept to a minimum, then long range overall planning, coupled with high standards of design, and sympathetic management at local, national and regional level, are essential.

The first chapter of this book began with a reference in relation to holidays and the Biblical story of the Creation, it is therefore perhaps appropriate to end with a quotation from the Koran, which could be regarded as a reference to travel and tourism.

'And God has made earth for you as a carpet spread out, that you may travel therein on spacious roads'. (Sura Noah 29).

Bibliography

AA tourist and holiday guides, Automobile Association, Publications Division, London.

The British Hotel through the Ages, M. C. Borer, Lutterworth, Guildford (1972).

British Railways Board – facts and figures, 2nd edn, BRB Public Affairs Dept., London (1980).

City Landscape, A. B. Grove and R. Cresswell (eds). Butterworths, London (1983).

Cooks Tours, E. Swinglehurst, Blandford Press, London

Design for Leisure Entertainment, Anthony Wylson, Butterworths, London (1980).

Design for Sport, Gerald A. Perrin, Butterworths, London (1981).

Environmental Revolution (A guideline for the new masters of the earth), Max Nicholson, Hodder & Stoughton, London.

Festivals and Saints Days, Victor J. Green, Blandford Press, London.

Guide to Fire Precautions Act; Hotels and Boarding Houses, HMSO, London (1971).

Highways in the Air, British Airways Public Relations, London.

History of Tourism, 3rd edn. Gilbert Signaux, Leisure Arts Limited, London (1979).

History of the Farmstead, John Weller, Faber & Faber Limited, London (1981).

Hotel, Motel, G. Alio, Hoepli, Milan (1970).

Hotels, motels & condominiums, Fred Lawson, The Architctural Press & Caterers Books International Inc., London (1976).

International Social Science Journal (The anatomy of tourism), Vol. XXXII, No. 1, 1980, UNESCO, Paris.

Man and Environment (crisis and the strategy of choice), Robert Arville, Penguin Books, London.

The Management of touring Caravans and Camping. (Planning Advisory Note), English Tourist Board, London. (1979).

The Microelectronic Revolution, Tom Forester (ed), Basil Blackwell, Oxford (1980).

Parcs et Chateaux de France, Commissariat General An Tourisme, Paris (1968).

Places for people, Jeanne M. Davern (ed), McGraw-Hill Inc., New York.

Planning, 9th edn. Edward D. Mills (ed), Butterworths, London.

Planning for tourism in England. (Planning Advisory Note), English Tourist Board, London (1978).

Preservation pays, Marcus Binney and Max Hanna, Save Britain's Heritage, London.

27 Principles for the development of tourism in mountain regions. Study No. 19, Council of Europe Study Series, Brussels.

Providing for disabled visitors, English Tourist Board, London (1977).

Rail topics No. 2 (List of Books on Railways), London Midland Region Public Relations, London.

Resort hotel planning and management, A. Abraben, Reinhold, New York (1965).

Saving old buildings, Sherban Cantacuzino and Susan Brandt, The Architectural Press, London (1980).

Skansen – Stockholm, The Skansen Foundation, Stockholm (1979).

Snowdon management scheme, Snowdonia National Park Information Service, Wales.

SWARA, The Journal of the East African Wildlife Society (Monthly).

Tourism, blessing and blight, George Young, Penguin Books, London.

Tourism, A. J. Burkhart and S. Medlik, Heineman, London.

Tourism and recreation development, Manuel Baud-Bovey and Fred Lawson, The Architectural Press and CBI Publishing Co. Inc., London (1977).

Tourism in Turkey, Ministry of Tourism and Information, Instanbul.

Treetops, Outspan & Paxtu, Jan Hemsing, Block Hotels (1974).

The Wildfowl Trust Brochure and Magazine, The Wildfowl Trust, Slimbridge, Glos.

National Trust Magazine, The National Trust, London (Quarterly).

Index

Addy Aldrich Rockafeller Folk Art Centre, 125
Africa, East, 65, 66, 81
Agriculture and tourism, 116–120
Air-conditioning, 135, 140
Air travel, history of, 4, 5, 11, 12
Aldeburgh Festival, 108
Alexandria-Troas, 58
Algrave, Portugal, 113
Amathus Beach Hotel, Cyprus, 74, 75
Amberley Chalk Pits Museum, Sussex, 126
Ambroseli camp site, Kenya, 39
Amorback Benedictine Abbey, Bavaria, 108
Arran, Island of, Scotland, 98
Arundel Nature Reserve, 84, 85
Arun flood plain, 84
Assisi, Italy, 106
Automobile Associations, 33
    United Kingdom, 116

Bahamas, The, 65
Beach Hotel, Camino Real, Cancun, Mexico, 70, 71
Beach Hotel, Jerba, Tunisia, 68, 69
Beaulieu Estate, Hampshire, 120, 126–128
Bedford, Earl of, 110
Bedroom design, 80
Belle-ile-en-mer holiday village, Bretagne, France, 62–64
Benin, 131
Bird watching, 54, 82–86, 90, 92
Blanes, Spain, 26
Bogmalo Beach Hotel, Goa, India, 76, 77
Borgaf Jall Ski Hotel, Sweden, 72, 73
Borodur, Indonesia, 20
Botswana, 83, 135, 138, 139
British Airways, 4
Brodick Information Centre, Scotland, 98–100
Broome Park, Kent, 103
Bryn Morfa caravan site, Wales, 41
Buildings, 37–39, 40, 41
    conservation of, 101–112
    construction of, 83
    materials, 135, 140, 141
Burgschenke Burg Guttenburg castle, Germany, 105
Butlin, Billy, 5

Cabins; *see* Holiday cabins
Cairo, Egypt, 24, 25

Camino Real, Mexico, 70, 71
Camping sites, 26, 37, 122
    control of, 38
    facilities at, 39
    number of, 37
    size of, 38
    urban, 38
Camps, holiday, 5
Canakkale Villa group, Turkey, 58, 59
Canterbury Cathedral, Kent, 14, 106
Caravanning, 26, 37, 122
Caravan sites, static, 40–44
Caribbean, 65, 70
    Tourist Association of, 133
Car parking, 31–33
    disabled persons, 78
    landscaping of, 33
    motels and, 78
Castles, 103–105
Cawdor Estate, Pembrokeshire, Wales, 117
Chateaux, 103–105
Chesterton, Elizabeth, 120
Chobe Game Lodge, Botswana, 83, 135, 138, 139
Christ Church Chapter House, Oxford, 107
Churches, 106–108
    government aid to, 107
    number of visitors to, 22
Club Mediterranée, 5, 6
Colonial Williamsburg, Virginia, USA, 121, 125
Cotylumbridge Highland Lodges, Aviemore, Scotland, 41
Communication,
    instant, 12
    satellites, 13
Conference centres, 66, 68, 76
Conservation, 81–83
    of buildings, 101–112
Cook, Thomas, 3
Corris Craft Centre, Wales, 130
Costa Brava, Spain, 25
Costa del Sol, Spain, 25
Cotswold Countryside Collection, 117
Country houses, 102–105
Country Parks, 120
Covent Garden, London, 108–111
Crafts and tourism, 128–130
Craft shops, 9, 10
Crikvencia, Yugoslavia, 133
Cultural centres 101; *see also* historic buildings
Cyprus, 74, 75

Danish Holiday Centre, Mellieha, Malta, 52, 53
Dansk Folke-ferie, 52
Day Study Centre, Witley, Surrey, 96, 97
Developing countries, 17, 19, 131
Disabled tourists, 35, 36, 78–81
    farm holidays, 118
    Wildfowl Trust Centres, 84, 86
Dubrodnik, Yugoslavia, 32
Durdanelles, Turkey, 58

Economic aspects, 15–21
Edinburgh, Scotland, 101
Egypt, 21, 24
Elderly tourists, 35, 113
Employment in tourism, 18
England, Richard, 22, 100
English Tourist Board, 9, 16, 37
Entrance doors, design, 79
Entrophication of lakes, 82
Environmental pollution, 22
Erosion, 23
European Architectural Heritage Year, 1975, 101

Fairs, 1
'Far-away places', 27, 28, 81–99
Farm buildings, 109, 116, 117
Farm holidays, 116–120
Federation for the Development of Utilitarian Handicrafts (FEDEAU), 129
Festavel Tourist Village, Mellieha, Malta, 45, 48, 49
Fishing facilities, 54, 70
Flevohof Recreational Farm, Holland, 117–119
'Flexi-time', 9
Floor finishes, 81
Folk museums, 120, 121
Foreign trade balance, 16
Forestry Commission, British, 41, 42
Fowler, Charles, 110
France,
    Belle-ile-en-mer, Bretagne, 62–64
    Port Grimaud, 64, 113
    Provence, 50, 51

Gallura, Sardinia, 56, 57
Gambia, 17

Game reserves, 19, 28, 66, 81, 82
  Nile Falls, 90, 91
  Semliki, 88, 89
  Treetops, Kenya, 82, 128
'Gast-Im-Schloss' organisation, 103, 105
Gites scheme, France, 116
Golf facilities,
  Algarve, Portugal, 113
  Broome Park, Kent, 103
  Camino Real, Mexico, 70
  Wellington Country Park, Hants, 122
Grand Tour, The, 2
Great Barn, The, Avebury, 117
Grouse shooting, 54

Handrails, 79
Hazelius, Arthur, 120
Historical sites, 101–112
  'alternative uses of,' 101, 102
  re-cycling of, 112
  visitors to, 102
Holiday cabins, 41
  Kernton forest, Cornwall, 42, 43
  Lochanhully, Scotland, 54, 55
Holiday camps, 5
Holiday villas at,
  Belle-ile-en-mer, France, 62, 63
  Canakkale, Turkey, 58, 59
  Danish, Mellieha, Malta, 52, 53
  Festaval, Mellieha, Malta, 48, 49
  Portmadoc, Wales, 60, 61
  Stazzo, Gallura, Sardinia, 56, 57
  Vilamoura, Algarve, Portugal, 46, 47
  Villa Group, Provence, 50, 51
'Honey potting', 125, 126, 128
Hotels, 24
  Amathus Beach, Cyprus, 74, 75
  Borgaf Jall, Sweden, 72, 73
  Camino Real, Mexico, 70, 71
  Feathers, The, Ludlow, 64
  Jerba Beach, Tunisia, 68, 69
  Kampala, International, 66, 67
  Mughal Sheraton, Agra, India, 65
  Oberoi, Goa, India, 76, 77
Hotels, facilities for,
  disabled persons, 78–81
  tourists, 64, 65
Housing kit, prefabricated, 144, 145

India, 76, 77, 136, 137
Indian Heritage Society Report, 1980, 24
Indonesia, 20
Information Centres, 83, 84, 92, 96, 98, 100
Infrastructure, tourist pressure on, 33, 34
International House of South Wales, Penarth, 114
International Labour Office, 129
International Union for Conservation and Natural Resources, 81
Ironbridge Gorge Museum Trust Shop, Telford, 105
Italy,
  Assisi, 106
  Rome, 14, 18
  Venice, 18, 19, 24

Jamaica, Toby Bay, 18
Japan, 82
Jerba, Tunisia, 68, 69
Johnson, Samuel, 2
Jones, Inigo, 110
Jumbo jet aircraft, 12

Kampala, Uganda, 66, 140
Kenya, 81, 82
  Ambroseli camp site, 39
  Folk museum, 125
  Game parks, 28, 82, 128
  Serena Beach Hotel, Mombasa, 142, 143
  wildlife in, 81
Kernton forest, Herodsfoot, holiday cabins, 42, 43
Kitchener, Lord, 103
Klostergut Jacobsberg Hotel, Germany, 108
Knole, Kent, 103
Kyoto, Japan, 15

Lake District, England, 26
Lanfant, Marie-Francoise, 21
Leisure patterns, 113
Leningrad, USSR, 101
Lifts, 80
Lightwater valley, Ripon, 120
Limassol, Cyprus, 74, 75
Litter, 26
Lochanhully, Scotland, 54, 55
Loch Rannoch Estate, Scotland, 105, 115
London Transport Museum, Covent Garden, 109
Longleat Safari park, 128
Lyons, Eric, 64

Madeley Court, Telford, 105
Majorca, 64
Malta, 52
Maltese General Workers Union, 52
Maltings, Snape, Suffolk, 108
Manasseh, Leonard, 120, 128
Martin Mere Wildfowl Refuge, Lancashire, 86, 87
Mellieha, Malta, 52
Mexico, 70, 71
Micro-electronics, 8–10
Mobility, 11, 12
Montagu, Lord, 101, 112
Moribihan, France, 62
Morocco, 17
Moscow, USSR, 101
Motels, 78
Motor transport, 11
Mount Fuji, Japan, 27
Mourne, mountains of, N. Ireland, 94, 103, 105
Multi-ownership holiday accommodation, 45, 103, 105, 114, 115

Nairobi National Park, 83, 100
National Centre of Scientific Research, Paris, 21
National Exhibition Centre, Birmingham, 33
National Motor Museum, Beaulieu, 120, 126
National Parks, 19, 28, 82, 83
National Parks Act, 1916, (USA), 83
National Trust, Great Britain, 22, 102, 103
  Witley Common Day Study Centre, 96
Nature trails, 84, 92, 122
Newcastle, N. Ireland, 94
New Hall School, Boreham, Essex, 114
Nile Falls National Park, Uganda, 90, 91
Nile, river, 90
Northern Ireland, 94
Northleach House, Cotswolds, 117
Norwich cathedral, 106

Orient Express, 11

Pabuka Lodge, Nile Falls, Uganda, 90, 91
Package holidays, 13
Paris, France, 18
Parthenon, Greece, 22
Pedestrianised zones, 31
Petrodvorets, USSR, 102
Physical impact of tourism, 22–28
Pisa, Italy, 101
'Planning for Tourism in England', 16
Planning tourism, 29–36, 132, 133
Plas Talgarth Estate, Wales, 116
Pollution, 22–24, 82
  from camping, 39
Pontin's Holiday Camp, Burnham-on-Sea, 6
Pony trekking, 54
Port Dinorwic, Wales, 60
Port Grimaud, France, 64, 113
Portmadoc holiday housing complex, Wales, 60, 61
Portmerion, Wales, 60
Portugal, 44, 46
  Algarve, 113
Provence, France, 50
Pyramids, Gizeh, Egypt, 17

Railways, 3, 11; see also Trains
Ramps, 79
Religious buildings, 106–108
Resort areas, 25
Restaurant facilities, 78
  Tollymore, N. Ireland, 94
Riding schools, 114
Rimini, Italy, 16
Risley Moss Nature Reserve, Cheshire, 92, 93
Road access, 82
Roads, 30
  bypasses, 29, 30
Road travel, 29–30
Rocky Mountain campsites, Canada, 26, 39
Rome, Italy, 14, 18
Ruffold Country Park, Nottinghamshire, 128

Sababurg Castle, Germany, 105
Sailing facilities, 60, 70, 74, 114
St. Bartholomew's Fair, 1
St. Fagan's Welsh Folk Museum, 121
St. Giles' Fair, 1
St. Marks, Venice, 112
St. Mary's Church, Castlegate, York, 107
St. Paul's Church, Covent Garden, 110
St. Paul's Church, Queensgate, Huddersfield, 107
Salina Palace, Malta, 25
Sardinia, 56, 57
Scarborough, 3
Scotland,
  Brodick Information Centre, 98–100
  Lochanhully, 54, 55
Scottish Tourist Board, 18, 131
Scott, Sir Peter, 81, 82
Seaside resorts, 2
Self-catering holidays, 44, 45
Semliki Game Reserve, Uganda, 88, 89
Serena, Beach Hotel, Kenya, 142, 143
Serengeti Game Park, 81
Service d'etudes d'amenagement touristique en espace rural (SEATER), 116
Services, 82
  for camping sites, 39, 41
Sevagram Guest House, Maharashtra, India, 136, 137
Sierra Leone, 17
  National Dance Company, 20

Sissinghurst Castle, Kent, 24
Skansen Folk Museum, Stockholm, 120, 121
Ski-ing facilities, 54, 72
Slimbridge Wildfowl Trust, 82
Snowdonia National Park, 26, 31
Solar energy, 82
Solar Tower, Villa Group, France, 50, 141
Spain, 25
Spas, 3
Spending patterns, 13, 14
Sport-based holidays, 113
Staircases, design, 79
Stazzo Pulcheddu, Sardinia, 64
Stazzo Holiday Housing, Sardinia, 56, 57
Strongborough Hall, Staffordshire, 117
Sweden, 26, 39, 72, 73

Taj Mahal, India, 23, 24
Thorndon hall, Essex, 103, 104
Tiger Tops, Nepal, 141
'Time sharing' accommodation, 45, 103, 105, 114, 115
Toilet facilities, 33
    for disabled, 80
Tollymore Cafe and Tourist Centre, N. Ireland, 94
Tourism, 6, 7,
    benefits, of, 21
    economic aspects of, 15–21
    employment in, 16
    objectives of, 8, 15
'Tourist Friends Association', Egypt, 21

Traffic,
    density, 26
    impact on countryside, 29
Trains,
    British Rail, Advanced Passenger, 11
    Japanese Bullet, 11
    Orient Express, 11
    Trans-Siberian Express, 29
Transport, urban, 24
Travel,
    alternative ways of, 141
    facilities, 11
Treetops Hotel, Kenya, 82, 128
Tunisia, 65, 68, 69
Turkey, 58, 59
Turkish Ministry of Tourism, 134

Uganda, 66, 88–91
Ulster Folk and Transport Museum, 121
UNESCO, 20, 21
United Nations Conference (Rome, 1963), 16
Universities, 113
Urban infrastructure problems, 24
USA, 78, 82
    cattle ranch holidays, 116
    time sharing, 114
USSR, 101, 107

Venic, Italy, 18, 19, 24
Verne, Jules, 5
Vienna, Austria, 18
Vilalara, Algarve, Portugal, 83
Vilamoura, Portugal, 44, 46, 47, 113

Villa Group, Provence, France, 50, 51
Villas; see Holiday Villas

Wakes weeks, 2
Waldeck Schloss, Germany, 105
Wales,
    Portmadoc, 60, 61
    Portmerion, 60
    Snowdonia,, 26, 31
Warrington New Town, 92
Warsaw, Poland, 102
Waste disposal, 82
Weald and Downland Open-air Museum, Sussex, 121
Wellington Country Park, Hampshire, 120, 122, 123
Westminster Abbey, London, 22
Wildfowl Trust (UK), 82, 83
    Arundel, 84, 85
    Martin Mere, 86, 87
Windsor Safari Park, 83, 100
Winter Sports, 54, 72, 113
Witley Common Information Centre, Surrey, 96, 97
Work patterns, 8, 9
World Bank, 16, 77, 132
World Tourist Organization (WTO), 6, 7, 132
World Wildlife Fund, 81

Yatri Nivas Guest House, India, 136, 137
York Minster, 106